I Do
What I Do

Select Praise for *I Do What I Do*

'What strikes you most about Raghuram Rajan is not his academic brilliance, open-mindedness or honesty of thought but how he blends all of these with simplicity of expression and disarming humility.' – *Times of India*

'Rajan is not loud; he is circumspect and there is a coherent pattern through all his speeches – taking forward the reform agenda in Indian banking and financial sector...By making his stance on demonetization public, he has possibly served a critical purpose of making clear that RBI did not support the move, it was at best a passive partner...Rajan's book clarifies that in February 2016 when the government asked for his views on demonetization, "in no uncertain terms" Rajan expressed his reservations against it, saying short-term economic costs would outweigh long-term benefits and there were "better alternatives to achieve the main goals" (unearthing black money, fighting terror finance and fake notes). When he was asked to prepare a note, he reiterated this, outlined the preparations needed for it and also what would happen if the preparation was inadequate.' – Tamal Bandyopadhyay, *Mint*

'A treasure trove of knowledge for an ardent follower of economics and politics. Dr Rajan tries to remove the complexities associated with economic theories and presents his ideas in an unembellished prose devoid of complex jargons. The book also offers simple nuggets of opinions and suggestions supplemented by equally interesting analogies.' – Nikunj Gandhi, *Free Press Journal*

'This book is not meant for Rajan's blind haters or equally blind admirers. It is for those who still have an open mind...It helps understand Rajan's stint in the central bank and his formidable legacy. This book is a must-read.' – Seetha, *Swarajya*

'An attempt by Rajan to give Indians a sense of what it was like to make policy at the RBI.' – Tushar Dhara, News18.com

'Rajan endorses an idea that is spoken in hushed tones – that the RBI should give advice but not insist that it be taken...The book gives us a sense of the issues that Rajan thinks are still important...He gives us an idea of how he steadied the foreign exchange boat, controlled inflation, re-energized the RBI's bank supervision functions and managed to hold off demonetization. But, as with the speeches of all governors, you have to read between the lines somewhat because they are not allowed to speak their minds.' – T.C.A. Srinivasa Raghavan, *India Today*

'Rajan writes with great clarity.' – Pulapre Balakrishnan, *Hindu*

'In a short span of three years as governor, Raghuram Rajan left his strong imprint on the Reserve Bank. He laid the base for a new monetary framework with inflation control as its focus. The articles and speeches included in this volume reveal Rajan's sharp mind, his deep scholarship and his ability to address practical problems with agility and wisdom.' – C. Rangarajan, former RBI governor

'Raghuram Rajan's daughter sent him a thumbs-down emoji when the media called him James Bond. He was no 007. But he sure defied conservatism and gave staid RBI a new, if short-lived, swagger. This book, packed with the weight of his intellect, charmingly convincing logic and down-to-earth dosa economics, is a welcome end to his one-year maun vrat. His advice to India watchers is simple: strip out both euphoria and despair in what you say about India, and you might find the truth!' – Shekhar Gupta, founder and editor-in-chief, ThePrint

'Rajan is not just a distinguished former RBI governor. He is also one of the world's foremost thinkers on the relationship between finance, capitalism and democracy. These clear, luminous speeches and essays provide a cogent introduction to his thinking and offer deep insights into our current predicament.' – Pratap Bhanu Mehta, Vice-Chancellor, Ashoka University

'Raghu is a rare individual, a brilliant intellectual, a fine administrator and someone always willing to talk truth to power. This collection of his writings and speeches over the last few years brings out another aspect – his ability to decipher and articulate the complex world of economics and central banking.' – Nandan Nilekani, co-founder of Infosys and founding chairman of UIDAI (Aadhaar)

I Do What I Do

On Reform, Rhetoric
and Resolve

Raghuram G. Rajan

HARPER
BUSINESS

An Imprint of HarperCollins *Publishers*

First published in hardback in India by Harper Business 2017
An imprint of HarperCollins *Publishers* India
4th Floor, Tower A, Building No. 10, DLF Cyber City,
DLF Phase II, Gurugram, Haryana – 122002
www.harpercollins.co.in

This edition published in India by Harper Business 2018

2 4 6 8 10 9 7 5 3 1

P-ISBN: 978-93-5302-488-8
E-ISBN: 978-93-5277-015-1

The following piece has been reproduced here with permission from *Foreign Affairs*: 'The True Lessons of the Great Recession'. The following pieces have been reproduced here with permission from *Straight Talk*: 'Risky Business: Skewed Incentives for Investment Managers May Be Adding to Global Financial Risk'; 'Clever Solution: But Will It Work?'; 'Assume Anarchy?'; 'Odious or Just Malodorous?'; 'The Great Game Again?'.

Raghuram G. Rajan asserts the moral right to be identified as the author of this work.

The views and opinions expressed in this book are the author's own and the facts are as reported by him, and the publishers are not in any way liable for the same.

Typeset in 11.5/14.5 Sabon Roman at
SÜRYA, New Delhi

Printed and bound at
Replika Press Pvt. Ltd.

MIX
Paper from
responsible sources
FSC® C016779
www.fsc.org

This book is produced from independently certified FSC® paper to ensure responsible forest management.

CONTENTS

SECTION II: THE GLOBAL FINANCIAL CRISIS

SECTION III: OCCASIONAL PIECES

INTRODUCTION

Early in my tenure as the Governor of the Reserve Bank of India (RBI), Krishan Chopra of HarperCollins asked me to write a book. He suggested putting together edited versions of my past articles and speeches under different themes. I pleaded that I was extremely busy, and simply did not have the time. As my term came to an end, however, I realized time would be less of a constraint. In the speeches I gave while at the RBI, I had been describing the reforms we were undertaking and the rationale behind them, both to build confidence amongst investors and to get support from the public. If I could link the speeches together in a book with commentary about what prompted each speech, I could give the youth of the country a feel for the excitement of working at the central bank. I hoped this would attract a few into the area of economics and finance, where India really needs more good people. Moreover, if I could describe the overall rationale for what had been done, completed reforms could stand a better chance of not being reversed, while incomplete reforms could be finished.

I did not want to intrude on my successor's initial engagement with the public, so I determined to stay silent on India for a year. This book will be published after that year is over. Also, while I have tried to explain my rationale for various speeches and actions through linking commentary, I have respected the privacy of conversations I had with various public figures. I have also added a short selection of some speeches and articles that I wrote, primarily while I was the Chief Economist at the International Monetary Fund, but also while at Chicago's Booth School of Business before I joined the RBI.

The title of this book reflects the serendipitous nature of public life. I enjoyed the give-and-take of press conferences after monetary policy meetings, especially because I knew most of the reporters. As one press conference was ending, I was asked (yet again) by a familiar face whether I was dovish like Yellen or hawkish like Volcker. I understood what the reporter was asking, but I wanted to push back on the attempt to pigeonhole me into existing stereotypes. Somewhat jokingly, I started in a James Bond-ish vein, 'My name is Raghuram Rajan...' To my horror, mid-sentence I realized I did not know how to end in a way that did not reveal more on monetary policy than I intended. So with TV cameras trained on me, I ended lamely '...and I do what I do'. For some reason, that sentence became the financial press headline the next day, with the details of our monetary policy relegated to the inside columns. The commentary on social media even reached my usually supportive daughter, who emphasized her negative reaction to my unwitting sentence with repeated thumbs-down emojis!

In a sense, though, the headline was apt. Two different governments had largely given me free rein at the Reserve Bank, reposing their trust in me. Knowing I had a three-year term, I could push hard for change. Eventually, the usual opposition from vested interests would build up, but I hoped the RBI would complete much of the needed reforms by then. And indeed it did.

I came into office during the currency crisis, when India was termed one of the Fragile Five. So my first task was stabilization. But right from the beginning, I realized that the prospect of financial sector reforms would be an aid to stabilization. With India making the transition from low-income to middle-income country, the need for these reforms was clear. Of course, reforms are an ongoing process, and they can be reversed. This was why it was important to embody the reforms in new institutional mechanisms, as well as build ownership of reforms within the RBI and amongst external stakeholders.

And that brings me to teamwork. This was not my first job in management. But I became head of an organization of 17,000 people, with assets of more than $400 billion. How does one manage such a large organization? Obviously with help. I have always found that the single most important task in management is to pick good deputies, and I managed to get very good ones. My role was to set the overall agenda (of course, in consultation with them), get the concurrence of the government, draw out the vast experience of my colleagues to fill out the details and rule out inadvisable steps, push and prod the organization where necessary so that we stuck to timelines, and then roll out the measures after engaging with stakeholders, including the public.

We did not undertake reforms by stealth. While the full import of some of the actions we took may not have been obvious early on, making it harder for opposition to crystallize, the roadmap for much of what we did was set by various RBI-appointed committees, advertised in public speeches, and then implemented after discussion with stakeholders. We were always willing to listen to alternative proposals from them, but any suggestion had to pass my test of economic or financial commonsense, and my colleagues' test of meeting sensible central and commercial banking practice, before it was accepted. By and large, these dual filters helped us screen out unhelpful suggestions.

Our reforms were guided by the need to increase the role of markets and improve competition, to ensure we had the right regulations and the regulations were enforced in a predictable and transparent way, and to do all this in a measured but steady way so that the system could adjust. As I will explain, this is broadly how we dealt with issues ranging from inflation management to resolving distressed loans. Throughout, our attempt was to institutionalize processes so that they would be both predictable and enduring. India is becoming a large middle income country, too complex and varied to be controlled centrally. The government will need to withdraw from occupying the commanding heights of the economy, confining itself to providing public goods and the governing framework, and leaving economic activity to the people. To harness their collective energy, India will need many such reforms in the years to come if it is to grow rapidly in a sustainable and equitable way.

My speeches were an essential part of the stabilization and

reform process, allowing me to explain the rationale for change to investors and the public, flag the building blocks of the reform, and draw in opinion leaders into the debate while the specific regulations were being drafted. The additional value of describing what we intended to do and delivering on it repeatedly was that it allowed the RBI to get credit for the intended reform from the market at the time of announcement, much before the time of delivery. This could prove crucial if markets became volatile again. Also, many speeches tried to educate the broader public on the underlying finance and economics. If someone got drawn by a speech into learning more, that was one more step towards spreading financial and economic literacy – I had what every teacher wants, a national platform, one I tried to use effectively and responsibly.

I also used my speeches to partly fulfil another important role the RBI has, that of managing macroeconomic risk for the country. This objective, as we will see, led to speeches that proved more controversial, perhaps because I was speaking outside the usual areas of central banking and regulation, and perhaps because some of my warnings were surprisingly seen as challenges to the government. Nevertheless, I saw these speeches as part of the Governor's responsibility as the primary technocrat managing macroeconomic risk for the country.

Being an academic, I wrote all my speeches myself. My wife, Radhika, suffered through early drafts of many speeches, offering constructive criticism. I then had the relevant subject matter expert at the RBI look at the speech to check for accuracy, followed by a read from my very able executive assistant (first, the ever-dependable Vivek Aggarwal who was succeeded by Vaibhav Chaturvedi). Finally, after Alpana Killawala, our Chief General Manager for Communications, took a pass screening for possible political controversy, I made final touches and delivered the speech.

Press attention was always intense, even in locales that the press were supposed to be excluded from – someone present would always be willing to speak to the press or post on social media. Much of the press attention was perhaps initially in the hope that I would offer tit-bits on the direction of future monetary policy, but as the press realized I did not speak on new policy outside monetary policy meetings, I like to believe that they came because the speeches were interesting. At any rate, press attention was a double-edged sword, as we will see. While it allowed me to get the RBI's messages out easily, a misunderstood speech or misinterpreted comment could make headlines and create unnecessary frictions. I saw this as an unavoidable cost of public engagement, but I did sometimes question whether the misinterpretation was accidental or deliberate.

The job of Governor is probably the most fulfilling job any Indian economist could aspire for. There were many days when I went home tired but happy that we had really made a difference. There are very few jobs in public administration where one can say this because one is always hemmed in by the need to get the concurrence of other organizations, and turf battles make it hard to move forward. At the RBI, on many issues the decision was ours, and ours alone, so progress was feasible and continuous. This also meant that the job weighed constantly on my mind, for I had to keep asking what more we could do, given the possibilities were endless. Putting a policy economist in the Governor's job is like letting a kid loose in a candy shop!

This is not to say that the job was always easy or enjoyable. While I enjoyed a good understanding with the political leadership – meeting regularly and cordially first with Prime Minister Dr Manmohan Singh and Finance Minister Chidambaram, and then when the government changed, with Prime Minister Narendra Modi and Finance Minister Jaitley – and while some bureaucrats were a delight to work with, the least pleasant aspect of my job was dealing with bureaucrats who were trying to undercut the Reserve Bank so as to expand their turf. In my last speech as Governor (see later), I offered suggestions to the government on how to reduce these unproductive frictions.

Any public job involves both undue praise and unfair criticism. It is human nature to think the latter dominates the former. Yet it is also the latter that is probably more useful in helping you sharpen your message. Much of the material in these speeches is an implicit response to critics, an attempt to explain why they do not have the full picture. To the extent that the criticism helped further public understanding through the clarifying speeches I gave in response, it had a silver lining. But over and above the ample rewards from the sense of personal fulfilment the job affords, I continue to be pleasantly over-compensated by the many students who tell me that they have been inspired to study economics and finance, the unknown passengers on planes who thank me for my work, and even by the security officer who stamps my boarding card as I leave India and asks me when I am coming back to work in the country.

As I indicated earlier, this is not a 'tell-all'. Before ending this introduction, there is one issue, however, on which I have been asked many questions, which I have resolutely refused to answer until my period of silence is over, and that is the demonetization that was announced in India in November 2016. The questions, which have reportedly also been asked by parliamentary committees, include when I knew about the possibility of demonetization and what my view on it was. The press, quoting government sources, have variously reported that I was against it (in the early days of the demonetization process) and that I was 'on board' (in the most recent reports).

My only public commentary on the issue of demonetization was in response to a question in August 2014 at the Lalit Doshi Memorial Lecture (see later). At that time, the matter had not been broached by the government. As the *Hindustan Times* reported*

> In August, at the annual Lalit Doshi memorial lecture, Rajan said, 'I am not quite sure if what you meant is demonetise the old notes and introduce new notes instead. In the past, demonetisation has been thought of as a way of getting black money out of circulation. Because people then have to come and say 'how do I have this 10 crores in cash sitting in my safe and

---

*http://www.hindustantimes.com/business-news/rajan-preferred-other-ways-over-demonetisation-to-tackle-black-money/story-vlTbd6oixy6M4DnH65dWxI.html

they have to explain where they got the money from. It is often cited as a solution. Unfortunately, my sense is, the clever find ways around it.'

Rajan said, 'Black money hoarders find ways to divide their hoard into many smaller pieces. You find that people who haven't thought of a way to convert black to white, throw it into the hundi in some temples. I think there are ways around demonetisation. It is not that easy to flush out the black money.'

A fair amount of unaccounted cash is typically in the form of gold and therefore even harder to catch, said Rajan, adding that he would focus more on incentives that lead to generation and the retention of black money. There were a lot of incentives on taxes and the current tax rate in the country was for the most part reasonable, he added.

Given that various stances have been attributed to me, including in Parliament, let me clarify. I was asked by the government in February 2016 for my views on demonetization, which I gave orally. Although there might be long-term benefits, I felt the likely short-term economic costs would outweigh them, and felt there were potentially better alternatives to achieve the main goals. I made these views known in no uncertain terms. I was then asked to prepare a note, which the RBI put together and handed to the government. It outlined the potential costs and benefits of demonetization, as well as alternatives that could achieve similar aims. If the government, on weighing the pros and cons, still decided to go ahead with demonetization, the note outlined the preparation that would be needed, and the time that preparation would take. The RBI flagged what would happen if preparation was inadequate.

The government then set up a committee to consider the issues. The deputy governor in charge of currency attended these meetings. At no point during my term was the RBI asked to make a decision on demonetization.

Enough said. Let me conclude this introduction with thanks. My wife was my constant support in Mumbai, as she has been all our life together. She could be relied upon to keep my feet firmly tethered to the ground, even while giving me the advice

I needed. My children, who came home occasionally during the holidays, endured the absence of their parents, and helped give me a sense of normalcy at home after being 'The Governor' in the office. My parents and parents-in-law were an unconditional source of comfort, as always. I owe a debt to my colleagues at the RBI, who worked tirelessly with me, and received my family with warmth into their midst. And, finally, I thank Krishan Chopra of HarperCollins, without whose perseverance this book would not have seen the light of day, Siddhesh Inamdar for his careful editing, and Rajinder Ganju for his typesetting.

Section I

RBI DAYS

CHAPTER 1

SETTING THE STAGE

I

I took over as the 23rd Governor of the Reserve Bank of India on 4 September 2013. The rupee had been in free fall in August, inflation and the current account deficit were high. Even though Mr Chidambaram, who had been brought back as Finance Minister in 2012 when Mr Pranab Mukherjee became the President of India, had taken an axe to the fiscal deficit, it was still large. With elections looming in May 2014, and the possibility of a hung parliament, investors were getting nervous. They were quick to label India one of the 'Fragile Five' emerging markets during the market volatility that followed Fed Chairman Ben Bernanke's hint in May 2013 that the Fed was likely to start the process of normalization of monetary policy. Having experienced the worst of that 'Taper Tantrum' while at North Block, and having seen measure after measure to stabilize the currency fall flat, I thought it was time to go all out. I wanted to send the message that India had strong institutions like the RBI that could push reforms forward even when Parliament was stalled, and international investors should not write India off.

My predecessor, Governor Subbarao, was gracious enough to allow me to spend most of August 2013 at the RBI, talking to my to-be colleagues and collecting possible ideas for reform measures. There were plenty of ideas floating around in the corridors of the Reserve

Bank, belying its reputation for staid conservatism. Where necessary, these were discussed with my colleagues in the finance ministry. I wanted to send four messages. First, we had to present a façade of confidence to assure the public and investors that the RBI knew what had to be done. Second, we would emphasize our commitment to bringing down inflation, which my friend, the Mexican central bank governor, Agustin Carstens, advised me, was in his long experience the best way to stabilize the currency. Third, we would signal the RBI could be bold and farsighted when the need arose – evidenced by the large number of measures that were announced, and our ability to look beyond the currency turmoil to discuss, for instance, the eventual internationalization of the rupee. Looking beyond the immediate problems would also suggest we were not overly pre-occupied with the current volatility. Finally, I wanted set standards for transparency and predictability, transparency through clear communication, and predictability by laying out what we at the RBI intended to do, so that we could be held to it.

My initial statement, which I read out on national TV, is reproduced here almost in its entirety, with only the description of some of the detailed measures dropped.

Statement on Taking Office, 4 September 2013

Good evening. I took charge this afternoon as the 23rd Governor of the Reserve Bank of India. These are not easy times, and the economy faces challenges. At the same time, India is a fundamentally sound economy with a bright future. Our task today is to build a bridge to the future, over the stormy waves produced by global financial markets. I have every confidence we will succeed in doing that. Today I want to articulate some first steps, concrete actions we will take, as well as some intentions to take actions based on plans we will formulate.

Before I turn to specifics, let me repeat what I said on the day I was appointed. The Reserve Bank is a great institution with a tradition of integrity, independence, and professionalism. I congratulate Dr Subbarao on his leadership in guiding the bank through very difficult times, and I look forward to working with the many dedicated employees of the RBI to further some of the important initiatives he started. I have been touched by the warmth with which the RBI staff have welcomed me.

To the existing traditions of the RBI, which will be the bedrock of our work, we will emphasize two other traditions that become important in these times: transparency and predictability. At a time when financial market are volatile, and there is some domestic political uncertainty because of impending elections, the Reserve Bank of India should be a beacon of stability as to its objectives. That is not to say we will never surprise markets with actions. A central bank should never say 'Never'! But the public should have a clear framework as to where we are going, and understand how our policy actions fit into that framework. Key to all this is communication, and I want to underscore communication with this statement on my first day in office.

MONETARY POLICY

We will be making the first monetary policy statement of my term on 20 September. I have postponed the originally set date a bit so that between now and then, I have enough time to consider all major developments in the required detail. I will leave a detailed explanation of our policy stance till then, but let me emphasize that the RBI takes its mandate from the RBI Act of 1934, which says the Reserve Bank for India was constituted

> 'to regulate the issue of Bank notes and the keeping of reserves
> with a view to securing monetary stability in India and generally
> to operate the currency and credit system of the country to its
> advantage;'

The primary role of the central bank, as the Act suggests, is monetary stability, that is, to sustain confidence in the value of the country's money. Ultimately, this means low and stable expectations of inflation, whether that inflation stems from domestic sources or from changes in the value of the currency, from supply constraints or demand pressures. I have asked Deputy Governor Urjit Patel, together with a panel he will constitute of outside experts and RBI staff, to come up with suggestions in three months on what needs to be done to revise and strengthen our monetary policy framework. A number of past committees, including the Financial Sector Legislative Reforms Committee (FSLRC), have opined on this, and their views will also be considered carefully.

INCLUSIVE DEVELOPMENT

I talked about the primary role of the RBI as preserving the purchasing power of the rupee, but we have two other important mandates; inclusive growth and development, as well as financial stability.

As the central bank of a developing country, we have additional tools to generate growth – we can accelerate financial development and inclusion. Rural areas, especially our villages, as well as small and medium industries across the country, have been important engines of growth even as large company growth has slowed. But access to finance is still hard for the poor, and for rural and small and medium industries. We need faster, broad-based, inclusive growth leading to a rapid fall in poverty.

The Indian public would benefit from more competition between banks, and banks would benefit from more freedom in decision making. The RBI will shortly issue the necessary circular to completely free bank branching for domestic scheduled commercial banks in every part of the country. No longer will a well-run scheduled domestic commercial bank have to approach the RBI for permission to open a branch. We will, of course, require banks to fulfil certain inclusion criteria in underserved areas in proportion to their expansion in urban areas, and we will restrain improperly managed banks from expanding until they convince supervisors of their stability. But branching will be free for all scheduled domestic commercial banks except the poorly managed.

There has been a fair amount of public attention devoted to new bank licences. The RBI will give out new bank licences as soon as consistent with the highest standards of transparency and diligence. We are in the process of constituting an external committee. Dr Bimal Jalan, an illustrious former Governor, has agreed to chair it, and the committee will be composed of individuals with impeccable reputations. This committee will screen licence applicants after an initial compilation of applications by the RBI staff. The external committee will make recommendations to the RBI Governor and Deputy Governors, and we will propose the final slate to the Committee of the RBI Central Board. I hope to announce the licences within, or soon after, the term of Deputy Governor Anand Sinha, who has been shepherding the process. His term expires in January 2014.

We will not stop with these licences. The RBI has put an excellent document on its website exploring the possibility of differentiated licences for small banks and wholesale banks, the possibility of continuous or 'on-tap' licensing, and the possibility of converting large urban co-operative banks into commercial banks. We will pursue these creative ideas of the RBI staff and come up with a detailed roadmap of the necessary reforms and regulations for freeing entry and making the licensing process more frequent after we get comments from stakeholders.

Finally, our banks have a number of obligations that pre-empt lending, and in fact, allow what Dr Rakesh Mohan, an illustrious former Deputy Governor, called 'lazy banking'. One of the mandates for the RBI in the Act is to ensure the flow of credit to the productive sectors of the economy. In this context, we need to reduce the requirement for banks to invest in government securities in a calibrated way, to what is strictly needed from a prudential perspective.

We also subject our banks to a variety of priority sector lending requirements. I believe there is a role for such a mandate in a developing country – it is useful to nudge banks into areas they would otherwise not venture into. But that mandate should adjust to the needs of the economy, and should be executed in the most efficient way possible. Let us remember that the goal is greater financial access in all parts of the country, rather than meeting bureaucratic norms. I am asking Dr Nachiket Mor to head a committee that will assess every aspect of our approach to financial inclusion to suggest the way forward. In these ways, we will further the development mission of the RBI.

RUPEE INTERNATIONALIZATION AND CAPITAL INFLOWS

This might be a strange time to talk about rupee internationalization, but we have to think beyond the next few months. As our trade expands, we will push for more settlement in rupees. This will also mean that we will have to open up our financial markets more for those who receive rupees to invest them back in. We intend to continue the path of steady liberalization.

The RBI wants to help our banks bring in safe money to fund our current account deficit. The Reserve Bank of India has been receiving requests from banks to consider a special concessional window for swapping Foreign Currency Non-Resident (FCNR) deposits that will be mobilized following the recent relaxations permitted by the bank. We will offer such a window to the banks to swap the fresh FCNR dollar funds, mobilized for a minimum tenor of three years and over, at a fixed rate of 3.5 per cent per annum for the tenor of the deposit.

Further, based again on requests received from banks, we have decided that the current overseas borrowing limit of 50 per cent of the unimpaired Tier I capital will be raised to 100 per cent and that the borrowings mobilized under this provision can be swapped with the RBI at the option of the bank at a concessional rate of 100 basis points below the ongoing swap rate prevailing in the market.

The above schemes will be open up to 30 November 2013. The RBI reserves the right to close the scheme earlier with due notice.

FINANCIAL INFRASTRUCTURE

Finance thrives when financial infrastructure is strong. The RBI has been working hard to improve the financial infrastructure of the country – it has made tremendous advances, for example, in strengthening the payment and settlement systems in the country. Similarly, it has been working on improving information sharing through agencies such as credit bureaus and rating agencies. I propose to carry on such work, which will be extremely important to enhance the safety and speed of flows as well as the quality and quantity of lending in the country.

On the retail side, I particularly want to emphasize the use of the unique identity, Aadhaar, in building individual credit histories. This will be the foundation of a revolution in retail credit.

For micro, small and medium firms (MSMEs), we intend to facilitate Electronic Bill Factoring Exchanges, whereby MSME bills against large companies can be accepted electronically and auctioned so that MSMEs are paid promptly. This was a proposal in the report of my Committee on Financial Sector reforms in 2008, and I intend to see it carried out.

Finance is not just about lending, it is about recovering loans also. We have to improve the efficiency of the recovery system, especially at a time of economic uncertainty like the present. Recovery should be focused on efficiency and fairness – preserving the value of underlying valuable assets and jobs where possible, even while redeploying unviable assets to new uses and compensating employees fairly. All this should be done while ensuring that contractual priorities are met. The system has to be tolerant of genuine difficulty while coming down hard on mismanagement or fraud. Promoters do not have a divine right to stay in charge regardless of how badly they mismanage an enterprise, nor do they have the right to use the banking system to recapitalize their failed ventures.

Most immediately, we need to accelerate the working of Debt Recovery Tribunals and Asset Reconstruction Companies. Deputy Governor Anand Sinha and I will be examining the necessary steps.

I have asked Deputy Governor Dr Chakrabarty to take a close look at rising Non Performing Assets (NPAs) and the restructuring/recovery process, and we too will be taking next steps shortly. RBI proposes to collect credit data and examine large common exposures across banks. This will enable the creation of a central repository on large credits, which we will share with the banks. This will enable banks themselves to be aware of building leverage and common exposures.

While the resumption of stalled projects and stronger growth will alleviate some of the banking system difficulties, we will encourage banks to clean up their balance sheets, and commit to a capital-raising programme where necessary. The bad loan problem is not alarming yet, but it will only fester and grow if left unaddressed.

We will also follow the FSLRC suggestion of setting up an enhanced resolution structure for financial firms. The working group on resolution regimes for financial institutions is looking at this and we will examine its recommendations and take action soon after.

This is part of my short-term time table for the Reserve Bank. It involves considerable change, and change is risky. But as India develops, not changing is even riskier. We have to keep what is good about our system, of which there is a tremendous amount, even while acting differently where warranted. The RBI has always changed when needed, not following the latest fad, but doing what is necessary. I intend to work with my excellent colleagues at the Reserve Bank, the senior management of which is represented around this table, to achieve the change we need.

Finally, a personal note: Any entrant to the central bank governorship probably starts at the height of their popularity. Some of the actions I take will not be popular. The governorship of the Central Bank is not meant to win one votes or Facebook 'likes'. But I hope to do the right thing, no matter what the criticism, even while looking to learn from the criticism – Rudyard Kipling put it better when he mused about the requirements of an ideal central banker in his poem 'If':

If you can trust yourself when all men doubt you,
But make allowance for their doubting too:

Kipling's reference to 'men' only dates these lines, but his words are clear.

We will fill in details of what we have announced shortly, and lay out a broader roadmap of reforms soon after. Appropriate notifications will be issued shortly. As this is under way, we will turn to preparing the mid-quarter policy statement.

II

My opening statement, which made headlines in the Indian papers the next day, had the desired effect – a public, desperate for good news, started believing that the Reserve Bank could provide some. The rupee stabilized as investors regained confidence.

While many elements of the package were important, one was particularly memorable because I was initially against it. It had been presented to me when I was in the finance ministry in North Block. Essentially, bankers told us they would bring plenty of dollars in as three-year foreign currency non-resident (FCNR) deposits, which they would convert to rupees and invest in India. In return, they wanted a cheap rate at which they could convert rupees back into dollars three years hence. So long as the Reserve Bank could be trusted to provide the forward dollars, this was a great deal for the banks – they got rupee interest income and a guaranteed cheap price at which they could swap maturing rupees back into dollars.

I did not think much of this scheme when I first heard of it, dismissing it as yet another clever ploy by bankers to get a subsidy from a country in trouble. But it refused to go away, and my old colleagues at the finance ministry thought it worth a try as the crisis of confidence worsened.

I too became more favourable after thinking carefully about it. First, I weighed the balance of risks. If we did not move the rupee back to fundamental value, every one-rupee rise in the dollar-rupee rate would costs us Rs 40,000 crores more in import costs. Assuming the rupee was undervalued by Rs 3 for a couple of years, this would mean a loss of lakhs of crores to national income. In contrast, even if the scheme was wildly successful in attracting inflows, the payout would only be in the tens of thousands of crores. Of course, there might be cheaper ways of restoring confidence but it was not clear what they were. And time was of the essence.

Discussions with colleagues at the RBI had thrown up another rationale. The bankers who proposed the scheme were saying that if the money came in, the rupee would appreciate, and it would cost us less to offer the forward subsidy. This was self-serving and not quite right. What was right was that if we changed the narrative on India, and the rupee continued appreciating between the point when the money came in and the point we covered our liabilities to the bankers in forward markets, it would cost us significantly less. In fact, we might even make money on the deal. But what if the rupee plunged after the dollars flowed in? There were no certainties here.

The bottom line was that the scheme was a measured risk, with a probability that the RBI would lose money, a certainty that the bankers would make money, but also a reasonable chance that the country would be significantly better off. Policy making is about deciding in the face of uncertainty, after weighing the alternatives as best as one can. Having obtained the concurrence of the finance ministry, the RBI Governor had to decide. I chose to go ahead with it.

The FCNR scheme drew in $26 billion, more than any of us anticipated. But, equally important, confidence picked up, the rupee continued strengthening beyond when the money came in, partly because the global investor mood as well as Indian electoral projections also changed, and we covered our forward swaps cheaply. The rupee became one of the most stable emerging market currencies for a while.

Of course, in hindsight it seems like it was the obvious thing to do because it worked. The reality is we will never know for certain whether it was the key! Perhaps it was the other elements of the package such as the determination we expressed on controlling inflation, perhaps it was everything together. Autobiographies are always written as if the author had it all mapped out with perfect foresight, ignoring the risks and uncertainties at that time. This misleads, as much as those beautiful photographs of a past holiday abstract from the heat, the mosquitoes, and the lack of connectivity. Policy making invariably involves taking measured risks in the face of uncertainty, for one has neither a prior template nor the luxury of indecision.

As an aside, that initial speech also had some unintended collateral effects. I became a 'rock star' central bank governor, the James Bond or Ranbir Kapoor of central banking, depending on which paper you read – this was an image I tried hard to downplay because not only was it far from the prosaic reality, but also I wanted the focus to be on the RBI's innovative but reliable work. Perhaps the article that did the most to ensure I would have a fan following was a send-up of the incoming governor by the courageous though risqué columnist Shobhaa Dé. Years into my term, I finally met her and her charming daughter at an official party, and I was delighted to find that she was as embarrassed as I was about meeting in person after her piece. We had a good laugh about it. Kindling the press's interest unsheathed a double-edged sword, as we will see later, but it was by and large a helpful part of my mission.

With the currency more stable, attention could now shift to other reforms. These reforms were often discussed threadbare in the Senior Management Committee of the Reserve Bank, where groups made presentations on proposed directions, and the entire senior staff consisting of the Governor, Deputy Governors, and Executive Directors debated the issues. A variety of very useful ideas came up in these discussions, which sometimes took on the character of a university seminar, with argument and counter-argument. Unlike a university seminar, however, we needed decisions at the end of meetings! The meetings were also a way to keep all our senior staff abreast of important developments, and for them to have ownership of the reforms (both to the financial system and the RBI's internal functioning).

I got a chance to articulate our thinking on 15 November 2013 at the Bankcon Conference. I stressed five pillars around which our reform efforts were structured. This then became an easy way to explain our strategy to the many visitors we had, as well as to organize thinking within the RBI. In the speeches and texts that are reproduced here, I have edited the original text only to eliminate repetition or to improve clarity.

The Five Pillars of RBI's Financial Sector Policies

I want to focus on what we at the Reserve Bank are doing to improve the financial system. We plan to build the Reserve Bank's developmental measures over the next few quarters on five pillars. These are:

1. Clarifying and strengthening the monetary policy framework.
2. Strengthening banking structure through new entry, branch expansion, encouraging new varieties of banks, and moving foreign banks into better regulated organizational forms.
3. Broadening and deepening financial markets and increasing their liquidity and resilience so that they can help allocate and absorb the risks entailed in financing India's growth.
4. Expanding access to finance to small and medium enterprises, the unorganized sector, the poor, and remote and underserved areas of the country through technology, new business practices, and new organizational structures; that is, financial inclusion.
5. Improving the system's ability to deal with corporate distress and financial institution distress by strengthening real and financial restructuring as well as debt recovery.

Let me elaborate on each of these measures a little.

First, we are among the large countries with the highest consumer price inflation in the world, even though growth is weaker than we would like it to be. Much of the inflation is concentrated in food and services. Our households are turning to gold because they find financial investments unattractive. At the same time, many industrial corporations are complaining about high interest rates because they cannot pass through their higher costs into higher prices for their products.

We can spend a long time debating the sources of this inflation. But ultimately, inflation comes from demand exceeding supply, and it can be curtailed only by bringing both in balance. We need to reduce demand somewhat without having serious adverse effects on investment and supply. This is a balancing act, which requires the Reserve Bank to act firmly so that the economy is disinflating, even while allowing the weak economy more time than one would normally allow for it to reach a comfortable level of inflation. The weak state of the economy, as well as the good kharif and rabi harvest, will generate disinflationary forces that will help, and we await data to see how these forces are playing out. No single data point or number will determine our next move.

I think the market understands what we are trying to do. But we do need a more carefully spelled out monetary policy framework than we have currently. Action on the framework will follow the submission of the Dr Urjit Patel Committee report, which is expected by end-December 2013.

Second, we have already announced measures to free bank branching, and to incentivize foreign banks to incorporate domestically. Going forward, we have to give our public sector banks, which are a national asset, the means to improve their competitiveness. Many of them have made enormous strides in the last decade – for instance, the extent to which they have digitized their operations is extremely praiseworthy – but because competition in the banking sector is likely to increase in the next few years, they cannot rest on their laurels. In the coming months, we will discuss with stakeholders in public sector banks about what needs to be done to further improve their stability, efficiency and productivity.

Third, we need to enlist markets in the aid of banking. Liquid markets will help banks offload risks they should not bear, such as interest rate or exchange risk. They will also allow banks to sell assets that they have no comparative advantage in holding, such as long-term loans to completed infrastructure projects, which are better held by infrastructure funds, pension funds, and insurance companies. Liquid markets will help promoters raise equity which is sorely needed in the Indian economy to absorb the risks that banks otherwise end up absorbing. Rather than seeing markets as being inimical to the development of the banking sector, we have to see them as complementary – of course, this requires you bankers to build on your risk management capabilities so that you can use markets effectively.

In the coming weeks, we will roll out more recommendations of the Gandhi Committee report to improve the liquidity and depth of the government securities (G-Sec) market. We will then turn to money markets and corporate debt markets. We will introduce new variants of interest rate futures and products like inflation-indexed certificates, and work to improve liquidity in derivative markets.

Fourth, we have to reach everyone, however remote or small, with financial services. Financial inclusion does not just mean credit for productive purposes, it means credit for health care emergencies or to pay lumpy school or college fees. It means a safe means of remunerated savings, and an easy way to make payments and remittances. It means insurance and pensions. It means financial literacy and consumer protection.

We have made great strides in inclusion, but we are still some distance from our goal. We have adopted a branch-based strategy for inclusion, but it is not enough. Too many poor people in so-called 'over-banked' urban areas still do not have access to banking services. We have many experiments under way to use technology, mobile phones, new products such as mobile wallets, and new entities such as business correspondents to link people up to the formal financial system. Much as with cell phones where we created a frugal Indian model, we need a frugal, trustworthy, and effective Indian model for financial inclusion. The Dr Nachiket Mor Committee is helping us think through possible models, and I am hopeful that when we outline measures based on its recommendations, our fine banks, Non-Bank Finance Companies (NBFCs), information technology companies and mobile players will rise to the occasion. At a more detailed level, we have set up committees like the Sambamurthy Committee to advise us on how to expand mobile banking in India through encrypted SMS-based funds transfer in any type of handset.

I should emphasize the need for banks like the ones represented in this room to move beyond simply opening bank accounts to ensuring that poor customers are confident and comfortable enough to use them. Innovation in reaching out to the underserved customer, rather than simply posting higher numbers in branches or bank accounts opened, has to be part of our efforts.

And last but not least, we have to deal better with distress; The natural, and worst, way for a bank management with limited tenure to deal with distress is to 'extend and pretend' – to evergreen the loan, hope it recovers by miracle, or that one's successor has to deal with it. The natural incentive for a promoter to deal with distress is to hold on to equity and control despite having no real equity left, and to stand in the way of all efforts to resolve the underlying project while hoping for an 'act of God' to bail him out. Not all bankers and promoters succumb to these natural incentives, but too many do.

We have to ensure that the system recognizes financial distress early, takes steps to resolve it, and ensures fair recovery for lenders and investors. We could wish for a more effective judicial process or a better bankruptcy system, but while we await that, we have to improve the functioning of what we have. In the next few weeks, we will announce measures to incentivize early recognition, better resolution, and fair recovery of distressed loans. We will focus on putting real assets back to work in their best use. Here again, you bankers have a critical role to play by fighting the natural incentives that are built into the system. You have to help those with genuine difficulty while being firm with those who are trying to milk the system. The RBI will help you with every means at our disposal.

Let me conclude. We are going through a period of great cynicism about what India can do. That cynicism does not just permeate the foreign press and their audiences, but also infects our domestic debate. Every policy is greeted with suspicion and scrutinized for evidence of malfeasance. With no upside to making decisions, it is no wonder that decision making has slowed. The solution, however, cannot come through inaction but through action, action that is, and is seen to be, purposeful, unbiased, and effective. No doubt mistakes will be made, but if the weight of clean actions builds up, the miasma of suspicion that pervades our society today will ebb. The Reserve Bank of India intends to play its part in making this happen.

CHAPTER 2

HAWKS, DOVES, OR OWLS

I

My initial focus was, of course, on inflation. Whenever you want to embark on a set of actions in public life in India, it helps to have a report recommending the actions. The report indicates that wise people have thought deeply about the problem, and helps give the actions legitimacy. On monetary policy, our go-to report was the Dr Urjit Patel Committee report, which I described in my opening statement. My hope, which I shared with Dr Patel, was that we would get a roadmap much like the Dr Sukhamoy Chakravarty report was for monetary policy in the 1980s, and I was not disappointed. My task was now to figure out how to implement recommendations that could be implemented, and how to modify what could not.

One important recommendation was seemingly innocuous and technical. We moved from targeting Wholesale Price Index (WPI) inflation, which was not what the consumer experienced, to targeting Consumer Price Index (CPI) inflation, which was more closely related to the inflation in the basket of goods they bought in their daily lives. This step was a fundamental change in monetary policy – consumer price inflation had been much higher than wholesale price inflation for some time, which meant that interest rates would have to go higher and stay higher for longer if we had to curb CPI inflation. Would our industrialists, who had benefited from the era of cheap negative real interest rates, understand that that era was over, and that the much abused saver would now get a better deal? Would the Industrialists protest?

Another important step was to embark on the road to targeting inflation. We set out on a glide path to bring down inflation into the target range suggested by the Urjit Patel Committee Report, with clear milestones every year. We met each milestone we had set for ourselves, even though many thought it would be impossible. As we met milestones, we pressed for a formal inflation management agreement with the government, in an attempt to institutionalize and make more credible the fight against inflation. With the good offices of mandarins in the finance ministry, this agreement was signed.

We also modernized our liquidity operations, including how we conducted money market operations, with the intent of deepening our money markets. Term repos and term reverse repos were introduced, and eventually, we announced a move away from the practice of keeping the entire banking system in liquidity deficit, which seemed to create unnecessary problems in the money markets, to keeping it liquidity neutral.

Finally, together with the government, we designed the framework for an independent monetary policy committee, which would take over the setting of policy from the Governor. A committee would bring more minds to bear on policy setting, preserve continuity in case a member had to quit or retire, and be less subject to political pressure, which was why I supported this move strongly. I was the last Governor to set policy individually (albeit with full consultation with my colleagues). The Government nominated its appointees to the monetary policy committee soon after I left office, and my successor Dr Urjit Patel's first policy was with the full monetary policy committee.

I set the parameters of our fight against inflation in a speech to the Fixed Income Money Market and Derivatives

Association of India (FIMMDA) in February 2014. I sought to pinpoint the sources of inflation, especially food inflation, and why bringing it under control was in the farmer's interest. This was an extremely important point to make to the then governing UPA regime, which had a constituency that believed significantly higher food prices were in the farmers' interest.

More generally, the way to fight inflation, given the inconclusive skirmishes we had had in the recent past, was to signal that we were determined to bring it under control. But we also needed to do it in a way that could be tolerated by the Indian economy, which has many people with minimal cushions against adversity – I felt right from the beginning that doing a 'Volcker', that is, raising interest rates so high that demand collapsed, was simply not right for the Indian economy. However, I was sure that the heavily indebted interests would soon gather to oppose the RBI's agenda, and that any government's tolerance for tight monetary policy would wane. So we had to show results quickly. My speeches on inflation tried to explain our stance to the general public, even while trying to build public support in an environment that was sceptical that the RBI could control inflation.

Fighting Inflation

As you know, the Reserve Bank of India was constituted 'to regulate the issue of Bank notes and the keeping of reserves with a view to securing monetary stability in India and generally to operate the currency and credit system of the country to its advantage'. Implicit in these words are the core purposes of the RBI: to foster monetary and financial stability conducive to sustainable economic growth, and to ensure the development of an efficient and inclusive financial system.

Note that the RBI is committed to getting the strongest growth possible for India – there is no difference between us and the finance ministry on this. We believe the best way we can foster sustainable growth in the current situation, other than through developing the financial sector, is through monetary stability – by bringing down inflation over a reasonable period of time. More specifically, we intend to bring CPI inflation down to 8 per cent by January 2015 and 6 per cent by January 2016.

There are a number of points here that need elaborating. First, are we choosing to tackle inflation at the expense of growth? Most people believe there is a short-run trade-off between growth and inflation. By raising interest rates, the RBI causes banks to raise rates and thus lowers demand; firms do not borrow as much to invest when rates are higher and individuals stop buying durable goods against credit and, instead, turn to save. Lower demand growth leads to a better match between demand and supply, and thus lower inflation for the goods being produced.

Relatedly, if lower rates generate higher demand and higher prices for goods, people may produce more of those goods, believing that they are getting more revenues. But because all goods are going up in price, high inflation reduces what they can buy out of the revenues. Following the saying, 'You can fool all the people some of the time', bursts of inflation can generate growth for some time. Thus, in the short run, the argument goes, higher inflation leads to higher growth.

But as the public gets used to the higher level of inflation, the only way to fool the public again is to generate yet higher inflation. The result is an inflationary spiral which creates tremendous costs for the public. Therefore, economists have argued – and a number of Nobel prizes have been given for the ideas contained in the previous paragraphs – that the best way for the central bank to generate growth in the long run is for it to keep inflation low and steady.

And if the public starts expecting that inflation will stay low, the central bank can cut interest rates significantly, thus encouraging demand and growth. Indeed, the reason the Malaysian Central Bank can keep rates low today to foster growth is because it has fought the battle against inflation and convinced its citizens that, if need be, it will smote the inflationary beast again if it rears its head.

Put differently, in order to generate sustainable growth, we have to fight inflation first. Let me also add that greater public faith that inflation will be low will add stability to our currency, and prevent the kind of gyrations we saw last summer. Exchange rate stability is central to business interests.

If we have to bring down inflation, we have to start today. We cannot wait till the public's expectations of higher inflation get more entrenched, and the inflationary spiral gains momentum. This is why we have raised interest rates three times since September.

But what about industrialists who tell us to cut rates? I have yet to meet an industrialist who does not want lower rates, whatever the level of rates. But will a lower policy interest rate today give him more incentive to invest? We at the RBI think not. First, we don't believe the primary factor holding back investment today is high interest rates. Second, even if we cut policy rates, we don't believe banks, who are paying higher deposit rates, will cut their lending rates. The reason is that the depositor, given her high inflationary expectations, will not settle for less than the rates banks are paying her. Inflation is placing a floor on deposit rates, and thus on lending rates.

Currently, therefore, we do not believe the policy rate is at a level where it can affect demand significantly, one way or the other. We do believe, however, that as inflation comes down because of the weak economy and strong food production, the policy rate will become a stronger influence on bank interest rate setting, and will start influencing demand.

A more important source of our influence today, however, is expectations. If people believe we are serious about inflation, and their expectations of inflation start coming down, inflation will also come down. Of course, many people form expectations simply by extrapolating the most recent or most salient experience they have. So we also need to take advantage of the current episode of food price disinflation to bring down expectations – yet another reason for acting now.

Let us turn from answering those who want us to go slow to those who want us to do more. If we think inflation is so important, why don't we 'do a Volcker' and try and bring down inflation quickly by raising rates sky high? Of course, if we do raise policy rates substantially, banks will also have to raise rates to match us. While this may lead to a collapse in demand and bring inflation down quickly, it will cause significant damage to the economy – remember the severe recession Volcker's Fed brought about and the Savings and Loan Crisis that followed?

A developing country is not in the same resilient position as the United States. Rather than administer shock therapy to a weak economy, the RBI prefers to dis-inflate over time rather than abruptly, while being prepared to do what is necessary if the economy deviates from the projected inflation path. As of now, we believe the rate is appropriately set.

Then there are those who believe we are moving too independently. All we have done thus far is to adopt the reasonable suggestion of the Patel Committee that we focus on CPI inflation rather than WPI inflation as our primary objective. The Patel Committee has also suggested a time horizon to glide down to 6 per cent inflation that seems doable without extreme hardship. If the eventual decision of the government, in consultation with the Reserve Bank, is to adopt the recommendations of the Mistry Committee, the Committee on Financial Sector Reforms, the Financial Sector Legislative Reforms Committee (FSLRC) and the Patel Committee, and focus on some form of an inflation objective, it would be good for the medium-term inflation target to be set by the executive or legislature, advised by the Reserve Bank.

The Patel Committee report is out there for public comment and debate, and once we collect and analyse comments, we will take an internal view and then start deliberations with the government. All this said, international experience suggests that, ideally, once the central bank's objective is given, and the operational target fixed, the government should leave the technocrats in the central bank to do their job.

Finally, does the Patel Committee intend to turn the RBI into inflation 'nutters' focused on bringing down inflation to the exclusion of all else, including financial stability? Of course not! Medium-term flexible inflation targeting means that the monetary policy committee focuses on inflation over the medium term, being concerned about too high, as well as too low, inflation.

That means it may be willing to overlook temporary inflation spikes (such as this November's inflation numbers) but also raise rates when sustained low interest rates and low inflation increase threats to financial stability – because a financial crisis could lead to deflation. In other words, the monetary policy committee will not put on blinkers and see just the inflation number. A number of emerging markets have adopted some form of targeting, while 'non-targeters' like the Federal Reserve target inflation in all but name, including putting a number to its goal of price stability.

In the remaining time, I want to present one more issue that has many commentators exercised – they say the real problem is food inflation, how do you expect to bring it down through the policy rate? The simple answer to such critics is that core CPI inflation, which excludes food and energy, has also been very high, reflecting the high inflation in services. Bringing that down is centrally within the RBI's ambit. But I will argue that monetary policy is not irrelevant even in controlling food inflation, though clearly, the government also has an important role to play.

I. ROLE OF FOOD PRICES IN THE HIGH INFLATION EXPERIENCE OF RECENT YEARS

Headline inflation measured by the new CPI has remained in double digits during April 2012 to January 2014, averaging 10 per cent over this period. Food inflation, which has a weight of 47.6 per cent in the index, has contributed the largest share of headline inflation. Food inflation itself has stayed in double digits throughout this period, edging down to 9.9 per cent only in January 2014.

2. WHY ARE FOOD PRICES HIGH?

Although domestic production has increased steadily, barring reversals in 2009-10 and 2012-13, this has not been reflected in a softening of food prices. Let us try and understand why.

GROWING PROSPERITY AND DIETARY SHIFTS

Data on household consumption expenditure show that the share of food in overall consumption has been declining during the last decade, but at a milder pace than the significant relative increase in food prices. This suggests that demand is relatively less elastic to price changes. Despite the decline in overall consumption share, per capita food consumption in real terms has increased, particularly in rural areas. There has also been a distinct shift in dietary patterns towards protein-rich items and other high value foods. These items, in turn, have been contributing significantly to overall food price increases in the recent period.

OTHER POSSIBLE CAUSES OF HIGH FOOD PRICE INFLATION

A. MINIMUM SUPPORT PRICE

One obvious cause for higher food price inflation that analysts have pointed to is higher minimum support prices (MSP). The minimum support price is set by the government on the recommendations of the Commission on Agricultural Costs and Prices (CACP), based on a variety of factors including primarily the cost of production and price trends in the market (domestic and international). The crops covered under MSP scheme constitute more than a third of the category 'primary articles' in the WPI. Since minimum support prices are intended to be a floor for market prices, and have sometimes directly set the market price when increases have been substantial, for key crops the rate of price inflation seems to relate to the increase in MSP in recent years.

Another way of saying this is that there has been a shift in the relative price of agricultural commodities, engineered by the rise in MSPs. If the idea is to get more food production to meet the rising demand we documented, this seems to be just what is needed. If we plot the ratio of WPI of food to WPI of non-food items over time, it suggests an appreciable improvement in terms of trade for agriculture.

But when we look at the ratio of changes in input cost over the changes in the output price of agricultural commodities received on the basis of CACP data, it has remained flat, indicating that the gains from MSP increases have not accrued to the farm sector in full measure because the costs of inputs have been rising. This may indicate why production growth has not been stronger. What could explain this?

One explanation could be that MSPs also drive input costs, so increasing MSPs is like a dog chasing its tail – it can never catch it. Another could be that since rice and wheat are the primary food commodities procured at the MSP, production is distorted towards rice and wheat, leading to a sub-optimal production mix by farmers – too much rice and wheat, and too little of other needed commodities. Both these explanations would suggest the need for more moderation as the government sets the MSPs in coming months.

It is useful, though, to look at the details of the cost increases. Prices of agricultural inputs, including wages, have recorded a sharp increase during 2008-09 through 2012-13 in comparison with the preceding five years (2004-05 to 2007-08). Perhaps the most significant increase has been in rural wages. Nominal rural wages have grown at a sharp pace during the last five years. Because so many Indian workers are at subsistence wages, higher food prices do drive rural wages higher, and there is some evidence for this before 2007. From 2007 onwards, however, econometric tests suggest causality has flowed from wages to prices, underscoring the role of rural wages as a major determinant in food price increases. So why has rural wage growth been so strong?

B. MAHATMA GANDHI NATIONAL RURAL EMPLOYMENT GUARANTEE ACT (MGNREGA)

A sharp pickup in rural wages was seen after the rural employment guarantee programme (assuring 100 days of employment to every household whose adult members volunteer to do unskilled manual work) was enacted. MGNREGA may have contributed to the bargaining power of rural workers, but careful econometric studies suggest that it accounts for only a small fraction of the rural wage increase, and indeed, any effect is waning. That said, the indexation of MGNREGA wages suggests its effects in pushing rural wage inflation will not disappear entirely.

C. RURAL LIQUIDITY AND CREDIT

There has been an increase in liquidity flowing to the agricultural sector, both from land sales, as well as from a rise in agricultural credit. More availability of funds to the farmer has fostered substantial private investment in agriculture, but may also have pushed up rural wages.

D. LABOUR SHIFTING TO CONSTRUCTION

The labour force has been moving from agriculture to non-agriculture sectors, particularly construction. This would have the effect of pulling up rural labourers' wages (due to scarcity), especially in the labour supplying states. Total agricultural labour declined from 259 million in 2004-05 to 231 million in 2012-12. Agriculture, which accounted for 60 per cent of total employment in 1999-2000, now accounts for less than 50 per cent.

E. FEMALE PARTICIPATION

One of the more interesting possible explanations for the rise in rural wages is the changing female participation in rural markets. The female participation rate is down in all the age categories. Improved living standards could lead rural families to withdraw women from the labour force. Also, higher prosperity could lead to greater investment in educating girls (for the age group 10 to 24) again leading to lower participation in the workforce.

3. TO SUMMARIZE

In sum then, when we examine food inflation, a substantial portion stems from an increase in food production costs, primarily rural wage inflation. Some of that is an increase in real wages, needed to attract labour to agriculture, away from construction, education, household work, or MGNREGA.

If, however, wages elsewhere also go up, the necessary shift in relative wages to keep agricultural work attractive will not take place, and we will continue to have a wage spiral. Also, some of the agricultural wage growth may be because of more liquidity flowing into rural areas. Somewhat paradoxically, to contain food inflation and get a strong increase in food production, we need to

(i)   Contain the rise in wages elsewhere so that relative wages in agriculture can rise without too much overall increase in wages.

(ii)   Contain any unwarranted rise in rural wages as well as the rise in other agricultural input costs (though not through subsidies) so that the farmer gets a higher return.

(iii) Allow food prices to be determined by the market and use minimum support prices to provide only a lower level of support so that production decisions do not get distorted or the price wage spiral accentuated. This means limiting the pace of MSP increases going forward.

(iv)   Reduce the wedge between what the farmer gets and what is paid by the household by reducing the role, number, and monopoly power of middlemen (amend Agricultural Produce Market Committee – APMC – Acts), as well as by improving logistics.

(v)   Improve farm productivity through technology extension, irrigation, etc.

Note that of these steps, monetary policy has a direct role in (i) and (ii) by slowing the demand for labour as well as anchoring inflation expectations, and thereby moderating wage bargaining. Indeed, with the slowdown in the urban economy, there is some evidence now that rural wage growth is slowing.

Finally, our food prices have largely caught up with global prices. Given that global food prices have been moderating, such moderation should feed through to domestic food prices –

provided we do not intervene to prevent the feed-through of global prices, and do not intervene in limiting exports or imports.

Let me emphasize that the RBI welcomes rural prosperity and wants to help increase rural productivity through appropriate credit and investment. But recent inflation has not helped strengthen the hand of the farmer, so the fight against inflation is also in the farmer's interest.

To sum up,

- As prosperity has increased the demand for food, we have needed more food production (or imports).
- Higher agricultural commodity prices should have incentivized farmers to produce significantly more.
- They have, but not enough. Part of the reason may be that farmer earnings are being eaten away by higher costs, most important of which is wages.
- To limit the rise in rural wages, given that it has to rise relative to other wages to attract labour into agriculture, wages elsewhere should not rise as much.
- Monetary policy is an appropriate tool with which to limit the rise in wages, especially urban ones.
- The slowdown in rural wage growth may be partly the consequence of tighter policy limiting wage rise elsewhere.
- Of course, monetary policy's effectiveness in containing other price and wage increases (such as services prices, which are an important part of the CPI index) is far less controversial.

The RBI believes its fight against inflation will have traction, despite food being an important component of the CPI.

As I talked to people around the country, I discovered that as inflation came down and banks lowered deposit rates, savers were unhappy – even though inflation had fallen much more than the rates on deposits. Earlier, they argued, they got paid 10 per cent on their fixed deposits at banks, now they got 8 per cent. Was that fair? I had to explain that it was indeed, because inflation had come down faster, so the real returns (in terms of goods and services they could purchase) on their savings were now higher. To illustrate the point, I gave way to my inner teacher in the C.D. Deshmukh Lecture delivered at the NCAER in January 2016. The press soon termed this 'Dosanomics', though it was really just an example.

Dosanomics

Industrialists grumble about high rates while retirees complain about the low rates they get today on deposits. Both overstate their case, though, as I have said repeatedly, the way to resolve their differences is to bring CPI inflation steadily down.

The typical letter I get (from the retiree) goes, 'I used to get 10 per cent earlier on a one-year fixed deposit, now I barely get 8 per cent', please tell banks to pay me more else I won't be able to make ends meet'. The truth is that the retiree is getting more today but he does not realize it, because he is focusing only on the nominal interest he gets and not on the underlying inflation which has come down even more sharply, from about 10 per cent to 5.5 per cent.

To see this, let us indulge in Dosa economics. Say the pensioner wants to buy dosas and at the beginning of the period, they cost Rs 50 per dosa. Let us say he has savings of Rs 1,00,000. He could buy 2,000 dosas with the money today, but he wants more by investing.

At 10 per cent interest, he gets Rs 10,000 after one year plus his principal. With dosas having gone up by 10 per cent in price to Rs 55, he can buy 182 dosas approximately with the Rs 10,000 interest.

Now what happens when inflation comes down? At 8 per cent interest, he gets Rs 8,000 in interest. With dosas having gone up by 5.5 per cent in price, each dosa costs Rs 52.75, so he can now buy only 152 dosas approximately with the interest payment. So the pensioner seems right to complain: with lower interest payments, he can now buy less.

But wait a minute. Remember, he gets his principal back also and that too has to be adjusted for inflation. In the high inflation period, it was worth 1,818 dosas, in the low inflation period, it is worth 1,896 dosas. So in the high inflation period, principal plus interest are worth 2,000 dosas together, while in the low inflation period it is worth 2,048 dosas. He is about 2.5 per cent better off saving in the low inflation period in terms of dosas.

This is a long-winded way of saying that inflation is the silent killer because it eats into pensioners' principal, even while they are deluded by high nominal interest rates into thinking they are getting an adequate return. Indeed, with 10 per cent return and 10 per cent inflation, the deposit is not giving you any real return net of inflation, which is why you can buy only 2,000 dosas after a year of saving, the same as you could buy immediately today. In contrast, when inflation is 5.5 per cent but the interest rate you are getting is 8 per cent, you are earning a real rate of 2.5 per cent, which means 2.5 per cent more dosas, as we have seen. So while I sympathize with pensioners, they certainly are better off today than in the past.

III

CPI inflation was 4.39 per cent in September 2016 when I ended my term, down from 10.5 per cent in September 2013 in the beginning of my term.* We were well on our way to meeting the third signpost on our glide path, 5 per cent inflation by March 2017 (which was indeed achieved by my successor). As I ended my tenure, I thought it was very important to communicate once again the reasons why we fought inflation, and why the battle could never be fully over, and why the fight needed to continue. I wanted to explain why the fight was important for sustainable growth, and why we had institutionalized the fight through a monetary policy framework agreed with the government, and an independent monetary policy committee appointed largely by the government. This was in a speech delivered at the Tata Institute of Fundamental Research (TIFR) on 20 June 2016.

The Fight against Inflation: A Measure of Our Institutional Development

In my speech today, I thought I would describe our efforts to build a different kind of institution, not one that delves into the deepest realms of outer space or into the tiniest constituents of an atom, but one that attempts to control something that affects your daily life; inflation. There are parallels between the institution building you have done at TIFR, and what we are setting up to control inflation, though clearly our efforts are much

---

*https://dbie.rbi.org.in/DBIE/dbie.rbi?site=home

less tied to investigating the very fabric of the universe and more towards influencing human behaviour. Ultimately, both require a fundamental change in mindset.

THE COSTS OF INFLATION

High inflation has been with us in India for the last four decades. Most recently, we have experienced an average of more than 9 per cent inflation between 2006 and 2013.

What are the costs of having high inflation? Clearly, everyone understands the costs of hyperinflation, when prices are rising every minute. Money is then a hot potato that no one wants to hold, with people rushing straight from the bank to the shops to buy goods in case their money loses value along the way. As people lose faith in money, barter of goods for goods or services becomes the norm, making transacting significantly more difficult. For instance, how much of a physics lecture would you have to pay a taxi driver to drive you to Bandra; moreover would the taxi driver accept a physics lecture in payment?; perhaps you would have to lecture a student, and get the student to sing to the taxi driver...you get the point, transacting becomes difficult as hyperinflation renders money worthless.

Hyperinflation also has redistributive effects, destroying the middle class's savings held in bonds and deposits. The horrors of hyperinflation in Austria and Germany in the 1920s still make scary reading.

So, clearly, no one wants hyperinflation. But what if inflation were only 15 per cent per year? Haven't countries grown fast over a period of time despite high inflation? The answer is yes, but perhaps they could have grown faster with low inflation. After all, the variability of inflation increases with its level, as does the dispersion of prices from their fundamental value in the economy. This makes price signals more confusing – is the price of my widget going up because of high demand or because of high generalized inflation? In the former case, I can sell more if I produce more, in the latter case I will be left with unsold inventory. Production and investment therefore become more risky.

Moreover, high and variable inflation causes lenders to demand a higher fixed interest rate to compensate for the risk that inflation will move around (the so-called inflation risk premium), thus raising the cost of finance. The long-term nominal (and real) interest rates savers require rise, thus making some long-duration projects prohibitively costly.

These effects kick in only when inflation is noticeably high. So it is legitimate to ask, 'At what threshold level of inflation does it start hurting growth?' Unfortunately, this question is hard to answer – developing countries typically have higher inflation, and developing countries also have higher growth. So one might well find a positive correlation between inflation and growth, though this does not mean more inflation causes more growth. For this reason, the literature on estimating threshold effects beyond which inflation hurts growth is both vast as well as inconclusive. Most studies find that double-digit inflation is harmful for growth but are fuzzier about where in the single digits the precise threshold lies.

THE INFLATION TARGET

Nevertheless, given the limited evidence, why do most countries set their inflation target in the low single digits – 2 to 5 per cent rather than 7 to 10 per cent? Three reasons come to mind. First, even if inflation is at a moderate level that does not hurt overall growth, the consequences of inflation are not evenly distributed. While higher inflation might help a rich, highly indebted, industrialist because his debt comes down relative to sales revenues, it hurts the poor daily wage worker, whose wage is not indexed to inflation. Second, higher inflation is more variable. This raises the chance of breaching any given range around the target if it is set at a higher level. To the extent that a higher target is closer to the threshold where the consequences on growth are adverse, this makes it more likely the country will exceed the threshold and experience lower growth. Third, inflation could feed on itself at higher levels – the higher the target, the more chances of entering regions where inflation spirals upwards.

The received wisdom in monetary economics today is therefore that a central bank serves the economy and the cause of growth best by keeping inflation low and stable around the target it is given by the government. This contrasts with the earlier prevailing view in economics that by pumping up demand through dramatic interest rate cuts, the central bank could generate sustained growth, albeit with some inflation. That view proved hopelessly optimistic about the powers of the central bank.

Put differently, when people say 'Inflation is low, you can now turn to stimulating growth', they really do not understand that these are two sides of the same coin. The RBI always sets the policy rate as low as it can, consistent with meeting its inflation objective. Indeed, the fact that inflation is fairly close to the upper bound of our target zone today suggests we have not been overly hawkish, and were wise to disregard advice in the past to cut more deeply. If a critic believes interest rates are excessively high, he either has to argue the government-set inflation target should be higher than it is today, or that the RBI is excessively pessimistic about the path of future inflation. He cannot have it both ways, want lower inflation as well as lower policy rates.

At the same time, the RBI does not focus on inflation to the exclusion of growth. If inflation rises sharply, for instance, because of a sharp rise in the price of oil, it would not be sensible for a central bank to bring inflation within its target band immediately by raising interest rates so high as to kill all economic activity. Instead, it makes sense to bring inflation back under control over the medium term, that is, the next two years or so, by raising rates steadily to the point where the bank thinks it would be enough to bring inflation back within the target range. Let me emphasize that this is not a prediction of either the path of oil prices or a forecast of our monetary actions, lest I read in the paper tomorrow 'RBI to raise rates'. More generally, the extended glide path over which we are bringing inflation in check appropriately balances inflation and the need for reasonable growth.

ARGUMENTS AGAINST WHAT WE ARE DOING

There are many who believe we are totally misguided in our actions. Let me focus on four criticisms. First, we focus on the wrong index of inflation. Second, we have killed private investment by keeping rates too high. Somewhat contradictorily, we are also hurting the pensioner by cutting rates too sharply. Third, monetary policy has no effects on inflation when the economy is supply constrained, so we should abandon our attempt to control it. Fourth, the central bank has little control over inflation when government spending dominates (what in the jargon is called 'fiscal dominance').

THE WRONG INDEX

Historically, the RBI targeted a variety of indicators, putting a lot of weight on the Wholesale Price Inflation (WPI). Theoretically, reliance on WPI has two problems. First, what the common citizen experiences is retail inflation, that is, Consumer Price Inflation (CPI). Since monetary policy 'works' by containing the public's inflation expectations and thus wage demands, Consumer Price Inflation is what matters. Second, WPI contains a lot of traded manufactured goods and commodity inputs in the basket, whose price is determined internationally. A low WPI could result from low international inflation, while domestic components of inflation such as education and health care services as well as retail margins and non-traded food are inflating merrily to push up CPI. By focusing on WPI, we could be deluded into thinking we control inflation, even though it stems largely from the actions of central banks elsewhere. In doing so we neglect CPI, which is what matters to our common man, and is more the consequence of domestic monetary policy.

THE EFFECTIVE REAL INTEREST RATE, INVESTMENTS, AND SAVINGS

Of course, one reason critics may advocate a focus on WPI is because it is low today, and thus would mean low policy rates.

This is short-sighted reasoning for when commodity prices and global inflation picks up, WPI could well exceed CPI [*Author's note: This, in fact, was the case at the time this book was put together*]. There is, however, a more subtle argument; the real interest rate is the difference between the interest rate a borrower pays and inflation – it is the true cost of borrowing in terms of goods like widgets or dosas. If policy interest rates are set to control CPI, they may be too high for manufacturers who see their product prices appreciating only at the WPI rate. I am sympathetic to the argument, but I also think the concern is overblown. Even if manufacturers do not have much pricing power because of global competition, their commodity suppliers have even less. So a metal producer benefits from the fall in coal and ore prices, even though they may not get as high a realization on metal sales as in the past. The true measure of inflation for them is the inflation in their profits, which is likely significantly greater than suggested by WPI.

A second error that is made is to attribute all components of the interest rate paid by the borrower to monetary policy. For heavily indebted borrowers, however, a large component of the interest rate they pay is the credit risk premium banks charge for the risk that they may not get repaid. This credit risk premium is largely independent of where the RBI sets its policy rate.

So when someone berates us because heavily indebted industrialists borrow at 14 per cent interest with WPI at 0.5 per cent, they make two important errors in saying the real interest rate is 13.5 per cent. First, 7.5 per cent is the credit spread banks charge for the risk of default, and would not be significantly lower if we cut the policy rate (at 6.5 per cent today) by another 100 basis points. Second, the inflation that matters to the industrialist is not the 0.5 per cent at which their output prices are inflating, but the 4 per cent at which their profits are inflating (because costs are falling at 5 per cent annually). The real risk-free interest rate they experience is 2.5 per cent, a little higher than elsewhere in the world, but not the most significant factor standing in the way of investment. It would be far more effective for borrowers to bring down their rates by improving their repayment behaviour and thus bringing down the credit risk premium than to try and push the RBI to lower rates unduly.

The policy rate in effect plays a balancing act. As important as real borrowing rates are for the manufacturer, real deposit rates are for the saver. In the last decade, savers have experienced negative real rates over extended periods as the CPI has exceeded deposit interest rates. This means that whatever interest they get has been more than wiped out by the erosion in their principal's purchasing power due to inflation. Savers intuitively understand this, and had been shifting to investing in real assets like gold and real estate, and away from financial assets like deposits. This meant that India needed to borrow from abroad to fund investment, which led to a growing unsustainable current account deficit.

In recent years, as we fought against inflation, we cut the policy rate only when we thought depositors could expect a reasonable positive real return on their financial savings. This has helped increase household financial savings relative to their savings in real assets, and helped bring down the current account deficit. At the same time, I do get a lot of heart-rending letters from pensioners complaining about the cut in deposit rates. The truth is they are better off now than in the past, as I tried to explain in a previous lecture, but I can understand why they are upset when they see their interest income diminishing.

The bottom line is that in controlling inflation, monetary policy makers effectively end up balancing the interests of both investors and savers over the business cycle. At one of my talks, an industrialist clamoured for a 4 per cent rate on his borrowing. When I asked him if he would deposit at that rate in a safe bank, leave alone invest in one of his risky friends, he said 'No!' Nevertheless, he insisted on our cutting rates significantly. Unfortunately, policy makers do not have the luxury of inconsistency.

SUPPLY CONSTRAINTS

Food inflation has contributed significantly to CPI inflation, but so has inflation in services like education and health care. Some argue, rightly, that it is hard for the RBI to directly control food demand through monetary policy. Then they proceed, incorrectly, to say we should not bother about controlling CPI inflation. The reality is that while it is hard for us to control food demand, especially of essential foods, and only the government can influence food supply through effective management, we can control demand for other, more discretionary, items in the consumption basket through tighter monetary policy. To prevent sustained food inflation from becoming generalized inflation through higher wage increases, we have to reduce inflation in other items. Indeed, overall headline inflation may have stayed below 6 per cent recently even in periods of high food inflation, precisely because other components of the CPI basket such as 'clothing and footwear' are inflating more slowly.

FISCAL DOMINANCE

Finally, one reason the RBI was historically reluctant to lock itself into an inflation-focused framework is because it feared government overspending would make its task impossible. The possibility of fiscal dominance, however, only means that given the inflation objective set by the government, both the government and the RBI have a role to play. If the government overspends, the central bank has to compensate with tighter policy to achieve the inflation objective. So long as this is commonly understood, an inflation-focused framework means better coordination between the government and the central bank as they go towards the common goal of macro stability. I certainly believe that the responsible recent budget did create room for the RBI to ease in April.

PRAGMATIC INFLATION FOCUS

As you will understand from all that I have been saying, monetary policy under an inflation-focused framework tries to balance various interests as we bring inflation under control. In doing so, we have to have a pragmatic rather than doctrinaire mindset.

For example, emerging markets can experience significant capital inflows that can affect exchange rate volatility as well as financial stability. A doctrinaire mindset would adopt a hands-off approach, while the pragmatic mindset would permit intervention to reduce volatility and instability. Nevertheless, the pragmatic mind would also recognize that the best way to obtain exchange rate stability is to bring inflation down to a level commensurate with global inflation.

Similarly, while financial stability considerations are not explicitly in the RBI's objectives, they make their way in because the RBI has to keep growth in mind while controlling inflation. So if the RBI's monetary policies are contributing to a credit or asset price bubble that could lead to a systemic meltdown and growth collapse, the RBI will have to resort to corrective monetary policy if macro-prudential policy alternatives are likely to prove ineffective.

THE TRANSITION TO LOW INFLATION

The period when a high inflation economy moves to low inflation is never an easy one. After years of high inflation, the public's expectations of inflation have been slow to adjust downwards. As a result, they have been less willing to adjust their interest expectations downwards. Household financial savings are increasing rapidly as a fraction of overall household savings, but not yet significantly as a fraction of GDP. Some frictions in the interest rate-setting market do not also help. Even while policy rates are down, the rates paid by the government on small savings are significantly higher than bank deposit rates, as are the effective rates on tax free bonds. I am glad the government has decided to link the rates on small savings to government bond rates, but these rates will continuously have to be examined to ensure they do not form a high floor below which banks cannot cut deposit rates. All in all, bank lending rates have moved down, but not commensurate with policy rate cuts.

The wrong thing to do at such times is to change course. As soon as economic policy becomes painful, clever economists always suggest new unorthodox, painless pathways. This is not a problem specific to emerging markets, but becomes especially acute since every emerging market thinks it is unique, and the laws of economics operate differently here. Flipping through a book of cartoons by that great economist, R.K. Laxman, I found one that indicated the solution for every ill in 1997, when the cartoon was published, as now, is for the RBI to cut interest rates by a hundred basis points. Arguments change, but clever solutions do not.

Decades of studying macroeconomic policy tells me to be very wary of economists who say you can have it all if only you try something out of the box. Argentina, Brazil, and Venezuela tried unorthodox policies with depressingly orthodox consequences. Rather than experiment with macro-policy, which brings macro risks that our unprotected poor can ill afford, better to be unorthodox on microeconomic policy such as those that define the business and banking environment. Not only do we have less chance of doing damage if we go wrong, but innovative policy may open new paths around old bottlenecks. Specifically, on its part the RBI has been adopting more liberal attitudes towards bank licensing, towards financial inclusion, and towards payment technologies and institutions in order to foster growth.

INSTITUTION BUILDING

Let me return to institution building. We had gotten used to decades of moderate to high inflation, with industrialists and governments paying negative real interest rates and the burden of the hidden inflation tax falling on the middle-class saver and the poor. What is happening today is truly revolutionary – we are abandoning the ways of the past that benefited the few at the expense of the many. As we move towards embedding institutions that result in sustained low inflation and positive real interest rates, this requires all constituencies to make adjustments. For example, if industrialists want significantly lower rates, they have to support efforts to improve loan recovery so that banks and bond markets feel comfortable with low credit spreads. The central and state governments have to continue on the path of fiscal consolidation so that they borrow less and thus spend less on interest payments. Households will have to adjust to receiving lower nominal rates on deposits, but must recognize that they are also receiving higher real rates which gives their savings higher purchasing power. They will find it worthwhile to save more to finance the enormous investment needs of the country.

Adjustment is difficult and painful in the short run. We must not get diverted as we build the institutions necessary to secure a low inflation future, especially because we seem to be making headway. The government has taken the momentous step of both setting a CPI-based inflation objective for the RBI as well as a framework for setting up an independent monetary policy committee. In the days ahead, a new Governor, as well as the members of the committee, will be picked. I am sure they will internalize the frameworks and institutions that have been set up, and should produce a low inflation future for India.

The rewards will be many. Our currency has been stable as investors have gained confidence in our monetary policy goals, and this stability will only improve as we meet our inflation goals. Foreign capital inflows will be more reliable and increase in the longer maturity buckets, including in rupee investments. This will expand the pool of capital available for our banks and corporations. The government will be able to borrow at low rates, and will be able to extend the maturity of its debt. The poor will not suffer disproportionately due to bouts of sharp inflation, and the middle class will not see its savings eroded. All this awaits us as we stay the course.

IV

I rarely expressed in public my deeper concern that some of the criticism was from quarters that were motivated by their interests rather than economic logic. But in my last speech on inflation, delivered at the RBI on Statistics Day, 26 July 2016, I wondered why uninformed critics were getting so much air time. An excerpt from that speech follows, which ends welcoming the institutionalization of the fight against inflation. Perhaps, years from now, we will wonder why any of this was worth debating.

Debate without Theory or Evidence

Why is it that as we seem to be bringing inflation under control, public voices to abandon the fight are loud? Why is the debate uninfluenced by the data? I don't know for sure but let me hazard a guess; is it possible the political economy of inflation is different from the received wisdom we were taught in class as students?

Specifically, despite all the political breast-beating about inflation and worries about its pernicious effect on the weaker sections of society, there seems to be surprisingly little public anxiety about inflation so long as it stays in the high single digits. Industrialists welcome negative real rates of interest for obvious reasons – it keeps their cost of funding low. Many middle-class savers value the high nominal interest rates on their fixed deposits, not realizing that their principal is eroding significantly every year. The Keynesian economist is happy because monetary policy is extremely accommodative. The analysts cheer every cut in interest rates, no matter the consequences to inflation, because markets are assumed to have a Pavlovian positive response to rate cuts. Even the poor are inured to their fate of seeing real incomes erode, and are only aggrieved when the price of some food staple skyrockets. Interestingly, short-term spikes in food staples are not really controllable by monetary policy, which then leads to the incorrect generalization that since monetary policy cannot control the politically most important aspects of inflation, it cannot control inflation in general.

With no powerful and vocal political constituency getting agitated about generalized inflation so long as it is only moderately high, opponents of disinflationary policies are free to frame the debate as they wish. The persuasive way is to claim that interest rates are hurting growth. The argument is hard to refute because there is always some sympathetic borrower who is paying seemingly excessive rates. The high prevailing borrowing rate of some small borrower – say 15 per cent today – is held out as Exhibit A of the central bank's inconsiderate policies, never mind that the rate charged includes the policy rate of 6.5 per cent plus an additional spread of 8.5 per cent, consisting of a default risk premium, a term premium, an inflation risk premium, and the commercial bank's compensation for costs, none of which are directly affected by the policy rate.

The press is constantly urged to frame the debate as inflation versus growth, and with inflation still only moderately high, only the excessively conservative central bank could be against growth! Never mind that overly accommodative policy today will set up inflation for the future; never mind that the last forty years of economic theory and practice suggests that the best way central banks can support growth over the medium term is by keeping inflation low and stable.

The reality, of course, is that high inflation is not stable. As we have seen in India's own past, and in other emerging markets, moderately high inflation tends quickly to become very high inflation. The currency then becomes volatile, leading occasionally to external stress. After all, one of the reasons we were termed the Fragile Five in the summer of 2013 was because of our high inflation. Moreover, the saver eventually recognizes that high inflation erodes the value of his financial savings and switches to real assets like gold. Since we do not mine gold in the country, this also puts pressure on the current account.

In sum, the fragilities associated with high inflation accumulate, and eventually could lead to crisis. However, the belief that there is a strong powerful domestic constituency against inflation in India, which was drummed into our heads as students, may be a myth, certainly at moderately high levels of inflation. Without any political push back as inflation rises, what is to ensure macroeconomic stability?

Unlike more authoritarian Asian economies that used severe administrative measures to deal with bouts of high inflation during their growth phase, our democratic structure rightly does not permit such measures. So it is better that we tackle inflation upfront by building the necessary institutions. Perhaps this is why successive governments, in their wisdom, have given the RBI a measure of independence. Certainly, such concerns would support the current government's decision to enshrine its commitment to low inflation through a formal inflation target and the creation of a monetary policy committee.

Postscript: Now that the government has set up a monetary policy committee and given it an inflation target, it would be appropriate for current and future governments to let the appointed experts on the committee decide.

CHAPTER 3

MAKING THE BANKING SECTOR MORE COMPETITIVE

I

The second of the five pillars was to create a more competitive and vibrant banking system. Liberal economists in India though the best way to fix the state-owned portion of the banking system was to privatize it. So long as the public sector banks (PSBs) had an umbilical cord attached to the central government treasury, they would not have the discipline to reform, or so they argued. Others felt that so long as governance in the public sector banking system was improved, there was no need for privatization. Public sector banks could be an important vehicle to implement the government's mandates intended to achieve inclusion and development goals.

My own perspective was somewhere in the middle. I did not believe privatization would be easy or fix the problems of all public sector banks. Perhaps one could start by privatizing one bank and drawing lessons from it – IDBI Bank was often mentioned as a possible candidate because privatization did not require legislative change. Be that as it may, I also felt many of the potential benefits of privatization could be achieved if PSB governance could be improved substantially. At the same time, I did not believe that it was possible to force government mandates only on the public sector banks, especially as the banking sector became increasingly competitive. If the government were, however, to pay banks for carrying out its mandates, there was no reason why private sector banks could not participate. At any rate, knowing that there was little appetite in either the UPA government or the NDA government for the liberal agenda, wholesale privatization was off the table. Within the parameters set by the government, the RBI had to do the best job it could in reforming the banking sector.

In addition to working with the government on PSB reform, my focus was on freeing up entry into the banking system, especially for new banks that might target underserved clients, so that there would be more competition and better service for all customers. In the Annual Day lecture at the Competition Commission of India on 20 May 2014, I got a chance to explain the RBI's strategy. I discussed the two grand bargains that underlay the past, and why that had to change. Many of the possibilities discussed in this speech were later translated into policy action. The work on banking reform was led by a succession of very able deputy governors, Anand Sinha, R. Gandhi, and N.S. Vishwanathan, aided by executive directors of the calibre of B. Mahapatra and Sudarshan Sen.

Competition in the Banking Sector: Opportunities and Challenges

Competition is the life force of a modern economy – it replaces dated and inefficient methods while preserving valuable traditions; it rewards the innovative and energetic and punishes the merely connected; it destroys the stability of the status quo while giving hope to the young and the outsider. True competition eliminates the need for planners, for as gravity guides water through the shortest path, competition naturally guides the economy to the most productive route.

Healthy competition is not just the best way to grow but also the best way to include all citizens; what better way to get needed services to a poor housewife than to encourage providers to compete for her money? What better way to uplift a member of a backward community than for private employers to compete to hire her for a good job?

Healthy growth-inducing inclusive competition does not, however, emerge on its own. Without intervention, we get the competition of the jungle, where the strong prey on the weak. Such competition only encourages a certain kind of winner, one who is adapted to the jungle rather than the world we want to live in. In contrast, healthy competition needs the helping hand of the government; to ensure the playing field is level, that entry barriers are low, that there are reasonable rules of the game and clear enforcement of contracts, and that all participants have the basic capabilities such as education and skills to compete.

Governments have historically found it difficult to ensure such healthy competition because intervention has to be just right. Governments typically are tempted to go beyond intervening to create a fair competitive environment, and instead have turned to determining winners and losers themselves. This typically has not worked out well. With this caveat, the creation of a healthier, more competitive environment in India could be the government's most important contribution to sustainable economic growth in India over the medium term. And the Competition Commission will be a central player in this endeavour. Whether in questioning existing government monopolies or the excessive market power of private players, you will be a key institution in the years to come. And for the sake of our country, I wish you the very best of success.

Today, I want to focus on the coming competitive environment in the banking sector. At the Reserve Bank of India, we have spent a few months thinking about how we see that shaping up, and I want to share that vision with you. My intent here is to further the debate rather than to announce any final decisions.

THE GRAND BARGAINS

The degree of competition in the banking sector in India is best seen as the product of two grand bargains. The first was between successive governments and the banks, whereby banks got privileged access to low-cost demand and time deposits, to the central bank's liquidity facilities, as well as some protection from competition, in return for accepting obligations such as financing the government (through the Statutory Liquidity Ratio or SLR), helping in monetary transmission (through maintaining the Cash Reserve Ratio or CRR), opening branches in unbanked areas and making loans to the priority sector.

The second grand bargain was between the public sector banks (PSBs) and the government, whereby these banks undertook special services and risks for the government, and were compensated in part, by the government standing behind the public sector banks. As India has developed, both these bargains are coming under pressure. And it is development and competition that is breaking them down.

Today, the investment needs of the economy, especially long-term investment in areas like infrastructure, have increased. The government can no longer undertake these investments. Private entrepreneurs have been asked to take them up. To create space for financing these investments, the government has to pre-empt less of the banking system's assets. But the nature of financing required is also changing. Private investment is risky, so there has to be more risk-absorbing financing such as from corporate bond markets and from equity markets. As more sources of financing emerge, not only will banks no longer be able to have a monopoly over financing corporations and households, they will also have to compete for the best clients, who can access domestic and international markets.

Similarly, deposit financing will no longer be as cheap, as banks will have to compete with financial markets and real assets such as housing for the household's savings. As households become more sophisticated, they will be unwilling to leave a lot of money in low-interest-bearing accounts. Of course, households will still be willing to accept low interest rates in return for liquidity. So privileged access to the central bank's liquidity windows will allow banks to offer households these liquidity services safely and get a rent, but this advantage will also become eroded as new payments institutions and technologies emerge.

The first grand bargain – cheap deposits in return for financing the government – is therefore being threatened from both sides. Deposits will not continue to be cheap, while the government cannot continue to pre-empt financing at the scale it has in the past if we are to have a modern entrepreneurial economy. This is yet another reason why fiscal discipline will be central to sustainable growth going forward.

Public sector banks (PSBs) are, if anything, in a worse position than private sector banks, which is why the second bargain is also under threat. As low-risk enterprises migrate to financing from the markets, banks are left both with very large risky infrastructure projects and with lending to small- and medium-sized firms. The alternative to taking these risks is to plunge into very competitive retail lending, so public sector banks may have little option, especially if the government pushes them to lend to infrastructure. Many of the projects being financed today, however, require sophisticated project evaluation skills and careful design of the capital structure. Successful lending requires the lender to act to secure his position at the first sign of trouble, otherwise the slow banker ends up providing the loss cover for more agile bankers, or for unscrupulous promoters. To survive in the changing business of lending, public sector banks need to have strong capabilities, undertake careful project monitoring, and move quickly to rectify problems when necessary.

In the past, PSBs had the best talent. But today, past hiring freezes have decimated their middle-management ranks, and private banks have also poached talented personnel from PSBs. PSBs need to be able to recruit laterally, while retaining the talent they have, but to do so they need to be able to promise employees responsibility as well as the freedom of action. Unfortunately, employee actions in public sector banks are constrained by government rules and second-guessed by vigilance authorities, even while pay is limited. It will be hard for public sector banks to compete for talent. If, in addition, these banks are asked to make sub-optimal decisions in what is deemed the public interest, their performance will suffer more than in the past. This will make it hard for them to raise funds, especially capital. With the government strapped for funds, its ability to support the capital needs of public sector banks as part of the second grand bargain is also coming into question.

We cannot go backwards to revive the two bargains – that means reversing development and bottling the genie of competition, neither of which would be desirable for the economy even if feasible. Instead, the best approach may be to develop the financial sector by increasing competition and variety, even while giving banks, especially public sector banks, a greater ability to compete. Let me be more specific.

INCREASING COMPETITION IN BANKING

The Reserve Bank of India is committed to freeing entry in banking. We just announced two new commercial bank licences after a rigorous vetting process. We are examining this experience, and after making appropriate changes, will announce a more regular process of giving licences – what has been termed licences on tap.

Because of the public's trust in banks and the presence of universal deposit insurance, we have to be careful in giving out the normal commercial bank licences. To be absolutely confident of the capabilities and integrity of applicants, we give licences only to those who have a proven track record and reasonable capital. But what of those who have no track record or no large capital base but do have capabilities? And what of those who see value in doing only one part of the banking business such as payments?

The RBI can take more of a chance with new players if they get the licence to open only a small bank or to conduct only one segment of banking business. Such differentiated licences – licences with restrictions on the geographical reach or the products offered by a new bank – can generate more organizational variety and efficiency. Small banks tend to be better at catering to local needs, including needs of small and medium businesses. A payments bank, which will take deposits and offer payment and remittance services but be constrained to invest all its funds in safe instruments such as government securities, could be very synergistic with other existing services. For example, the proposed Post Bank could start as a payment bank, making use of post office outlets to raise deposits and make payments.

Key in any new structure is that there should be no arbitrage possibilities hurting the current banking system. Today, a commercial bank can convert itself into a payment bank by maintaining 100 per cent SLR margins. Of course, it may not want to, because it seeks to make more money through corporate lending, but this possibility indicates regulations will not favour a payments bank unduly. Some of my colleagues believe a payments bank will be unviable, while others believe that it will skim the cream of banking business away from regular commercial banks. We can debate this issue for a long time, or we can experiment by allowing a few payments banks and monitoring their performance. The RBI proposes to discuss further steps with stakeholders in this regard.

If payments banks are successful, they will allow us to steadily reduce some of the obligations we impose on commercial banks. For instance, as payments banks hold government securities for liquidity purposes, we can reduce the quantity of government securities we ask commercial banks to hold as part of SLR.

While on the issue of bank obligations, there is an area where they do seem to be at a disadvantage vis-à-vis other financial institutions – in the raising and lending of long-term money. This becomes especially important for infrastructure, where banks can be essential in early stage construction financing. Since construction lasts for five to seven years, banks should be able to raise long tenor money for these purposes. But if they raise such money today, they immediately become subject to CRR and SLR requirements, and any lending they do attracts further priority sector obligations. To the extent that banks raise long-term bonds and use it for infrastructure financing, could we relieve them of such obligations? This will immediately put them on par with other financial institutions such as insurance companies and finance companies in funding long-term infrastructure.

The priority sector obligation will probably be necessary for some more time in a developing country like ours, though we need to deliberate more on what sectors should constitute priority as the economy develops. But even without entering this potentially contentious debate, can we allow banks to fulfil existing norms more efficiently? For instance, if one bank is more efficient at rural lending, can it over-achieve its obligations and then 'sell' its excess to another bank that is an underachiever? We are examining such possibilities.

Finally, we have had only limited success in achieving inclusion when it is seen as a mandate. Banks sometimes open branches in remote areas but the officers that staff them do not really reach out to the local population; banks open no-frills accounts but many lie dormant... The reality is that if the mandate is unprofitable, banks will find ways to avoid them. Not all forms of inclusion can be made profitable, but we should give banks the freedom to try new approaches, perhaps drawing in other institutions that can traverse the last mile to the underserved where necessary. The RBI will come out with new relaxations on business correspondents shortly. Also, some of the entities that become payments banks may be very well suited to support or substitute commercial banks in reaching remote areas.

In sum, then, we can increase competition in the banking sector while, at the same time, strengthening banks by reducing the burden of obligations on them. In this way, they will be able to contribute to sustainable growth even after the breakdown of the first grand bargain.

FREEING PUBLIC SECTOR BANKS TO COMPETE

Let us turn next to the public sector banks. There are well-managed public sector banks across the world, and even in India today. So privatization is not necessary to improve the competitiveness of the public sector. But a change in governance, management, and operational and compensation flexibility are almost surely needed in India to improve the functioning of most PSBs, as the Dr P.J. Nayak Committee has just reiterated.

A number of eminently practicable suggestions have been made to reform PSBs, such as creating a holding company to hold government PSB shares, increasing the length of PSB CEO tenures, breaking up the position of Chairman and CEO, bringing more independent professionals on bank boards and empowering boards with the task of selecting the CEO, becoming more selective in cases that are followed up for vigilance investigations...

We need to examine all these ideas carefully, many of which will help give public sector banks the flexibility to compete in the new environment. Let us remember that what is at stake is not just the tremendous amount of national value that is represented by public sector banks but future financing and investment in our economy.

If public sector banks become competitive, and especially if they do so by distancing themselves from the influence of the government without sacrificing their 'public' character, they will be able to raise money much more easily from the markets. Indeed, the better performers will be able to raise more, unlike the current situation where the not-so-good performers have a greater call on the public purse. Competition will improve efficiency. The second grand bargain will also become irrelevant.

CONCLUSION

The banking sector is on the cusp of revolutionary change. In the next few years, I hope we will see a much more varied set of banking institutions using information and technology to their fullest, a healthy public sector banking system, distant from government influence but not from the public purpose, and deep and liquid financial markets that will not only compete with, but also support, the banks. Such a vision is not just a possibility, it is a necessity if we are to finance the enormous needs of the real economy. As India resumes its path to strong and sustainable growth, it is the RBI's firm conviction that the Indian banking sector will be a supportive partner every inch of the way.

II

At the FICCI-IBA Annual Banking Conference on 16 August 2016, I went over some of the reforms we had introduced. As we will see, bankers had become focused on cleaning up the bad debt on their books. While this was important, I urged the banking sector to look ahead, beyond the problems of bad debts, to focusing on growth. I addressed, once again, the challenges faced by Public Sector Banks, and what they needed to do.

Interesting, Profitable, and Challenging: Banking in India Today

These are interesting, profitable, and challenging times for the financial sector. Interesting because the level of competition is going to increase manifold, both for customers as well as for talent, transforming even the sleepiest areas in financial services. Profitable because new technologies, information, and new techniques will open up vastly new business opportunities and customers. Challenging because competition and novelty constitute a particularly volatile mix in terms of risk. In this talk, I will speak about how we see these aspects at the central bank.

INTERESTING AND PROFITABLE

Over the next year, seventeen new niche banks will begin business. In addition, licensing for universal banks is now on tap, so fit and proper applicants with innovative business plans and good track records will enter. Fintech will throw up a variety of new ways of accessing the customer and serving her, so new institutions

57

that we have little awareness of today will soon be a source of competition. These will finally draw customer sectors, firms, and individuals without access today into the formal financial system. Those customers that are already being served will be spoiled for choice.

For the service provider, even though greater competition will tend to reduce spreads, new customers and new needs will increase volumes. Moreover, risk and cost reduction through information technology and risk management techniques will tend to increase effective risk-adjusted spreads. In sum then, despite increased competition, profitability can increase. The comparative advantage of banks may lie in their access to lower cost deposit financing, the data they have on customers, the reach of their network, their ability to manage and warehouse risks, and their ability to access liquidity from the central bank. These should then be the basis for the products they focus on.

Perhaps a couple of examples would be useful. India will have enormous project financing needs in the coming days. Even though bankers are very risk averse today, and few projects are coming up for financing, this will change soon. What is in the pipeline is truly enormous – airports, railway lines, power plants, roads, manufacturing plants, etc. Bankers will remember the period of irrational exuberance in 2007-08 when they lent without asking too many questions. I am hopeful that this time will be different.

Here are ways it can be different and risks lowered. First, significantly more in-house expertise can be brought to project evaluation, including understanding demand projections for the project's output, likely competition, and the expertise and reliability of the promoter. Bankers will have to develop industry knowledge in key areas since consultants can be biased.

Second, real risks have to be mitigated where possible, and shared where not. Real risk mitigation requires ensuring that key permissions for land acquisition and construction are in place upfront, while key inputs and customers are tied up through purchase agreements. Where these risks cannot be mitigated, they should be shared contractually between the promoter and financiers, or a transparent arbitration system agreed upon. So, for instance, if demand falls below projections, perhaps an agreement among promoters and financiers can indicate when new equity will be brought in and by whom.

This leads to the third element of project structuring – an appropriately flexible capital structure. The capital structure has to be related to residual risks of the project. The more the risks, the more the equity component should be (genuine promoter equity, not fake borrowed equity, of course), and the greater the flexibility in the debt structure. Promoters should be incentivized to deliver, with significant rewards for on-time execution and debt repayment. Where possible, corporate debt markets, either through direct issues or securitized project loan portfolios, should be used to absorb some of the initial project risk. More such arm's length debt should typically refinance bank debt when construction is over. Some of the measures taken to strengthen corporate debt markets, including the new bankruptcy code, should make all this possible.

Fourth, financiers should put in a robust system of project monitoring and appraisal, including, where possible, careful real-time monitoring of costs. For example, can project input costs be monitored and compared with comparable inputs elsewhere using IT, so that suspicious transactions suggesting over-invoicing are flagged?

And finally, the incentive structure for bankers should be worked out so that they evaluate, design, and monitor projects carefully, and get significant rewards if these work out. This means that even while committees may take the final loan decision, some senior banker ought to put her name on the proposal, taking responsibility for recommending the loan. IT systems within banks should be able to pull up overall performance records of loans recommended by individual bankers easily, and this should be an input into their promotion.

Note that none of this is really futuristic, but it requires a much stronger marriage between information technology and financial engineering, with an important role for practical industry knowledge and incentive design. There are also inputs to making project loans more profitable – such as the availability of Current and Savings Accounts deposits – that will accrue to the banks that build out their IT to access and serve the broader saver cheaply and effectively. Few banks have the in-house talent to do all this now, but preparation is imperative.

An area of more intensive use of IT and analysis is customer loans, which is my second example. It seems today that, having abandoned project loans, every bank is targeting the retail customer. Clearly, the risks in this herding will mount over time, as banks compete for less and less creditworthy customers. But some of this risk can be mitigated if they do sufficient due diligence.

New means of credit evaluation are emerging. For example, some lenders are examining not just credit histories from the credit bureau but mining their own data and also data from social media posts by the applicant to see how reliable they might be. Various forms of crowdfunding, intermediated by peer-to-peer lenders, also claim superior credit evaluation. Of course, much of the hoopla surrounding these new forms of lending has yet to be tested by a serious downturn, and it is unclear how responsibilities for recovery will devolve between intermediary and investor at such times.

Nevertheless, in this Information Age, not only are there more data with which to determine a loan applicant's creditworthiness, it is also possible to track their behaviour for early warning signs of stress. Furthermore, in this interconnected world, a borrower's inability to hide adverse information such as default when tagged by a unique ID constitutes a big incentive to repay.

Importantly, banks no longer have a monopoly over all credit-related data; some IT companies may do a better job in pulling together even the bank's data, in addition to trawling for other available data, and analysing it all to make better lending and monitoring decisions. Loan applications and decisions are now being made entirely online, without a borrower having to step into a branch. Alliances between IT companies and banks are likely to increase significantly.

The bottom line is that competition is increasing, and ways of delivering financial services are changing tremendously. Banks have to discover strategies to use their traditional, although eroding, advantages such as convenience, information, and trust to remain on the competitive frontier. Competition and innovation constitute a particularly volatile mix in terms of risk challenging banks' traditional risk management capabilities. They are also a challenge to the regulator, who wants the best for the customer (and therefore wants to encourage competition and experimentation), while maintaining systemic stability (and thus wants to understand risks before they get too large or widespread).

THE AUTHORITIES' DILEMMA

Before turning to how the banks should respond to these competitive and technological forces, let us ask how these forces affect the regulatory compact. Ideally, the authorities should ensure their actions are institution, ownership, and technology neutral so as to ensure that the most efficient customer-oriented solutions emerge through competition. However, if the authorities deliberately skew the playing field towards some category of institutions and away from others, competition may not produce the most efficient outcome.

Banks in India have been subject to the grand bargain, whereby they get the benefits of raising low-cost insured deposits, liquidity support and close regulation by the central bank (I am sure some of you see this as a cost) in return for maintaining reserves with the central bank, holding government bonds to meet SLR requirements, and lending to the priority sector.

In addition, public sector banks are further subject to government mandates such as opening PMJDY accounts, or making MUDRA loans [*Author's note: These were loans to small and medium enterprises*]. They are also subject to hiring mandates, in particular the need to hire through open all-India exams rather than from specific campuses or from the local community, and to meet various government diversity mandates. In part compensation, public sector banks do get more government deposits and business, and are backed by the full faith and credit of the government. While it is unclear whether the cost of the mandates outweigh the benefits, they do skew the competitive landscape.

Authorities like the central bank and the government should, over the medium term, reduce the differences in regulatory treatment between public sector banks and private sector banks, and more generally, between banks and other financial institutions.

Some of the differences between public sector banks and private banks can be mitigated if the government pays an adequate price for mandates. If, for example, when every direct benefit transfer is paid a remunerative price, all banks have an incentive to undertake the business and open basic customer accounts. The most efficient bank will garner more business, and the payment can be gradually reduced over time, commensurate with the accrued efficiencies.

Some of the mandates will also become less costly with new techniques. For example, banks are finding ways to make MSME loans more remunerative by decreasing transactions costs. Similar techniques could be brought to agricultural loans, especially as farm productivity increases. Wider use of credit information bureaus and collateral registries should also help improve credit evaluation and lower the cost of repossession. This should make it easier to meet priority sector norms. The cost has been further reduced through the introduction of tradeable priority sector lending certificates, whereby the most efficient lenders can sell their over-performance, while the inefficient ones can compensate for underperformance by buying certificates.

Nevertheless, over time, differences should be reduced further. This is why, for example, the Reserve Bank has been reducing Statutory Liquidity Ratio requirements steadily, and allowed over half of the SLR holdings to meet the Basel-mandated Liquidity Coverage Ratio. But we are also trying to shape mandates to new technologies and approaches. For example, it is mandated that a quarter of a bank's branches should be opened in underserved areas. But what exactly qualifies as a branch? Could we accept alternative definitions of a branch so long as they meet the needs of the population for a regular outlet for banking business? Of course, all villages would love to have a full service brick and mortar bank branch. However, if the cost is currently prohibitive, can we accept alternatives that do much of what is needed? An internal RBI committee is looking at these issues.

In sum, mandates should increasingly be paid for, and are becoming easier to achieve as the institutional and technological underpinnings of financial services improve. As competition increases, however, the authorities should ask how long mandates should continue, and keep targeting them better towards the truly underserved. They should also withdraw any preferential treatment, to the extent feasible, at a commensurate pace.

Let me now turn to how banks respond to the emerging competitive challenges. I will talk specifically about public sector banks, which perhaps face the greatest challenges.

CHALLENGES FACED BY PUBLIC SECTOR BANKS

The most pressing task for public sector banks is to clean up their balance sheets, a process which is well under way. A parallel task is to improve their governance and management. Equally important is to fill out the ranks of middle management that have been thinned out by retirements, and to recruit talent with expertise in project evaluation, risk management, and IT, including cyber security.

(i) Governance

The Bank Board Bureau (BBB), composed of eminent personalities with integrity and domain experience, has taken over part of the appointments process in public sector banks. There are two ways the government still plays a role. First, the final decision on appointments is taken by the Appointments Committee of the Cabinet. Second, appointments of non-official directors onto bank boards still lie outside the BBB. As the BBB gains experience, it would make sense to allow these decisions also to be taken by it.

Over time, as the bank boards are professionalized, executive appointment decisions should devolve from the BBB to the boards themselves, while the BBB – as it transforms into the Bank Investment Company (BIC), the custodian for the government's stake in banks – should focus only on appointing directors to represent the government stake on the bank boards. It is important that bank boards be freed to determine their strategies. Too much coaching by central authorities will lead to a sameness in public sector banks that successive Gyan Sangams [*Author's note: An annual government conference to deliberate public sector bank strategy*] have criticized.

Management efforts to tighten practices are also needed. Far too many loans are done without adequate due diligence and without adequate follow up. Collateral when offered is not perfected, assets given under personal guarantees not tracked, and post-loan monitoring of the account can be lax. The lessons of the recent past should be taken seriously, and management practices tightened. A more stringent approach to evaluating and recovering large loans will give bank management the credibility when they go to their staff with plans for cost rationalization.

(ii) Talent

The middle-management ranks of public sector banks are being thinned by retirements. In addition, they need experts in specific areas like project evaluation and risk management. At the same time, banks have to reduce bloated cost structures. All public sector entities across the world tend to pay more than the private sector to lower level employees, and less than the private sector to higher level employees. This makes it hard for them to attract top talent, but makes it easier to attract good people at lower levels.

Rather than seeing these as difficulties, perhaps they can be opportunities. In the RBI, we find that our compensation packages enable us to attract very highly qualified applicants at the Class III level. Perhaps part of the solution is to enable such new hires, with technology and training, to do far more responsible work than they were given in the past, and give them a brighter prospect of movement up the officer ranks. Banks can also use the opportunity offered by retirements to reorient hiring towards the skills they need, and to offer attractive rapid career progression supported by strong training programmes to new hires – with thinning middle management, the mix of experience and capabilities should shift towards capabilities.

And to get talent in specialized areas like project evaluation, risk management, and IT, they may have to hire laterally in small doses. While contractual hires are currently permitted, better personnel would be attracted only by a strong prospect of career progression internally. Banks will have to think about how to enable this.

One of the difficulties public sector banks have is court judgments that prohibit hiring from specific campuses. This leads to anomalies like the public-sector-bank-supported National Institute of Bank Management sending most of its high quality graduates to work for private sector banks. Public sector banks can petition the courts to allow some modicum of campus hire, especially when the campus chooses openly through a national exam. Another alternative is to make bank entrance exams much less onerous to take, with applications, tests, and results, wherever possible, available quickly and online. The banks then have an easier task of persuading students on elite campuses to take the exam. We are following this latter course at the RBI.

To have local information, be comfortable with local culture, be locally accepted, and be competitive in low-cost rural areas, PSBs will have to have more freedom to hire locally, and pay wages commensurate with the local labour market. Alternatively, they will have to be much more effective in using technology to reduce costs. Finally, as banks adopted differentiated strategies, they should move away from common compensation structures and common promotion schemes across all public sector banks.

While one of the strengths of the public sector sometimes is the absence of pay and promotion that is very sensitive to performance, too little sensitivity can also be a problem as high performers get demotivated, and the slothful are not penalized. An increased emphasis on performance evaluation, including identifying low performers with the intent of helping them improve, may be warranted. In addition, rewards like Employee Stock Ownership Plans (ESOPs) that give all employees a stake in the future of the bank may be helpful. With PSB shares trading at such low levels, a small allocation to employees today may be a strong source of motivation, and can be a large source of wealth as performance improves.

(iii) Customers

Public sector banks enjoy trust with customers. An emphasis on customer service and customer-centric advice may allow them to recapture low-cost customer deposits that are migrating elsewhere. Public sector banks should take the lead in emphasizing the RBI's five-point Charter of Consumer Rights. While it is understandable that with stressed balance sheets public sector banks do not want to make too many loans to sectors in difficulty, it is less clear why their deposit growth is faltering, for the low-cost deposit franchise will be the key to their future success.

(iv) Structure

Some banks may be best off focusing on local activity, and in effect, becoming small finance banks. Others may be best off merging with other banks so as to obtain scale and geographic diversification. As banks get cleaned up, and their boards are strengthened, their boards should focus on appropriate structure as part of an overall rethink on strategy.

None of these changes are easy, but they are also not impossible. It requires work with the unions, persuading them of the need for change that benefits all, especially the long-term future of the bank. Since each bank has different challenges and probably different solutions, as these solutions emerge it may also be the occasion to rethink the collective bargaining approach across the public sector bank universe that now prevails.

BACK TO THE AUTHORITIES

Today, a variety of authorities – Parliament, the Department of Financial Services, the Bank Board Bureau, the board of the bank, the vigilance authorities, and of course various regulators and supervisors including the RBI – monitor the performance of the public sector banks. With so many overlapping constituencies to satisfy, it is a wonder that bank management has time to devote to the management of the bank. It is important that we streamline and reduce the overlaps between the jurisdictions of the authorities, and specify clear triggers or situations where one authority's oversight is invoked.

In particular, we have to move much of the governance to the bank's board, with the government exercising its control through its board representatives (chosen by the BBB), keeping in mind the best interests of the bank and the interests of minority shareholders. Wherever possible, public sector bank boards should be bound by the same rules as private sector bank boards – one reason why the RBI has recently withdrawn the Calendar of Reviews PSBs were asked to follow. Similarly, board membership of public sector banks should pay as well as private sector banks if they are to attract decent talent.

As boards take decisions, the Department of Financial Services could move to (i) a programme role: for example, ensuring government programmes such as PMJDY are well designed, appropriately remunerated to banks, and progress monitored (ii) a coordinating role: for example, ensuring financial institutions join a common KYC registry and (iii) a developmental role: revitalizing institutions like the Debt Recovery Tribunals through appropriate legislation. The RBI would perform a purely regulatory role, and withdraw its representatives on bank boards – this will require legislative change. Over time, the RBI should also empower boards more, for instance, offering broad guidelines on compensation to boards but not requiring every top compensation package be approved.

Given strong oversight from the bank's board, the CVC and CAG would get involved only in extraordinary situations where there is evidence of malfeasance, and not when legitimate business judgment has gone wrong.

I have focused on the challenges public sector banks face meeting the new competitive environment, as well as some possible solutions. These should be viewed as opening a discussion rather than the formal views of the RBI. That I have not discussed the challenges private banks will face is not because I think they are perfectly positioned but because they are not as constrained as the public sector banks. But before I end, let me emphasize an immediate area of action for all.

With changes in technology, cyber security, both at the bank level and at the system level, has become very important. I think it would be overly complacent for anyone of us to say we are well prepared to meet all cyber threats. A chilling statement by an IT expert is 'We have all been hacked, the only question is whether you know it or you don't'. While the statement may be alarmist, it is an antidote to complacency. We all have to examine our security culture. Too many access points are left unmonitored, too many people share passwords or have easily penetrated passwords, too little surveillance is maintained of vendors and the software they create. The RBI is working on upgrading the capabilities of its inspectors to undertake bank system audit as well as to detect vulnerabilities in them. The RBI is also in the process of setting up an IT subsidiary, which will be able to recruit directly from industry, and will give the Reserve Bank better ability to manage and supervise technology. I would urge all of you to take a fresh look at your systems, and more important, of the cyber culture within your bank.

Postscript: Many of the suggestions in this speech are still relevant. In particular, the governance of public sector banks can be improved only when the government distances itself fully from the banks, creates a transparent and professionalized process for appointing its directors on the boards (not dominated by governing party favourites or current or retired government bureaucrats), and allows bank boards both autonomy as well as accountability in picking and compensating bank management. Unless public sector banks are run like normal corporations, they will not be competitive in the medium term. I have a simple metric of progress here: We will have moved significantly towards limiting interference in public sector banks when the Department of Financial Services (which oversees public sector financial firms) is finally closed down, and its banking functions taken over by bank boards and the Bank Board Bureau.

CHAPTER 4

BROADENING AND DEEPENING MARKETS

I

As we gained confidence that the volatility engendered by the 'Taper Tantrum' in summer 2013 would not re-emerge, we could focus on broadening and deepening our debt, derivatives, and exchange markets. Once again, liberal economists wanted a 'big bang' removal of all constraints on market participation. This was all very well in an economy that had well-functioning institutions such as a bankruptcy procedure, so that those who took excessive risks would get their just deserts. In an economy where such institutions were in the process of being developed, a 'big bang' reform entailed uncertain benefits and likely costs. I preferred to follow the RBI's traditional course of steady liberalization, only asking questions of my colleagues continually of what the rationale behind rules were, and urging them to up the pace of change.

In these reforms, Deputy Governor H.R. Khan was a pillar of strength, both with his intimate knowledge of the markets, and with his determination that the RBI needed to liberalize steadily. Executive Directors like G. Padmanabhan, Chandan Sinha, G. Mahalingam, Rajeshwar Rao, and R. Kanungo provided strong support. A speech to the Foreign Exchange Dealers Association of India (FEDAI) on 26 August 2016 summarizes our thinking and what we did.

Strengthening Our Debt Markets

I want to speak today about debt markets and associated derivatives; why we need them to be deep and liquid, why, in addition to central and state governments, we need riskier firms and projects to be able to access the bond markets for funds, why we need to encourage product innovation, and finally the dilemmas that regulators like the RBI face. In the process, I hope to touch on some of our recent successes, as well as failures, and our ambitions for the future.

There are three important reasons why debt markets have become a lot more attractive in recent months. First, we finally have a framework that commits us to low and stable inflation. Yes, July's inflation reading was a high 6.07 per cent, but I have no doubt that inflation will fall in the months ahead. The key point is that market participants know that the Monetary Policy Committee has to maintain low and stable inflation, certainly over the next five years for which its remit has been set, and it will do what it takes. This lowers the inflation risk premium, and thus reduces the nominal fixed interest rate for everyone, from the government to the riskiest borrower. In this regard, I am confident that Dr Urjit Patel, who has worked closely with me on monetary policy for the last three years, will ably guide the Monetary Policy Committee going forward in achieving our inflation objectives.

A second development has been the reluctance of public sector banks (PSBs) to lend, and together with private sector banks, the reluctance to fully pass through past policy rate cuts into bank lending rates. Short-term market rates, however, have seen full pass-through. No wonder highly rated firms are bypassing banks to borrow from the commercial paper (CP) markets, with outstanding commercial paper having more than doubled in the last two years to over 3 lakh crores.

But what of lower rated firms? Unfortunately, the difficulty of debt recovery in India has meant that credit spreads are wider than elsewhere. This is where the third notable development comes in. Recent reforms of the Securitization and Reconstruction of

Financial Assets and Enforcement of Security Interest (SARFAESI) Act and Debt Recovery Tribunals as well as the new Bankruptcy Code will help enhance the prospects of repayment, thus reducing credit spreads.

Given these developments, what should the objectives of fixed income market regulation be?

THE OBJECTIVES OF MARKET REGULATION

As a developing country regulator, the RBI is focused on enhancing growth while maintaining stability. In the past, this has meant that the RBI has moved cautiously on liberalizing fixed income and derivatives markets. What is there about these markets for central banks to worry about?

Typically, three issues. We have always worried that markets attract speculators, and that in thin markets, the speculative element can move market prices away from fundamentals. This is certainly a concern, but we should also remember that not all speculators think the same way. So long as there is no concerted move to manipulate markets (and this concerted manipulation can be prevented by regulation), the varied opinions of speculators can provide liquidity, which in turn can make the markets more immune to manipulation. In other words, excessive fear of speculation in markets is self-fulfilling – it renders markets illiquid and prone to manipulation.

Second, markets can be a source of competition for established institutional players. For instance, as I noted above, high quality corporate credits can migrate from banks to debt markets. This may push banks into higher risk lending. Once again, there is merit in these concerns. However, too much can also be made of them. After all, banks are supposed to lend to riskier clients that need monitoring and hand-holding, while markets are supposed to lend to clients who do not need such attention. Moreover, the problem in India is too much risk ends up on bank balance sheets, either directly or indirectly. For example, Non-Bank Finance Companies (NBFCs) are supposed to take on greater risk, such as loans to real estate developers, because their liabilities are longer term. In actuality, though, many have substantial borrowings from banks. It would be better from the perspective of systemic risk if they replaced bank financing with market borrowing. More generally, some of the very large single and group exposures of banks should be brought down by forcing large borrowers to raise more market financing.

Third, we worry about unbridled innovation that attempts to get around prudential and supervisory norms and ends up creating uncertain valuations and systemic risk. For instance, the fixed income products and derivatives structured around housing mortgage pools in the United States became hard to value as house prices turned down. This was a primary factor in the Global Financial Crisis. Once again, though, financial innovation has been useful in opening credit to the hitherto underserved – the unfortunately named 'junk' bonds have indeed facilitated the growth of a variety of enterprises and sectors, most recently shale oil. While regulators have to weigh carefully the benefits versus the systemic risks posed by every new product, we cannot simply ban all innovation just because it makes us feel safer.

The broader point is that a measured and well-signalled liberalization of fixed income and derivative markets will probably allow us to reap the benefits of deeper and more liquid markets, while minimizing the risks associated with speculation, competition, and innovation. Over the last few years, we have had to proceed somewhat cautiously on market development because we worried about creating vulnerabilities when global financial markets were fragile. But as macroeconomic stability has strengthened, the movement has always been forward. Yesterday's announcements of additional market reforms were simply the next steps in steady, measured liberalization. Let me explain.

PARTICIPATION

Greater participation adds liquidity. Over the years, we have tried to enhance participation.

Most recently, even though retail investors form a small part of the global fixed income market, we are working to enhance their access to the institution-dominated screen-based NDS-OM market [*Author's note: A market for government bonds hosted by the RBI*] so that they can trade government securities, and also so that they can use their de-materialized accounts to do so. However, in markets that require sophisticated understanding, such as complex derivatives, we continue to be careful about broadening retail access.

We can be more relaxed about institutional participation. Foreign Portfolio Investors (FPIs) will now have direct access to a variety of markets including NDS-OM , corporate bond trading and perhaps other market segments going forward.

One reason we limited institutional participation in the past was to prevent speculation. So, for example, we required participants to be long an underlying exchange asset, say dollars, in order for them to take a short position in financial markets, and vice-versa. But sometimes the volume of importers hedging prospective imports by buying dollars forward far outweighs the volume of exporters, who hedge future receipts by selling dollars forward. To satisfy the net demand for forward dollar hedging, typically banks have taken the other side. However, to ensure bank stability, we have limited the extent of open positions that banks can hold.

There is a cost to these limits. Every time the market gets imbalanced, exchange rates have to move substantially to equalize temporary imbalances between demand and supply, even if unwarranted by medium-term fundamentals. This puts more pressure on the central bank to intervene.

We can certainly increase bank open position limits, and will do so over time, but it would not be prudent to place all the exchange risk on banks. A better option would be to allow more players to hold open positions without an underlying, with some limits so that we do not get excessive speculation or attempts at manipulation by single traders. This can rectify market imbalances, improving exchange market liquidity and depth, without imposing large demands on banks or on the RBI. The RBI took a fundamental step in this direction yesterday by allowing a moderate open position to all market participants. Based on experience, the RBI will decide further moves.

Finally, not all participation adds to liquidity and depth in Indian markets. For example, some foreign organizations have suggested allowing trading of domestically issued Indian securities abroad, only reporting the trades domestically. Unfortunately, this could subtract trading on Indian exchanges, and thereby diminish liquidity. We have suggested to such organizations that they either conduct their trades on the Indian exchanges, or that they direct their clients to Masala bonds [*Author's note: These are rupee-denominated bonds issued in foreign locales that are discussed later in the speech*]. The former is still under discussion.

INNOVATION

Financial innovation is sometimes seen in a bleak light as a way to evade or avoid taxes and regulations. Properly done, however, financial innovation can slice and dice risks so that they are placed on the right shoulders. One example of such an instrument is interest rate futures, where after an overhaul in 2013-14, the last twelve months' average daily trading volume was close to Rs 23 billion (despite falling in recent months). An investor, bank, or corporation can use the IRF market to gain or shed interest exposures as they desire. The key to the success of this market has been to allow the design of the relevant instrument to be governed by market participants, while ensuring regulatory concerns are satisfied. We are proceeding in a similar way with money market futures contracts.

Not all innovative instruments have been successful. Inflation Indexed Bonds (IIBs) tied to the Wholesale Price Index (WPI) have not been very popular because the RBI has moved away from a focus on the WPI to a focus on CPI. Even the market for CPI indexed IIBs has been lukewarm. The moderate investor interest perhaps reflects the disinflationary environment, where inflation protection is less sought after. Also, unlike the more tax-protected Gold Monetization Bonds, the CPI indexed IIBs are not fully tax protected against inflation. Going forward, a level playing field on taxes is warranted for all instruments, so that instruments do not gain favour simply because they get better tax treatment.

The lesson from these examples is that financial innovation needs support, not to create tax or regulatory arbitrage, but so that appealing features are encouraged. Innovation also requires tinkering, to modify what does not work until something more appealing can be found – the first versions of Interest Rate Futures were not attractive, but later versions have succeeded. This is why the RBI has moved to a sandbox approach, where we are liberal towards early product innovations so long as they are not clearly problematic, regulating more carefully only when interest picks up and the product looks like it might become of systemic importance.

Finally, an important function for the regulator in encouraging financial innovation is to create the necessary infrastructure. For instance, a number of financial contracts are structured off benchmarks. RBI has encouraged the setting up of the Financial Benchmarks India Pvt. Ltd which is building a series of market benchmarks. I am hopeful that these will soon be used in innovative financial contracts.

INTERNATIONALIZATION

As a current account deficit country, India needs financing from abroad. Ideally, we would like to attract risk capital, which is in short supply in this country. This means encouraging Foreign Direct Investment, as well as equity investment. Foreign investors can also help deepen debt and derivative markets as they contribute to price discovery and liquidity.

Not all domestic entities should issue claims held by foreign investors. Ideally, of course, companies should be left to make decisions about what currency they borrow in, and how much they hedge, but given our weak bankruptcy system, there is moral hazard built into unhedged foreign borrowing – if the rupee appreciates, the promoter takes all the upside associated with paying the low dollar interest rate and the now-lower principal, if the rupee depreciates, the occasional unscrupulous promoter goes to his Indian bankers and asks them to bail him out. This is why the issuance of short-term dollar or yen-denominated debt by infrastructure companies, if left unhedged, could be severely problematic in case of rupee depreciation.

Therefore, we have encouraged companies that do not have foreign exchange earnings to either issue long-term dollar bonds, fully hedged shorter term bonds, or rupee-denominated Masala bonds abroad. The first issues recently of Masala Bonds reflect a coming of age of Indian debt that has been insufficiently remarked upon – for the first time in recent decades, the rupee's value is trusted enough in international markets that corporations can issue there in domestic currency. Going forward, we hope a more vibrant Masala bond market abroad will complement a vibrant domestic corporate bond market.

Even though FDI flows are enough to cover our current account deficit, we are also encouraging inflows into the debt markets to improve depth and liquidity. We have progressively expanded FPI limits in government debt, and recently specified how these limits will expand for the foreseeable future. We have also opened up investment in state government debt, and laid out the medium-term plan for those limits also. In general, our aim is to liberalize steadily, but in a thoughtful way, continuously asking how further liberalization will strengthen our domestic markets.

We have not been persuaded by every market plea. For example, a number of investment banks want a dollar-denominated G-Sec issued internationally – ostensibly to create a benchmark dollar yield curve for Indian instruments. While I agree such an instrument would be attractive for investors in the yield-starved world, I am not persuaded it is useful for India. When much of the emerging world would love to move from issuing dollar debt to issuing in its own currency so as to avoid currency risk, I don't see why we should move the other way. Instead, let us build out an international quasi-sovereign rupee yield curve, so that rupee issuances can be priced easily. It is with this in mind that we have allowed banks to issue Masala bonds yesterday, with bank bonds being a good quasi-sovereign proxy.

LIQUIDITY

Of course, not all parts of the rupee yield curve are liquid, even in the domestic G-Sec market. At the very short end, we are trying to bring more liquidity and better pricing through the auctioning of term repos. At the longer end, we have been trying to focus on more illiquid securities in our open market operations so that the term curve evens out. We are also proposing to encourage market making in specific G-Sec instruments by involving primary dealers.

One way to bring liquidity to corporate debt is to enable them to be used as collateral in repo transactions with the central bank, with appropriate haircuts, of course. As banks become able to borrow against their high quality corporate bonds, yields will fall, and more issuers will come to the market. With this in mind, we have initiated the process with the government to amend the RBI Act to allow the RBI to conduct repos of corporate bonds with banks and other financial institutions.

RATINGS, CONTINGENT SUPPORT, AND SUPPLY

The ratings put out by credit rating agencies are important in assuring arm's length investors about corporate credit quality. In order for their ratings to be accurate, agencies need both up-to-date information, as well as good analysis. Agencies have asked the RBI to give them information about corporate bank borrowings. Since these are available from the credit information bureaus (CIBs), the RBI has suggested the credit-rating agencies become members of CIBs. I do hope that incidents where a highly rated corporate bond plummets without warning into default will become increasingly rare as rating agencies exercise due diligence.

Some have argued that the easy access to bank cash credit keeps large corporations from going to the money and bond markets for funds. This phenomenon also raises bank exposures to single names or groups, increasing their risk concentration. While, as suggested earlier, we are seeing some movement of corporations to the money and bond markets in this period of bank stress, we will nudge corporations further by imposing higher provisioning and capital requirements for banks on such corporate lending when exposures become large.

Many of the measures proposed so far will enhance the attractiveness of highly rated corporate bonds to investors. But infrastructure projects that need substantial amounts of financing may not start out highly rated. To enable such entities to issue, we have allowed banks to offer credit enhancement to such bonds. We have been careful to set the capital requirement for such credit enhancement commensurate with the risk banks are taking on so that there is no arbitrage. Yesterday's announced measures should make it easier for banks to offer appropriate amounts of credit enhancement.

One area that needs greater clarification is obligations of state governments as well as state-government guaranteed obligations. In order for state government obligations to have zero risk weight, and have the highest rating, it is important that there be no explicit or implicit default or restructuring of such obligations. While a restructuring may seem like a way to postpone obligations, its ramifications, not just for the yield the market will demand of the particular state government issuer in the future but also for the yields on obligations of other state governments, are large enough that such actions should continue to remain 'unthinkable'.

REGULATIONS

We are conscious of the limitations placed on netting of derivative contracts, and thus the higher associated capital requirements on banks. The issue has been taken up with the government, and we hope to amend the RBI Act to make such netting possible. As with the tax issues associated with securitization, which have recently been addressed by the government, resolving this issue should lead to substantial market activity.

Finally, while the RBI is a liberalizer, we have to be careful not to relax prudential regulations simply because an entity or activity is deemed of national importance. Dispensation on prudential regulation is the wrong instrument to favour such activities. A nationally important activity such as infrastructure may be very risky. To require lower provisions, or to allow higher leverage or ECBs for such activities, may increase systemic risk. In the long run, the activity may be damaged by the regulatory dispensation (too many infrastructure projects that do not have dollar earnings will be financed with dollar or yen loans and cannot repay) and stability may also be compromised. It is far better for the government to directly subsidize such activities if it deems them important than for the RBI to sacrifice systemic stability on the altar of national importance.

CONCLUSION

Let me conclude. While the RBI has been cautious in reforming during the recent period of global market turmoil, it has not stood still. Market reforms have proceeded at a steady measured pace. Observers may be impatient, but my belief is that steady and irreversible reform and 'mini Bangs' like yesterday's rather than 'Big Bang' is the need of the hour. As global conditions become less uncertain, the pace of reform can pick up. The lessons we have learnt during this period on what works will be invaluable then.

CHAPTER 5

FINANCIAL INCLUSION

I

Financial inclusion was the fourth pillar of our strategy. I believed it was critical for sustainable growth, as is clear in the speeches I gave on the political economy of our development (reproduced later). In the Gadgil Lecture delivered on 13 February 2014, I set out some of what we intended to do, based on the Dr Nachiket Mor Committee report, which had just been submitted to the RBI.

Financial Inclusion: Technology, Institutions and Policies

The Dr Nachiket Mor Committee Report has given the RBI much food for thought on the issues of financial inclusion. I want to reflect on the recommendations, even while putting some additional issues on the table.

Financial inclusion is about (a) the broadening of financial services to those people who do not have access to financial services sector ; (b) the deepening of financial services for people who have minimal financial services; and (c) greater financial literacy and consumer protection so that those who are offered the products can make appropriate choices. The imperative for financial inclusion is both a moral one as well as one based on economic efficiency. Should we not give everyone that is capable the tools and resources to better themselves, and in doing so, better the country?

Last week, I met with some members of Ela Bhatt's Self-Employed Women's Association. In a room full of poor but confident women entrepreneurs, I asked how many borrowed from moneylenders before they came to SEWA. About half the women raised their hands. When asked how many thought of approaching a regular bank before they came to SEWA's cooperative bank, not one raised her hand. Interestingly, many of them said that the loan from SEWA freed them from the moneylender's high interest rate, which gave them enough to service SEWA's loan fully even while focusing on other productive activities. I have heard this from other micro-entrepreneurs – the highest return initial investment is often to free oneself of the clutches of the moneylender. Despite this high return from the delivery of credit to the poor, and despite much of our financial inclusion efforts being focused on credit, we still reach too few of the target population. So there is much more to be achieved.

We have tried to effect inclusion in the past through mandates – whether it be through direction on branch opening or on lending to priority sectors. That we are still far short of our goals has led some critics to suggest we should abandon mandates because the market will take care of needs; if the poor have demand for financial services, the critics say, providers will emerge to supply it. Markets do respond to need, and competition is a very healthy force for improvement, but market functioning can be impeded by poor infrastructure, uneven regulation, natural or regulatory monopolies, and even cartelization. ·

While enlisting competitive forces wherever possible to compete for the bottom of the pyramid's business, as a development central bank we also need to offer a supportive hand. By putting in place the right infrastructure and enabling regulation, we have to encourage the development of the products, institutions, and networks that will foster inclusion.

Let us start with products. We have been trying for decades to expand credit. We have focused much less on easing payments and remittances or on expanding remunerative savings vehicles or on providing easy-to-understand insurance against emergencies. Perhaps we should try to expand financial inclusion by encouraging these other products, and allow credit to follow them rather than lead. Indeed, many successful organizations working with the poorest of the poor try to get them to put aside some money as savings, no matter how little, before giving them loans. Some of our self-help groups (SHGs) work on this principle. Not only does the savings habit, once inculcated, allow the customer to handle the burden of repayment better, it may also lead to better credit allocation. With the power of information technology, perhaps the analysis of the savings and payment patterns of a client can indicate which one of them is ready to use credit well.

One roadblock to access, even to something as simple as a universal basic savings account, is Know Your Customer (KYC) requirements. Experts have emphasized the need to make it far simpler to open basic accounts, and have suggested minimizing the required documentation. In an effort to do so, the Dr Nachiket Mor Committee recommends requiring proof of only a permanent address. This is nevertheless more onerous than current RBI norms, which allow an applicant to self-certify her address and other details for accounts below Rs 50,000. But despite the RBI's exhortations, few banks have reduced their demand for documentation – they fear that they will be held responsible if something goes wrong, no matter what the regulatory norms. The acceptance of third-party KYC certification is particularly difficult.

Today, stringent KYC norms keep too many out of the banking system, and lead to unnecessary harassment for others. Banks may adopt these norms more because of regulatory or legal liability than to safeguard against true criminal or terrorist activity. Can't we do better? Some bankers suggest that by monitoring activity patterns in accounts carefully, even while putting some limits on basic accounts (such as holding a large value cheque for a few days before it is cashed), much of the suspicious activity can be detected and stopped. Could we allow a commercial bank some regulatory dispensation in case there is minor mischief in some low value accounts, provided the bank has a reliable system in place to detect greater mischief? Could the gains in easing widespread access to safe accounts outweigh the costs of minor fraud? How can we get entities within the system to rely on each other's KYC, without the process having to be continuously repeated? How can technology assist in effectively addressing the above issues? These are questions we have to examine and address.

The broader issue is whether through sophisticated state-of-the-art technology, we can offer customers products that are simple, low cost, and easy to use. We have done this with mobile phones, can we do it with banking? Payments may be another obvious product. I should note that our payments infrastructure in India is very advanced. We have three large RBI technology centres devoted to supporting payments and robust payment and settlement networks for both large value and small transactions. We have introduced an additional factor of authentication for all e-commerce transactions – which makes these transactions more secure – and are swiftly moving to Chip and PIN technology for credit card transactions. SMS alerts for bank and credit card transactions are an important advance relative to even the United States, where thieves find it easy to bill thousands of dollars to your credit card even before you know it is stolen. All this means that we have the infrastructure to provide cheap and safe payments and remittances. What we need are non-governmental players to utilize this infrastructure to provide the products and access that people want.

With over 900 million mobile phones, the potential for mobile banking as a delivery channel for financial services is a big opportunity in India. We have consciously adopted the bank-led model for mobile banking, while the non-banks, including mobile network operators, have been permitted to issue mobile wallets, where cash withdrawal is not permitted as of now. The key to cheap and universal payments and remittances will be if we can find a safe way to allow funds to be freely transferred between bank accounts and mobile wallets, as well as cashed out of mobile wallets, through a much larger and ubiquitous network of business correspondents. The Dr Nachiket Mor Committee suggests the creation of Payment Banks as a step towards this goal.

Other suggestions include interoperable business correspondents who will get the scale economies to serve in remote locations, and the usage of NBFCs as banking correspondents. We will examine all this.

In the meantime, interesting solutions are emerging. Cashing out is important for remittances, because we have a large recipient population in the country, most of whom do not have access to formal banking services. We have recently approved the in-principle setting up of a payment system which will facilitate the funds transfer from bank account holders to those without accounts through ATMs. Essentially, the sender can have the money withdrawn from his account through an ATM transaction. The intermediary processes the payment, and sends a code to the recipient on his mobile that allows him to withdraw the money from any nearby bank's ATM. The system will take care of necessary safeguards of customer identification, transaction validation, velocity checks, etc. We need more such innovative products, some of which mobile companies are providing.

In India, despite the high mobile density, it is also a reality that most of the handsets are very basic ones and many of the mobile connections are prepaid subscriptions. These are important constraints. We have a great opportunity for banks and telecom service providers to come together to deliver mobile banking services of all kinds in a seamless and secure manner to their customers. In the next few months, we will accelerate the dialogue between key players.

One of the difficulties the poor and small businesses have in accessing credit is the lack of information about them, both upfront as they are being evaluated for credit, and after lending where the lender has to monitor them. If savings and payments products are sold widely, and information, including payments to mobile companies, utility companies, as well as the government, collected, then the excluded can build information records that will help them access credit. If, in addition, negative information on defaults is shared in a fair and responsible way through the financial network, every individual borrower will have something at stake – their credit history – which can serve to encourage timely repayment. This, in turn, can improve the willingness of banks to lend.

Finally, let me turn to consumer literacy and protection. As we reach more and more of the population, we have to be sure that they understand the products they are being sold and have the information to make sensible decisions. Caveat emptor or let the buyer beware is typically the standard used in financial markets – that is, so long as the buyer is not actively misled, she is responsible for researching her product choices and making purchase decisions. While this puts a lot of burden on the buyer to do due diligence, it also gives her a lot of freedom to make choices, including of course the freedom to make bad choices.

But with poorly informed and unsophisticated investors, we should consider the Dr Nachiket Mor Committee's recommendation of setting some guidelines on what products are suitable for different categories of investors. Broadly speaking, the more complicated the product the more sophisticated should be the target customer. Should we move to a norm where a suite of simple products is pre-approved for dissemination to all, but as products get more complicated, financial sector providers bear more and more responsibility to show that the buyer was sophisticated and/ or appropriately counselled before she purchased?

Of course, the longer run answer is for customers to become more savvy. Can the technology sector help educate people in financial matters? After all, finance is not something most people learn in schools, but it is something they encounter every day in the world. Low cost but high quality distance finance education is something the country very much needs and we look to entrepreneurs here to think of innovative ways to provide it.

Before I conclude, one caveat. Technology can magnify the reach of finance for bad purposes as well as good. Many of you must receive frequent emails, purportedly from me, informing you of a large sum of money that awaits you at the RBI, and urging you to send me your account details so that I can transfer the money to you. Let me assure you that the RBI does not give out money, I do not send these emails, and if you do fall for such emails, you will lose a lot of money to crooks and be reminded of the adage – if anything looks too good to be true, it probably is not true.

Of course, technology can also offer answers to check fraud. Can we enlist social media in enabling the public to identify fraud and help regulation? How can we do this in a responsible way? Again, these are questions at this point, but I am sure we will find the answers.

Let me conclude. Technology, with its capacity to reduce transaction costs, is key to enabling the large volume low-ticket transaction that is at the centre of financial inclusion. By collecting and processing large volumes of data easily, technology can also improve the quality of financial decision making. When products have network effects, technology can ensure not just interoperability, key to obtaining the benefits of networking, but also security, key to maintaining the confidence of people and preventing them from withdrawing from the formal financial system once again. I sincerely hope the successful ICT industry will partner with the finance industry to revolutionize financial inclusion in this country.

II

I summarized what we were doing on inclusion in a speech in Hyderabad on 18 July 2016 delivered to the National Seminar on Equity, Access, and Inclusion. During my term, I was trying to move us away from a belief that mandates to the public sector banks would solve the problem of inclusion. Every uncompensated unprofitable mandate was effective only so long as the bureaucracy and the regulator monitored the banks closely. However, if banks could game the monitor and avoid the mandate, they would. This was understandable since, ultimately, we held even public sector bank CEOs responsible for profits.

To end this cat and mouse game, I wanted us to focus more on creating an enabling environment where the poor customer was seen as attractive, and worth serving, even while we had safeguards in place to prevent her from being exploited. I have to admit our success here was mixed – even as the RBI tried to create the enabling environment, the government seemed more convinced that mandates like the Jan Dhan Yojana and the Mudra scheme (for small loans) would work better. Of course, the two could co-exist. The government was probably right that in the short run, the public sector banks could be pushed to deliver specific mandates. So, for example, they could be enlisted to open accounts for the poor. However, for sustainable broad-based inclusion, where banks go beyond the mandate to actually serve the poor customer well, we have to create the right environment where inclusion is an attractive, though not exploitative, proposition. So, for example, it is important to compensate banks adequately for the transfer of government-provided direct benefits into newly opened accounts. If the accounts are even moderately profitable as a result, banks would have the incentive to improve the quality of their service and compete for the poor customer. In this vein, while supporting the government's agenda we also pushed for a change in the environment for inclusion.

The Changing Paradigm for Financial Inclusion

What are the economic impediments to greater financial inclusion? Perhaps the most important is the economic condition of the excluded. World over, the poor, the small, and the remote are excluded. It is not just because the financial system is underdeveloped, but because they are hard to service profitably. Nevertheless, this is not a reason to abandon hope, but to ask how we can overcome the impediments in the way of inclusion. The best way to characterize the impediments are through the acronym IIT: Information, Incentives, and Transaction Costs.

IIT

The excluded may live in remote areas or may belong to communities or segments of society that undertake economic activity informally – they do not maintain records or have signed contracts or documentation. They often do not own property or have regular established sources of income. As a result, a banker, especially if as is typical, he is not from the local region, will have difficulty getting sufficient information to offer financial products.

A second concern is incentives. For example, loans are easily available only if the lender thinks he will be repaid. When the legal system does not enforce repayment quickly or cheaply, and when the borrower does not have any collateral to pledge, the lender might believe that he will find it difficult to get repaid.

The third impediment is transactions costs. Since the size of transactions by the poor, or by micro farmers or enterprises is small, the fixed costs in transacting are relatively high. It takes as much time helping a client fill out the forms and to provide the necessary documentation if he is applying for a loan for Rs 10,000 as it takes to help another one borrow Rs 10 lakhs. A banker who is conscious of the bottom line would naturally focus on the large client in preference to the tiny one.

HOW DOES THE MONEYLENDER MANAGE?

One of the primary motivations for the country to push financial inclusion is to free the excluded from the clutches of the moneylender. How does the moneylender boldly lend where no banker dares to lend? Because he does not suffer the same impediments! Coming from the local community, the *sahukar* is well informed on what everyone's sources of income and wealth are, and how much they can repay. He is quite capable of using ruthless methods to enforce repayment. Moreover, the borrower knows that if he defaults on the sahukar, he loses his lender of last resort. So the borrower has strong incentives to pay. Finally, because the *sahukar* lives nearby and uses minimal documentation – after all, he is not going to use the courts to force repayment – loans are easily and quickly obtained. In an emergency or if the poor need to borrow on a daily basis, there are few more readily available alternatives than the moneylender. No wonder he has so many in his clutches.

How then should public policy approach this problem? I will now describe three approaches: mandates and subventions, transforming institutions, and moving away from credit.

APPROACH I: MANDATES AND SUBVENTIONS

One approach is to push formal institutions into reaching out to the excluded, even if it is unprofitable. This is why, for example, we mandate that banks allocate a certain fraction of their loans to the 'priority sector' and that they open 25 per cent of their branches in unbanked areas. There are also interest subventions that are made available for loans to particular sectors.

Furthermore, banks have been urged to open bank accounts for all under the Pradhan Mantri Jan Dhan Yojana (PMJDY), while today they are being exhorted to make loans to small businesses under the Mudra Scheme.

Because there are positive social benefits to financial inclusion that are not captured by the service provider (what economists call 'externalities'), such mandates are reasonable from a societal perspective. For instance, the higher familial and community status a farm worker gets from starting her own poultry farm and contributing to the family income may, on net, outweigh the costs the bank incurs on making the loan. The bank cannot monetize the status benefits, but a government can decide those benefits are worth generating and mandate them.

In a similar vein, there may be network benefits from universal access – for instance, direct transfer of benefits is easier when the vast majority of beneficiaries have a bank account, and the accounts themselves will be used heavily when account-to-account transfers are made easier through mobile phones via the soon-to-be-introduced Unified Payment Interface (UPI). Mandated account-opening essentially creates the universal network with its associated positive network externalities.

There are, however, a number of risks emanating from mandates. The first is that there is no market test of usefulness, and indeed, these may not be possible – how does one measure the value of the enhanced social status of the poultry farmer? So mandates are driven by the beliefs of the political leadership, and may persist a long time even if they are not effective. Furthermore, some vested interests may benefit from specific mandates and push for their perpetuation long after they have ceased being useful. Bankers themselves, seeing little profit in obeying the mandate, will try and 'achieve' it at least cost by targeting the most accessible and least risky in the eligible category, and even mislabelling normal activity so that it fits in the eligible list. Finally, some mandates fall primarily on the public sector banks. As competition reduces their profitability, their capacity to carry out mandates and still earn enough to survive diminishes.

So while acknowledging the value of mandates at the RBI, we

have tried to make them more effective. For example, the list of sectors eligible for priority sector treatment has been revised, with an emphasis on targeting the truly excluded. Specifically, the share of adjusted net bank credit (ANBC) that has to go to small and marginal farmers (including share croppers) is set at 8 per cent for March 2017, and that for micro enterprises set at 7.5 per cent. At the same time, the scope for banks to meet priority sector norms without lending to the truly excluded has been reduced. For example, large loans to firms producing agricultural products no longer qualify. Also, banks are now required to meet their targets at the end of every quarter, rather than at the end of the year, which reduces the scope for window-dressing with short-term end-of-year credit. Finally, Priority Sector Lending Certificates, which allow a lender to 'sell' any over-achievement in particular categories to others who are deficient, are now being traded, thus encouraging those who have a better capacity to make such loans to do so. All in all, the priority sector mandate is now not only better targeted at the truly excluded, but will be delivered more efficiently.

Mandates are not costless. Rather than forcing banks to recover costs by overcharging ordinary customers, or by demanding recapitalization by the government, better to bring the costs into the open by paying for the mandate wherever possible. So, for instance, accounts or cash machines opened in remote areas could attract a fixed subsidy, which would be paid to anyone who delivers them. Not only will the cost of the mandate become transparent and will be borne by the authorities, thus incentivizing them to make sensible decisions about how long to impose the mandate, the mandate can be delivered by the most efficient service providers, attracted by the subsidy. This is why the RBI today explicitly subsidizes cash recycling machines set up in underserved areas, and why central and state governments are paying banks for maintaining and servicing specified accounts. Going forward, narrow targeting of mandates to the truly underserved and explicit payment for fulfilling the mandate so that they are delivered by the most efficient should be the norm.

APPROACH 2: CREATING THE RIGHT INSTITUTIONS

As I argued earlier, the moneylender is particularly effective because he knows the neighbourhood and its people, and can make a good assessment of who is creditworthy. A large national bank with a local branch suffers from two infirmities. First, the branch manager has typically been recruited through an all-India exam, is from a different state, and is not intimately familiar with the local people. While many good branch managers do indeed learn about the community, some do not. The higher socio-economic status of bank officers also creates a distance with the poorer segments of the community, and their high salary makes many branches in remote areas economically unviable even if they could solicit business intelligently. Finally, given that the excluded do not have formal documents, bank managers in large banks with bureaucratic centralized procedures find it hard to provide effective service – how does one convey to head office the rationale for a loan to an intelligent, enthusiastic tribal who wants to set up a small shop, but who has no formal education or track record?

Local financial institutions, with local control and staffed by knowledgeable local people, could be more effective at providing financial services to the excluded. HDFC Bank, for example, has been very successful growing its loan portfolio in Kashmir by recruiting local youth as loan officers. Certainly, this is also the obvious lesson to be drawn from the success of microfinance institutions, who combine their local knowledge with stronger incentives for repayment through peer pressure and frequent collection of repayments. Indeed, this was also the rationale for local area banks and regional rural banks, and is a strong feature in the cooperative movement.

Yet, while there have been some grand successes among these institutions, each form has some deficiencies. Microfinance institutions do not have access to low-cost deposit financing, though securitization of loans has been a growing avenue of finance. Local area banks could not expand out of their area, exposing them to the geographical concentration risks.

Regional rural banks agitated for parity in salary structures with parent scheduled commercial banks, and having achieved parity, find that their costs are not optimally suited for the clientele they need to service. There are some very successful cooperative banks, on par with any universal bank, but far too many suffer from governance problems. The RBI has been engaged in bringing stronger governance to urban cooperative banks, but split supervision with state authorities limits how much it can do.

To provide an alternative institutional avenue for these categories of institutions to fulfill their mission, the RBI has created a new institution called the small finance bank, where 'small' refers to the kind of customer the bank deals with, not its size. With 75 per cent of the loans mandated to be below Rs 25 lakhs, the small finance bank is intended to provide services to the excluded. Thus far, the licences have been largely given to microfinance institutions and one local area bank, but there is no reason why these cannot be given to regional rural banks and cooperatives in the future. The hope is that these institutions will maintain a low cost structure, augmented by technology, to provide a menu of financial services to the excluded.

New institutions can also help ease the flow of credit. For instance, credit information bureaus have helped tremendously in solving both the information and incentive problem in retail credit. When an individual knows that a default will spoil their credit rating and cut off future access to credit, they have strong incentives to make timely payments. In rural India, we need to expand the reach of credit bureaus, including by bringing borrowing under self-help groups into their ambit. The use of Aadhaar in identifying individuals will also help eliminate duplicate records, while making existing records more accurate. Going forward, by the end of the year, the Credit Information Bureau of India will start providing individuals with one free credit report a year, so that they can check their credit rating and petition if they see possible discrepancies. An important proposal by the government is to give small businesses 'Udyog Aadhaar' numbers, which are unique IDs tied to both the entity as well as the promoter. Such IDs could allow small firms to build credit histories with credit bureaus, especially as the histories are tied to specific promoters.

Land is often the single most valuable source of wealth in rural areas. The digitization of land records, accompanied by a guarantee of certificates of final ownership by the state government, as proposed in Rajasthan, will ease the use of land as collateral against which funds can be borrowed. Even a formal recognition of share cropping agreements, as in the pattas registered by the state government in Andhra Pradesh, could ease access to credit for share croppers.

As a final example, MSMEs get squeezed all the time by their large buyers, who pay after long delays. All would be better off if the MSME could sell its claim on the large buyer in the market. The MSME would get its money quickly, while the market would get a claim on the better rated large buyer instead of holding a claim on the MSME. All this will happen as the three Trade-Receivables Discounting Systems (TReDS) which the RBI has licensed, start later this financial year. The key is to reduce transaction costs by automating almost every aspect of the transaction so that even the smallest MSMEs can benefit.

APPROACH 3: DON'T START WITH CREDIT

We have been trying for decades to expand credit. We have focused much less on easing payments and remittances, on expanding remunerative savings vehicles, or on providing easy-to-obtain insurance against crop failures. In the emerging financial inclusion paradigm, the government and the RBI are trying to expand inclusion by encouraging these other products, allowing credit to follow them rather than lead. Indeed, many successful organizations working with the poorest of the poor try to get them to put aside some money as savings, no matter how little, before giving them loans. Some of our self-help groups (SHGs) work on this principle. Not only does the savings habit, once inculcated, allow the customer to handle the burden of repayment better, it may also lead to better credit allocation.

Easy payments and cash out will make formal savings more attractive. Today, a villager who puts money into a bank has to either trudge the 'last miles' to the bank branch to take out her money, or wait for an itinerant banking correspondent to come by. We are engaged in strengthening the network of banking correspondents; by creating a registry of banking correspondents, giving them the ability to take and give cash on behalf of any bank through the Aadhaar Enabled Payment System (which will also give them adequate remuneration), and requiring that they are adequately trained in providing financial services. Cash-in-cash-out points will expand soon as the Postal Payment Bank and telecom-affiliated payment banks make post offices and telephone kiosks entry points into the financial system. Perhaps, most interestingly, transfers from bank account to bank account will become easier in a few weeks via mobile through the Unified Payment Interface. A villager needing to pay a shopkeeper only needs to know the latter's alias – say Ram@xyzbank.psp. He feeds that into his mobile app, writes the payment amount, puts in his password, and presses 'send' and the payment is made, with both getting messages to that effect. Neither needs to visit the bank to take out or deposit money, no point-of-sale machine is needed. With the price of smartphones falling sharply, we are on the verge of solving the last-mile problem.

With the power of information technology, perhaps the analysis of the savings and payment patterns of a client can indicate which one of them is ready to use credit well. Small businesses, which use the services of an online internet platform to sell, can establish a verifiable record of revenues that can form the basis for loans. Indeed, we are encouraged by the emergence of full-service entities that help the small business with marketing and logistics, while tying up with a finance company to provide the business with credit. This will help the carpet seller from Srinagar advertise his wares to the world, even while expanding his business. We also propose to encourage peer-to-peer lending platforms with light-touch regulation, anticipating that they may have innovative approaches to gathering the information necessary to lend.

SOME ISSUES

Having highlighted the various approaches to expand inclusion, let me now focus on some important issues that arise in managing the process. These are 1) Know your customer requirements 2) Encouraging competition to prevent exploitation 3) Ensuring some flexibility and forgiveness in financial arrangements 4) The need for skilling and support 5) Encouraging financial literacy and ensuring consumer protection.

KNOW YOUR CUSTOMER

Missing basic documentation is often an impediment to obtaining financial services. Knowing this, the Reserve Bank has steadily eased the required documentation for basic financial services. For instance, recognizing that proof of address is difficult, especially for those moving location, RBI requires only one document showing permanent address be presented. Current address can be self-certified by the account owner, preventing the considerable problems customers face when they migrate inside the country. Unfortunately, the RBI's instructions sometimes do not percolate to every bank branch – which leads to unnecessary harassment for consumers, as vividly described by a columnist recently. Going forward, we have asked the Indian Banks' Association to devise common account forms, where minimum RBI requirements will be printed on the back of the form. It will, for instance, become clear that a very basic account with some restrictions on amounts and transactions can be obtained with no official documents whatsoever. [*Author's note: KYC requirements were subsequently displayed prominently on the RBI website*].

COMPETITION TO PREVENT EXPLOITATION

As I have argued, the excluded are typically risky, as well as costly to service. At the same time, they are also liable to exploitation because they have so little access. Exploitation may come from a moneylender who charges usurious rates, or a banker demanding personal gratification for giving a government-subsidized loan. The fundamental way to deal with exploitation is to increase competition amongst suppliers of financial services. Regulation can help, but we should be careful that regulation does not shut out competition, thus enhancing exploitation.

Consider two examples:

Politicians are rightfully concerned about the poor being charged usurious rates. So they often ask regulators to set interest rate ceilings. Of course, a clever regulated lender can avoid interest rate ceilings through hidden and not-so-hidden fees for making the loan. But let us assume the even cleverer regulator can ferret out such practices (not always a valid assumption). Nevertheless, there is still a problem. The lender has to recoup not just the credit-risk margin which compensates him for the higher default risk of lending to those on the economic edge, but also the fixed costs of making, monitoring, and recovering small loans. If the interest rate ceiling is set too low, the regulated lender will not bother to lend since it is not worth his while. With competition from the regulated stifled, the poor borrower is left to the tender mercies of the rapacious, unregulated moneylender. So interest rate ceilings have to have a Goldilocks quality – not so high that they allow the uninformed poor to be exploited, and not so low that they kill any incentive the regulated might have to lend. This is the very thin line that the RBI has been following in setting interest rate ceilings for microfinance firms. As institutional frameworks develop to reduce risk in lending, and as competition amongst lenders increases, we can lower the maximum chargeable rate.

In a similar vein, our regulations sometime prohibit the taking of collateral for loans below a certain size to certain borrowers such as students or small businesses. However, if lenders are not forced to lend, the prohibition on taking collateral may lead to borrowers who can indeed offer collateral being denied a loan. The impossible trinity suggests that you cannot limit interest rates, prohibit the taking of collateral, and still expect the borrower to have the same level of access to loans. Put differently, unless a regulation mandates lending, which it rarely does, there is always a risk that ceilings on interest rates or prohibitions on taking collateral will cut off institutional lending to some of the eligible. Our regulations must be set bearing this in mind.

One reasonable compromise between protecting the poor and ensuring they have access is to allow only unsecured or collateral-free loans to qualify for priority sector treatment or interest subventions, but to also allow institutions to take collateral if offered on ordinary loans, provided they have a policy of charging lower rates on such secured loans. While this may force some who have collateral to pledge it even if they do not have to do so under current regulations (albeit with some compensation in terms of a lower borrowing rate), it mitigates the greater evil of those who have collateral to offer being denied credit altogether. This is certainly an issue we have to reflect on.

FLEXIBILITY AND FORGIVENESS

When people complain about the high cost of credit to small businesses, they do not realize the biggest component of interest costs is the credit risk margin, not the real policy rate. The credit risk margin is not under the control of the central bank, it has to be brought down by focusing on improving the lending institutional infrastructure, as I have argued earlier. However, even though a system that allows for strong enforcement of repayment reduces the credit risk margin lenders charge, it also imposes larger costs on unfortunate borrowers. So, for example, should a student who chose the wrong college for studies and ended up having to pay back huge loans with only a mediocre job be penalized for life? We need a system that has some flexibility in repayment, so that those who make bad choices or have bad luck can get some relief. At the same time, they should not escape all responsibility, else we will see people borrowing excessively and misusing the proceeds, knowing they can get away scot-free.

Keeping this in mind, our master circular on natural calamities allows banks to restructure agricultural loans without classifying them NPA, provided there are widespread crop losses in the local area. This prevents individuals from exploiting the system, while giving collective relief when the area is hit. Similarly, we have advocated that student loans be structured with an optional moratorium period, so that a borrower can survive periods of unemployment without being permanently labelled a defaulter. Going forward, we should accept the possibility of individuals, including farmers, declaring bankruptcy and being relieved of their debts, provided this remedy is used sparingly, and the individual chooses bankruptcy as a last choice, knowing he will lose assets and be excluded from borrowing for a period.

SKILLING AND SUPPORT

There is a widely perpetuated myth that access to financial services is all that is necessary to set a poor farm worker on her way to riches. This is simply not true. Clearly, access to institutional credit can help her pay back a moneylender, and thus give her some relief. Access to a bank account can allow her to put aside some savings, which protects them from the demands of needy relatives. But to generate income in a sustainable way, she needs help – in acquiring the skills necessary to raise chicken or cows or grow flowers, in marketing that product, and in learning how to manage funds. Often, credit offered without such support simply drives her further into debt.

Sometimes, people learn from neighbours as clusters start undertaking an activity. Sometimes people already know a marketable skill and only lack credit to buy the necessary raw material to produce or expand. More commonly, however, those who want to encourage micro-entrepreneurship have to work on a variety of supporting actions other than just credit, especially skilling. Fortunately, in India we have a flourishing NGO movement that often works with the government to provide the necessary support – as in the Jivika rural livelihoods programme in Bihar. Increasingly, some banks have adopted a holistic approach to support as they encourage micro-entrepreneurship. As the government's Skill India programme expands, it will produce more people who can use credit well. Stronger linkages between the programme and financial institutions will have to be built.

FINANCIAL LITERACY AND CONSUMER PROTECTION

Finally, as the excluded are drawn into formal financial services, they will encounter aggressive selling and in some cases outright mis-selling. At the Reserve Bank, we are conscious of our need to expand financial literacy so that the consumer is more aware. In the coming weeks, we will be launching a nationwide campaign trying to impart some basic messages on sound financial practice. We are also looking to have financial education included in the school curriculum across the country.

In 2015, the RBI came out with five principles that banks had to follow in dealing with customers. We asked banks to implement this Charter of Consumer Rights, and asked them to appoint an internal ombudsman to monitor the grievance redressal process. We now will examine how banks are faring, and whether further regulations are needed to strengthen consumer protection. We will especially focus on mis-selling of third-party products such as insurance, as well as the extension of adequate grievance redressal to rural areas, including through the RBI's ombudsman scheme.

CONCLUSION

The country has come a long way in the process of financial inclusion, but still has a way to go. We are steadily moving from mandates, subsidies, and reliance on the public sector banks for inclusion to creating enabling frameworks that make it attractive for all financial institutions to target the excluded, even while the interests of the excluded are protected through education, competition and regulation. I am confident that in the foreseeable future, we will bring formal financial services to every Indian who wants them. Financial inclusion will be an important element in ensuring access and equity, necessary building blocks for the sustainable growth of our country.

CHAPTER 6

THE RESOLUTION OF DISTRESS

I

The pillar where we made the least progress, despite the involvement of the best and the brightest in the RBI, was in getting the banks to recognize financial distress and deal with it. This was also the area where the prevailing mindset was shaped most by the existing weak institutional structure, making change very hard without changing institutions.

The problem was most acute in the public sector banks, which had the greatest risk appetites in 2007-09 when many of the bad loans were made. The public perception was that much of the problem was due to corruption, but while this could be true of some banks where the bad loans really accelerated in the terms of specific CEOs, I became convinced that there were other, perhaps more important, causes. These included the irrational exuberance and the tolerance for high promoter leverage among bankers after the successful lending experience in the period before the global financial crisis, the slowdown in government permissions in the wake of scandals post 2011, the mindset of bankers vis-à-vis promoters, and the lack of instruments for recovery when distress hit.

We could do little about the past, and public sector bankers (with the exception of a few CEOs) were becoming cautious about lending in any case, given the piling bad loan problems. We could urge the government repeatedly to deal with projects held up because of government inaction, but results here too were outside our control. Where we could have more effect was in changing the mindset of bankers, and giving them more instruments to act vis-à-vis large promoters. The intent here was not punishment – recognizing that public sector bank credit growth was slowing, I wanted to focus on putting projects back on track so that economic activity would not be hampered. Instead, the intent was to ensure that everyone absorbed a fair share of the losses, and these did not fall entirely on the banks. As for fraudulent promoters, I felt the investigative agencies should proceed against them separately, but their projects and workers should not be punished for promoter malfeasance.

Let me explain the problem of mindsets with an example. I remember early in my term a plane ride in which an articulate and competent public sector bank CEO happened to sit next to me. As we discussed the banking system, he described one notorious but prominent promoter who had been playing off one bank against another in an attempt to keep his failing enterprise afloat. The banker told me that the promoter had promised him repayment out of funds that were arriving but had diverted the funds to another enterprise. When he got to know of this, the banker told me that he was angrier than he had ever been before in his professional life. 'What did you do?' I asked the banker. 'I cut his credit line by 20 per cent,' came the answer. I did not know whether to laugh or cry.

In most countries with a strong financial system, broken promises by an incompetent borrower would be met with a complete cut-off of credit, and the initiation of recovery measures. In India, the worst this angry banker was willing to do was to cut future lending by a measly 20 per cent! Many promoters came from rich storied families, were well-connected and dominated the society pages. To ask the banker to get tough with the promoter was to ask him to take on an icon of society. Some bankers could do this with ease, many could not.

But there were two other impediments in taking action to restructure distressed projects to put them back on track. First, despite having some of the most draconian laws on the books in any country on recovering secured debt, these laws were effective only against small promoters, not against wealthy promoters who could hire the best lawyers to play the judicial system to stymie the recovery process. Second, bankers were always fearful of the investigative agencies, who could question a purely commercial decision where debt was written down, and thus ruin the banker's hope of a quiet and honourable retirement. This made bankers very reluctant to agree to the deep significant restructuring that was needed to set projects back on track – why take the risk when retirement was only six months away.

What this meant was a collective reluctance to recognize the problem – indeed, when I took over, we were only starting to implement a system to measure the aggregate exposure of the banking system to specific promoters and the status of those loans. Effectively, this meant a strong desire on the part of both bankers and promoters to repeatedly push the bad loan problem into the future, which meant the problem had already grown to a significant size. This was something we needed to change. The first step was to give bankers more instruments to deal with distress. The second was to stop the regulator acquiescing to the problem by engaging in regulatory forbearance (that is, agreeing to turn a blind eye to non-performing loans). The third was to force disclosure and provisioning for bad loans, so that everyone knew the extent of the problem, and it did not grow to an alarming size sight unseen. That would also ensure that the government could budget adequately for the growing hole in public sector bank balance sheets, and not be surprised suddenly.

My speeches and commentary in this area were intended to lay out areas of action, but also send a more subtle message. The promoters were not above the law, and should be treated as they deserved – some with compassion because of genuine difficulties outside their control, and others with harshness. I especially criticized promoters who lived the good life even while they had bled their companies dry. This was as much a message to the promoters and bankers as to my own junior staff – top management at the RBI would back them if they did their jobs.

Our staff worked hard and creatively to create resolution mechanisms and some incentive for promoters to pay back in a system where they had little incentive to do so and banks had every incentive to extend and pretend. Despite a slow and uneven legal system, and despite the absence of a functioning bankruptcy code during my term, we did manage to force banks to start recognizing problems, and did bring some promoters to the table to pay. Following our representation to the Prime Minister, the investigative agencies started proceeding on cases of outright fraud with additional vigour. However, all this is still work in progress, and much needs to be done.

My first major talk on the subject was the Kurien Lecture in November 2014.

Saving Credit

At a time when demand for bank credit is weak, even while we are likely to have enormous demand for it if investment picks up, we have to ask if India's system of credit is healthy. Unfortunately, the answer is that it is not. We need fundamental reforms starting with a change in mindset. A public lecture in the memory of a great Indian who did much to change our mindsets is a perfect place to make the case.

THE DEBT CONTRACT

The flow of credit relies on the sanctity of the debt contract. A debt contract is one where a borrower, be it a small farmer or the promoter of a large petrochemical plant, raises money with the promise to repay interest and principal according to a specified schedule. If the borrower cannot meet his promise, he is in default. In the standard debt contract through the course of history and across the world, default means the borrower has to make substantial sacrifices, else he would have no incentive to repay. For instance, a defaulting banker in Barcelona in mediaeval times was given time to repay his debts, during which he was put on a diet of bread and water. At the end of the period, if he could not pay he was beheaded. Punishments became less harsh over time. If you defaulted in Victorian England, you went to debtor's prison. Today, the borrower typically only forfeits the assets that have been financed, and sometimes personal property too if he is not protected by limited liability, unless he has acted fraudulently.

Why should the lender not share in the losses to the full extent? That is because he is not a full managing partner in the enterprise. In return for not sharing in the large profits if the enterprise does well, the lender is absolved from sharing the losses when it does badly, to the extent possible. By agreeing to protect the lender from 'downside' risk, the borrower gets cheaper financing, which allows him to retain more of the 'upside' generated if his enterprise is successful. Moreover, he can get money from total strangers, who have no intimate knowledge of his enterprise or his management capabilities, fully reassured by the fact that they can seize the hard collateral that is available if the borrower defaults. This is why banks offer to finance your car or home loan today at just over 10 per cent, just a couple of per centage points over the policy rate.

VIOLATING THE SPIRIT OF DEBT

The problem I want to focus on in this lecture is that the sanctity of the debt contract has been continuously eroded in India in recent years, not by the small borrower but by the large borrower.

And this has to change if we are to get banks to finance the enormous infrastructure needs and industrial growth that this country aims to attain.

The reality is that too many large borrowers do not see the lender, typically a bank, as holding a senior debt claim that overrides all other claims when the borrower gets into trouble, but as holding a claim junior to the borrower's own equity claim. In much of the globe, when a large borrower defaults, he is contrite and desperate to show that the lender should continue to trust him with management of the enterprise. In India, too many large borrowers insist on their divine right to stay in control despite their unwillingness to put in new money. The firm and its many workers, as well as past bank loans, are the hostages in this game of chicken – the promoter threatens to run the enterprise into the ground unless the government, banks, and regulators make the concessions that are necessary to keep it alive. And if the enterprise regains health, the promoter retains all the upside, forgetting the help he got from the government or the banks – after all, banks should be happy they got some of their money back! No wonder government ministers worry about a country where we have many sick companies but no 'sick' promoters.

Let me emphasize that I do not intend in any way to cast aspersions on the majority of Indian businesspeople who treat creditors fairly. I also don't want to argue against risk taking in business. If business does not take risks, we will not get architectural marvels like our new international airports, the 'developed-for-India' low-cost business model in the telecom sector, or our world-class refineries. Risk taking inevitably means the possibility of default. An economy where there is no default is an economy where promoters and banks are taking too little risk. What I am warning against is the uneven sharing of risk and returns in enterprise, against all contractual norms established the world over – where promoters have a class of 'super' equity which retains all the upside in good times and very little of the downside in bad times, while creditors, typically public sector banks, hold 'junior' debt and get none of the fat returns in good times while absorbing much of the losses in bad times.

WHY DOES IT HAPPEN?

Why do we have this state of affairs? The most obvious reason is that the system protects the large borrower and his divine right to stay in control.

This is not for want of laws. The Debts Recovery Tribunals (DRTs) were set up under the Recovery of Debts Due to Banks and Financial Institutions (RDDBFI) Act, 1993 to help banks and financial institutions recover their dues speedily without being subject to the lengthy procedures of usual civil courts. The Securitization and Reconstruction of Financial Assets and Enforcement of Security Interests (SARFAESI) Act, 2002 went a step further by enabling banks and some financial institutions to enforce their security interest and recover dues even without approaching the DRTs. Yet the amount banks recover from defaulted debt is both meagre and long delayed. The amount recovered from cases decided in 2013-14 under DRTs was Rs 30,590 crores while the outstanding value of debt sought to be recovered was a huge Rs 2,36,600 crores. Thus recovery was only 13 per cent of the amount at stake. Worse, even though the law indicates that cases before the DRT should be disposed off in six months, only about a fourth of the cases pending at the beginning of the year are disposed off during the year – suggesting a four-year wait even if the tribunals focus only on old cases. However, in 2013-14, the number of new cases filed during the year were about one and a half times the cases disposed off during the year. Thus backlogs and delays are growing, not coming down.

Why is this happening? The judgments of the DRTs can be appealed to Debt Recovery Appellate Tribunals, and while there are thirty-three of the former, there are only five of the latter. And even though section 18 of the RDDBFI Act is intended to prevent higher constitutional courts from intervening routinely in DRT and DRAT judgments, the honourable Supreme Court lamented on 22 January 2013 in the Union of India vs the DRT Bar Association case that

'It is a matter of serious concern that despite the pronouncements of this Court, the High Courts continue to ignore the availability of statutory remedies under the RDDBFI Act and SARFAESI Act and exercise jurisdiction under Article 226 for passing orders which have serious adverse impact on the right of banks and other financial institutions to recover their dues.'

The consequences of the delays in obtaining judgments because of repeated protracted appeals implies that when recovery actually takes place, the enterprise has usually been stripped clean of value. The present value of what the bank can hope to recover is a pittance. This skews bargaining power towards the borrower who can command the finest legal brains to work for him in repeated appeals, or the borrower who has the influence to obtain stays from local courts – typically the large borrower. Faced with this asymmetry of power, banks are tempted to cave in and take the unfair deal the borrower offers. The bank's debt becomes junior debt and the promoter's equity becomes super equity. The promoter enjoys riskless capitalism – even in these times of very slow growth, how many large promoters have lost their homes or have had to curb their lifestyles despite offering personal guarantees to lenders?

The public believes the large promoter makes merry because of sweet deals between him and the banker. While these views have gained currency because of recent revelations of possible corruption in banks, my sense is that Occam's Razor suggests a more relevant explanation – the system renders the banker helpless vis-à-vis the large and influential promoter. While we should not slow our efforts to bring better governance and more transparency to banking, we also need to focus on reforming the system.

Who pays for this one-way bet large promoters enjoy? Clearly, the hard working savers and taxpayers of this country! As just one measure, the total write-offs of loans made by the commercial banks in the last five years is 1,61,018 crores, which is 1.27 per cent of GDP. Of course, some of this amount will be recovered, but given the size of stressed assets in the system, there will be more write-offs to come. To put these amounts in perspective – thousands of crores often become meaningless to the lay person –

1.27 per cent of GDP would have allowed 1.5 million of the poorest children to get a full university degree from the top private universities in the country, all expenses paid.

THE CONSEQUENCES

Let me emphasize again that I am not worried as much about losses stemming from business risk as I am about the sharing of those losses – because, ultimately, one consequence of skewed and unfair sharing is to make credit costlier and less available. The promoter who misuses the system ensures that banks then charge a premium for business loans. The average interest rate on loans to the power sector today is 13.7 per cent even while the policy rate is 8 per cent. The difference, also known as the credit risk premium, of 5.7 per cent is largely compensation banks demand for the risk of default and non-payment. Since the unscrupulous promoter hides among the scrupulous ones, every businessperson is tainted by the bad eggs in the basket. Even comparing the rate on the power sector loan with the average rate available on the home loan of 10.7 per cent, it is obvious that even good power sector firms are paying much more than the average household because of bank worries about whether they will recover loans. Reforms that lower this 300 basis-point risk premium of power sector loans vis-à-vis home loans would have large beneficial effects on the cost of finance, perhaps as much or more than any monetary policy accommodation.

A second consequence is that the law becomes more draconian in an attempt to force payment. The SARFAESI Act of 2002 is, by the standards of most countries, very pro-creditor as it is written. This was probably an attempt by legislators to reduce the burden on DRTs and force promoters to pay. But its full force is felt by the small entrepreneur who does not have the wherewithal to hire expensive lawyers or move the courts, even while the influential promoter once again escapes its rigour. The small entrepreneur's assets are repossessed quickly and sold, extinguishing many a promising business that could do with a little support from bankers.

A draconian law does perhaps as much damage as a weak law, not just because it results in a loss of value on default but also because it diminishes the incentive to take risk. For think of a mediaeval businessman who knows he will be imprisoned or even beheaded if he defaults. What incentive will he have to engage in innovative but risky business? Is it any wonder that business was very conservative then? Indeed, Viral Acharya of NYU and Krishnamurthi Subramanian of ISB show in a compelling study that innovation is lower in countries with much stricter creditor rights. Or put differently, the solution to our current problems is not to make the laws even more draconian but to see how we can get more equitable and efficiency-enhancing sharing of losses on default.

A final consequence of the inequitable sharing of losses in distress is that it brings the whole free enterprise system into disrepute. When some businessmen enjoy a privileged existence, risking other people's money but never their own, the public and their representatives get angry. I have met numerous parliamentarians who are outraged at the current state of affairs. If the resolution of these issues is taken out of the realm of the commercial into the realm of the political, it will set back industrial growth. Reforms therefore assume urgency.

What we need is a more balanced system, one that forces the large borrower to share more pain, while being a little more friendly to the small borrower. The system should shut down businesses that have no hope of creating value, while reviving and preserving those that can add value. And the system should preserve the priority of contracts, giving creditors a greater share and greater control when the enterprise is unable to pay, while requiring promoters to give up more.

A BETTER BALANCE

How do we achieve this better balance?

- Let us start with better capital structures. The reason so many projects are in trouble today is because they were structured upfront with too little equity, sometimes borrowed by the promoter from elsewhere. And some promoters find ways to take out the equity as soon as the project gets going, so there really is no cushion when bad times hit. Lenders should insist on more real equity up front, and monitor the project closely to ensure it stays in. Promoters should not try and finance mega projects with tiny slivers of equity. We also need to encourage more institutional investors, who have the wherewithal to monitor promoters, to bring equity capital into projects.

- Banks need to react more quickly and in a concerted way to borrower distress. The longer the delay in dealing with the borrower's financial distress, the greater the loss in enterprise value. Some banks are more agile (and have better lawyers), so the promoter continues servicing them while defaulting on other banks. In the absence of an efficient bankruptcy process that brings lenders together, the RBI has mandated the formation of a Joint Lending Forum (JLF) of lenders when the first signs of distress are perceived. The JLF is required to find a way to deal with the distressed enterprise quickly, with options ranging from liquidation to restructuring. In this way, we hope to coordinate lenders and prevent the borrower from playing one off against the other.

- The government's plan to expand the number of DRTs and DRATs is timely, and will be most effective if also accompanied by an expansion in facilities, trained personnel, and electronic filing and tracking of cases, as suggested by the Supreme Court. Also

  □ Some monetary incentives to tribunals for bringing down the average duration of cases, without compromising on due process, could be contemplated.

  □ Some limit on the number of stays each party can ask for could also be thought of.

  □ Appeals to the DRAT should not be a matter of course. Indeed, DRATs should require borrower appellants to deposit a portion of the money ordered to be paid by the DRT as laid down in the law as a matter of course, rather than routinely waiving such deposits as is reported to be the current practice.

☐ It is worth examining if appellants should be made to pay the real costs of delay out of their own pockets if unsuccessful, where the costs include the interest costs of postponed payments.

- As suggested by the Supreme Court, Constitutional Courts should respect the spirit of the laws and entertain fewer appeals. It is hard to see what points of law or judicial administration are raised by the standard commercial case, and routine judicial intervention favours the recalcitrant borrower at the expense of the lender.

☐ Challenging the orders of DRT and DRAT before courts should be made costlier for the appellants. Courts should require them to deposit the undisputed portion of the loan before admitting the case so that routine frivolous appeals diminish.

- The system also needs professional turnaround agents who can step in in the place of promoters. Asset Reconstruction Companies (ARCs) were meant to do this, but they need more capital and better management capabilities. Also, there is a requirement that they hand the enterprise back to the original promoter once they have generated enough value to repay the original debts. Such a requirement is misconceived and needs to be repealed, else ARCs have little incentive to spend effort and money to turn around firms. They will simply be liquidators, as they have largely proven to be so far. I should mention that the RBI is open to more firms applying for licences as ARCs.

- The government is working on a new bankruptcy law, which is very much needed. Properly structured, this will help bring clarity, predictability, and fairness to the restructuring process.

FLEXIBILITY NOT FORBEARANCE

Finally, let me end on a current concern that pertains to the RBI's regulation that is not unrelated to the issues discussed in this lecture. Today, a large number of industries are getting together with banks to clamour for regulatory forbearance. They want the RBI to be 'realistic' and postpone any recognition of bad loans.

This is short-sighted, especially on the part of the banks. Today, the market does not distinguish much between non-performing loans and restructured loans, preferring to call them both stressed loans and discounting bank value accordingly. Mutilating Shakespeare, an NPA by any other name smells as bad! Indeed, because forbearance makes bank balance sheets opaque, they may smell worse to analysts and investors. The fundamental lesson of every situation of banking stress in recent years across the world is to recognize and flag the problem loans quickly and deal with them. So regulatory forbearance, which is a euphemism for regulators collaborating with banks to hide problems and push them into the future, is a bad idea.

Moreover, forbearance allows banks to postpone provisioning for bad loans. So when eventually the hidden bad loans cannot be disguised any more, the hit to the bank's income and balance sheet is larger and more unexpected. This could precipitate investor anxiety about the state of the bank, and in the case of public sector banks, leave a bigger hole for the government to fill. These are yet more reasons to end forbearance. Or put differently, forbearance is ostrich-like behaviour, hoping the problem will go away. It is not realism but naiveté, for the lesson from across the world is that the problems only get worse as one buries one's head in the sand.

At the same time, the banks have also been asking the regulator for greater flexibility to restructure loans so as to align them with the project's cash flows, and for the ability to take equity so as to get some upside in distressed projects. These are more legitimate requests as they imply a desire to deal more effectively with distress. The regulator has been reluctant to afford banks this flexibility in the past because it has been misused by bank management. Nevertheless, recognizing that it cannot micromanage the resolution of distress, the RBI is exploring ways to allow banks more flexibility in restructuring. This is a risk we are prepared to take if it allows more projects to be set on the track to recovery.

In sum, the RBI opposes forbearance which simply pushes problems into the future, while it will allow more flexibility so that problem loans can be dealt with effectively today. Let us also be clear that we will be watchful for misuse of flexibility and will deal severely with it if it occurs.

CONCLUSION

Let me conclude. Perhaps the reason we have been so willing to protect the borrower against the creditor is that the hated moneylender looms large in our collective psyche. But the large borrower today is not a helpless illiterate peasant and the lender today is typically not the *sahukar* but the public sector bank – in other words, we are the lender. When the large promoter defaults wilfully or does not cooperate in repayment to the public sector bank, he robs each one of us taxpayers, even while making it costlier to fund the new investment our economy needs.

The solution is not more draconian laws, which the large borrower may well circumvent and which may entrap the small borrower, but a more timely and fair application of current laws. We also need new institutions such as bankruptcy courts and turnaround agents. Finally, we need a change in mindset, where the willful or non-cooperative defaulter is not lionized as a captain of industry, but justly chastized as a freeloader on the hardworking people of this country. I am sure that is a change in mindset that Dr Verghese Kurien would approve of.

II

In the absence of a functioning bankruptcy code, the RBI put together a number of schemes to facilitate bank resolution of distress. We repeatedly re-examined the schemes to see how they could be tweaked to facilitate resolution. Unfortunately, with the exception of a few hard-charging and conscientious bankers, the general mood among the bankers was to continue to extend and pretend. They feared they would be held accountable for any concession they made, and constantly (and perhaps understandably) avoided taking decisions. In this environment, the idea of a bad bank, funded by the government, that would take the loans off their books, kept cropping up. I just saw this as shifting loans from one government pocket (the public sector banks) to another (the bad bank) and did not see how it would improve matters. Indeed, if the bad bank were in the public sector, the reluctance to act would merely be shifted to the bad bank. Why not instead infuse the capital that would be given to the bad bank directly into the public sector banks? Alternatively, if the bad bank were to be in the private sector, the reluctance of public sector banks to sell loans to the bad bank at a significant haircut would still prevail. Once again, it would solve nothing.

As we found banks reluctant to recognize problems, we decided not just to end forbearance but also to force them to clean up their balance sheets. The Asset Quality Review, initiated in 2015, was the first major exercise of this nature in India, ably led by Deputy Governor Mundra. I would especially highlight the role of two extremely polite and self-effacing but tough-as-nails ladies, Chief General

Manager Parvathy Sundar and Executive Director Meena Hemchandra, who really energized their staff and assured them of their support at every turn. The young team they put together was tireless, and made me aware once again of what we are capable of if we put our minds to it.

Every situation of banking sector stress I have ever studied was fixed only by recognizing the problem, resolving the bad loans, and recapitalizing the banks. India was no exception, but once again there were a bunch of critics who claimed that cleaning up the bad loan problem was what led to the slowing of credit by the public sector banks. In a speech in June 2016 in Bengaluru, I made the case for the clean-up once again by asking these critics to actually look at data, which showed the slowdown started before the clean-up, probably as banks became aware of the magnitude of the problem.

Resolving Stress in the Banking System

Ordinarily, in a city like Bengaluru, we would talk about startups. Today, however, I want to talk about the resolution of financial distress. I want to refute the argument that monetary policy has been too tight. Instead, I will argue that the slowdown in credit growth has been largely because of stress in the public sector banking, which will not be fixed by a cut in interest rates. Instead, what is required is a clean-up of the balance sheets of public sector banks, which is what is under way and needs to be taken to its logical conclusion. Specifically, I will describe what we have been doing in India to change the culture surrounding the loan contract. To start, let us look at public sector credit growth compared with the growth in credit by the new private banks [*Author's note: I have omitted the charts this talk was based on, but they are available at https://rbi.org.in/Scripts/BS_ SpeechesView.aspx?Id=1009*]

PUBLIC SECTOR LENDING VS PRIVATE SECTOR LENDING

The data indicate public sector bank non-food credit growth has been falling relative to credit growth from the new private sector banks since early 2014. This is reflected not only in credit to industry but also in micro and small enterprise credit. The relative slowdown in credit growth, albeit not so dramatic, is also seen in agriculture, though growth is picking up once again. Whenever one sees a slowdown in lending, one could conclude there is no demand for credit – firms are not investing. But what we see here is a slowdown in lending by public sector banks vis-à-vis private sector banks. Why is that?

The immediate conclusion one should draw is that this is something affecting credit supply from the public sector banks specifically, perhaps it is the lack of bank capital. Yet if we look at retail loan growth, and specifically housing loans, public sector bank loan growth approaches private sector bank growth. The lack of capital therefore cannot be the culprit. Rather than an across-the-board shrinkage of public sector lending, there seems to be a shrinkage in certain areas of high credit exposure, specifically in loans to industry and to small enterprises. The more appropriate conclusion then is that public sector banks have been shrinking exposure to infrastructure and industry risk right from early 2014 because of mounting distress on their past loans. Private sector banks, many of which did not have these past exposures, were more willing to service the mounting demand from both their traditional borrowers, as well as some of those corporates denied by the public sector banks. Given, however, that public sector banks are much bigger than private sector banks, private sector banks cannot substitute fully for the slowdown in public sector bank credit. We absolutely need to get public sector banks back into lending to industry and infrastructure, else credit and growth will suffer as the economy picks up.

These data refute another argument made by those who do not look at the evidence – that stress in the corporate world is because of high interest rates. Interest rates set by private banks are usually equal or higher than rates set by public sector banks.

Yet their credit growth does not seem to have suffered. The logical conclusion therefore must be that it is not the level of interest rates that is the problem. Instead, stress is because of the loans already on PSB balance sheets, and their unwillingness to lend more to those sectors to which they have high exposure.

There are two sources of distressed loans – the fundamentals of the borrower not being good, and the ability of the lender to collect being weak. Both are at work in the current distress.

THE SOURCES OF LENDING DISTRESS: BAD FUNDAMENTALS

Why have bad loans been made? A number of these loans were made in 2007-08. Economic growth was strong and the possibilities limitless. Deposit growth in public sector banks was rapid, and a number of infrastructure projects such as power plants had been completed on time and within budget. It is at such times that banks make mistakes. They extrapolate past growth and performance to the future. So they are willing to accept higher leverage in projects, and less promoter equity. Indeed, sometimes banks signed up to lend based on project reports by the promoter's investment bank, without doing their own due diligence. One promoter told me about how he was pursued then by banks waving cheque books, asking him to name the amount he wanted. This is the historic phenomenon of irrational exuberance, common across countries at such a phase in the cycle.

The problem is that growth does not always take place as expected. The years of strong global growth before the global financial crisis were followed by a slowdown, which extended even to India, showing how much more integrated we had become with the world. Strong demand projections for various projects were shown to be increasingly unrealistic as domestic demand slowed down. Moreover, a variety of governance problems coupled with the fear of investigation slowed down bureaucratic decision making in Delhi, and permissions for infrastructure projects became hard to get. Project cost overruns escalated for stalled projects and they became increasingly unable to service debt.

I am not saying that there was no malfeasance – the country's investigative agencies are looking into some cases such as those where undue influence was used in getting loans, or where actual fraud has been committed by diverting funds out of a company, either through over-invoicing imports sourced via a promoter-owned subsidiary abroad or exporting to related shell companies abroad and then claiming they defaulted. I am saying that, typically, there were factors other than malfeasance at play, and a number of genuine committed entrepreneurs are in trouble, as are banks that made reasonable business decisions given what they knew then.

THE SOURCES OF LENDING DISTRESS: POOR MONITORING AND COLLECTION

The truth is, even sensible lending will entail default. A banker who lends with the intent of never experiencing a default is probably over-conservative and will lend to too few projects, thus hurting growth. But sensible lending means careful assessment up front of project prospects, which I have argued may have been marred by irrational exuberance or excessive dependence on evaluations by others. Deficiencies in evaluation can be somewhat compensated for by careful post-lending monitoring, including careful documentation and perfection of collateral, as well as ensuring assets backing promoter guarantees are registered and tracked. Unfortunately, too many projects were left weakly monitored, even as costs increased. Banks may have expected the lead bank to exercise adequate due diligence, but this did not always happen. Moreover, as a project went into distress, private banks were sometimes more agile in securing their positions with additional collateral from the promoter, or getting repaid, even while public sector banks continued supporting projects with fresh loans. Promoters astutely stopped infusing equity, and sometimes even stopped putting in effort, knowing the project was unlikely to repay given the debt overhang.

The process for collection, despite laws like SARFAESI intended to speed up secured debt collection, has been prolonged and costly, especially when banks face large, well-connected promoters. The government has proposed reforms to the judicial process, including speeding up the functioning of the Debt Recovery Tribunals, which should make it easier for banks to collect, but those legislative reforms are before Parliament. Knowing that banks would find it hard to collect, some promoters encouraged them to 'double-up' by expanding the scale of the project, even though the initial scale was unable to service debt. Of course, the unscrupulous among the promoters continued to divert money from the expanded lending, increasing the size of the problem on bank balance sheets.

The inefficient loan recovery system then gives promoters tremendous power over lenders. Not only can they play one lender off against another by threatening to divert payments to the favoured bank, they can also refuse to pay unless the lender brings in more money, especially if the lender fears the loan becoming a Non-Performing Asset. Sometimes promoters can offer miserly one-time settlements (OTS) knowing that the system will ensure the banks have little ability to collect even secured loans, and that too after years. Effectively, loans in such a system become implicit equity, with a tough promoter enjoying the upside in good times, and forcing banks to absorb losses in bad times, even while he holds on to his equity.

CLEANING UP THE BANKS: PRINCIPLES

The world over, there are three cardinal rules when faced with incipient distress.

1) Viability does not depend on the debt outstanding, but on economic value. Debt may have to be written down to correspond to what is viable.

Because of changed circumstances, demand may be lower and project cash flows may be significantly lower than projected earlier. The project has economic value when completed – in the sense that operating cash flows are positive, but much less than the interest on the debt it carries. If the debt is not written down, the project continues as an NPA, even while the promoter, knowing it cannot repay, loses interest. If neglected, the project may stop generating any cash flows and the assets may depreciate rapidly. Excessive indebtedness can destroy value.

2) Complete projects that are viable, even if it requires additional funds infusion.

Stalled projects do not get any better over time. If there are small investments needed to complete the project, and the promoter has no funds, it may still make sense to lend to the project, even while writing down the overall debt. Essentially, the new loan makes it possible to generate operating cash flows to service some debt, even if not all the outstanding debt.

3) Don't throw good money after bad money simply because there is an unreliable promise that debt will become serviceable.

This is the opposite of (2). If the project is unviable, doubling its size does not make it any more viable. Promoters that have over-borrowed often propose an increase in scale so that the bank's outstanding debt and new loans will all become serviceable. Perhaps it would be better for the bank to write down its loans to the initial project, rather than going deeper into the hole because the promoter may incur new cost overruns as he expands. An incompetent or unreliable promoter will remain so even when scale expands.

BANK MORAL HAZARD

Unfortunately, the incentives built into the public sector banking system have made it more difficult for public sector bank executives to follow these principles (I should add that some private sector bank executives have also not been immune on occasion). The short tenure of managers means they are unwilling to recognize losses immediately, and more willing to postpone them into the future for their successors to deal with. Such distorted incentives lead to overlending to or 'ever-green' unviable projects. Unfortunately, also, the taint of NPA immediately makes them reluctant to lend to a project even if it is viable, for fear that the investigative agencies will not buy their rationale for lending. The absence of sound and well-documented loan evaluation and monitoring practices by banks makes such an outcome more likely. So excessive lending to bad projects and too little lending to viable ones can coexist.

THE REGULATOR'S DILEMMA

For the regulator who wants the banking system to clean up so it can start lending again, this creates a variety of objectives, which can be somewhat conflicting. First, we want banks to recognize loan distress and disclose it, not paper over it by ever-greening unviable projects. Loan classification is merely good accounting – it reflects what the true value of the loan might be. It is accompanied by provisioning, which ensures the bank sets aside a buffer to absorb likely losses. If the losses do not materialize, the bank can write back provisioning to profits. If the losses do materialize, the bank does not have to suddenly declare a big loss, it can set the losses against the prudential provisions it has made. Thus the bank balance sheet then represents a true and fair picture of the bank's health, as a bank balance sheet is meant to.

Second, we want them to be realistic about the project's cash generating capacity, and structure lending and repayment to match that.

Third, we want them to continue lending to viable projects, even if they had to be restructured in the past and are NPAs.

The problem is that any forbearance in labelling loans NPAs on restructuring makes it easier to avoid disclosure and indulge in ever-greening. On the other hand, strict disclosure and classification rules could imply a cessation of lending to even viable projects. There are no clean solutions here given the kind of incentives in the system, and given the absence of an operational bankruptcy code in India. Therefore, the RBI has had to adopt a pragmatic approach to the clean-up, creating new enabling processes.

THE RBI'S APPROACH

Our first task was to make sure that all banks had information on who had lent to a borrower. So we created a large loan database (CRILC) that included all loans over Rs 5 crores, which we shared with all the banks. The CRILC data included the status of each loan – reflecting whether it was performing, already an NPA or going towards NPA. That database allowed banks to identify early warning signs of distress in a borrower such as habitual late payments to a segment of lenders.

The next step was to coordinate the lenders through a Joint Lenders' Forum (JLF) once such early signals were seen. The JLF was tasked with deciding on an approach for resolution, much as a bankruptcy forum does. Incentives were given to banks for reaching quick decisions. We have also tried to make the forum more effective by reducing the need for everyone to agree, even while giving those who are unconvinced by the joint decision the opportunity to exit.

We also wanted to stop restructuring of unviable projects by banks who want to avoid recognizing losses – so we ended the ability of banks to restructure projects without calling them NPA in April 2015. At the same time, a number of long-duration projects such as roads had been structured with overly rapid required repayments, even though cash flows continued to be available decades from now. So we allowed such project payments to be restructured through the 5/25 scheme provided the long dated future cash flows could be reliably established. Of course, there was always the possibility of banks using this scheme to evergreen, so we have monitored how it works in practice, and continue tweaking the scheme where necessary so that it achieves its objectives.

Because promoters were often unable to bring in new funds, and because the judicial system often protects those with equity ownership, together with SEBI we introduced the Strategic Debt Restructuring (SDR) scheme so as to enable banks to displace weak promoters by converting debt to equity. We did not want banks to own projects indefinitely, so we indicated a timeline by which they had to find a new promoter.

All these new tools (including some I do not have the space to describe) effectively created a resolution system that replicated an out-of-court bankruptcy. Banks now had the power to resolve distress, so we could push them to exercise these powers by requiring recognition. This is what the Asset Quality Review, completed in October 2015 and subsequently shared with banks, sought to accomplish. Since then banks have classified existing distressed loans appropriately, and since March 2016 are looking at their weak-but-not-yet-distressed portfolio for necessary actions. There is a change in culture, and banks have been quite willing to get into the spirit of the AQR. Many have gone significantly beyond our indications in what they have cleaned up by the quarter ending March 2016. Of course, once the banks have properly classified a non-performing loan and provisioned against it, their incentive to ever-green or avoid writing down the debt to appropriate levels is diminished.

Nevertheless, clean-up is ongoing work. The SDR scheme dealt with weak promoters. But some promoters are competent even while their projects are overly indebted. The 'Scheme for Sustainable Structuring of Stressed Assets' (S4A) is an optional framework for the resolution of large stressed accounts. The S4A envisages determination of the sustainable debt level for a stressed borrower, and bifurcation of the outstanding debt into sustainable debt and equity/quasi-equity instruments which are expected to provide upside to the lenders when the borrower turns around. Thus capable-but-over-indebted promoters have some incentive to perform, and because the project is not deemed an NPA if adequate provisions are made, public sector banks continue lending to it if necessary.

Most recently, the government is contemplating a fund to lend into distressed situations, with significant participation by third parties, so that new loans can be made to viable distressed projects. Provided decision making is not dominated by banks whose very loans are distressed, this could be an effective vehicle to speed up resolution.

WHY SO MANY SCHEMES AND WHY THE CONSTANT TINKERING

The sources of borrower distress are many, and we have sought to provide lenders with a menu of options to deal with it, even while limiting their discretion to paper over the problem. Effectively the RBI has been trying to create an entirely new bad loan resolution process in the absence of an effective bankruptcy system. We have had to tinker, since each scheme's effectiveness, while seemingly obvious when designing, has to be monitored in light of the distorted incentives in the system. As we learn, we have adapted regulation. Our objective is not to be theoretical but to be pragmatic, even while subjecting the system to increasing discipline and transparency.

The good news is that banks are getting into the spirit of the clean-up, and pursuing reluctant promoters to take the necessary steps to rehabilitate projects. Indebted promoters are being forced to sell assets to repay lenders. We will shortly license a number of new Asset Reconstruction Companies (ARCs) to provide a deeper market for stressed assets. We are also working on a framework to enhance efficiency and transparency of price discovery in sale of stressed assets by banks to ARCs. Bank investors, after initially getting alarmed by the size of the disclosures, have bid up PSB bank shares. To the extent that these are still trading at a fraction of book value, there is still room for upward valuation if the banks can improve the prospects of recovery. The new schemes, as well as the improving economy, should help.

FRAUD AND WILFUL DEFAULT

Even while we make it easier for committed promoters to restructure when they experience bad luck or unforeseen problems, we should reduce the ability of the fraudster or the wilful defaulter, who can pay but simply is disinclined to do so, or the fraudster, to get away. This is why it is extremely important that banks do not use the new flexible schemes for promoters who habitually misuse the system (everyone knows who these are) or for fraudsters. The threat of labelling a promoter a wilful defaulter could be effective in the former case, and we have coordinated with SEBI to increase penalties for wilful defaulters. For fraudsters, quick and effective investigation by the investigative agencies is extremely important. We should send the message that no one can get away, and I am glad that the Prime Minister's Office is pushing prosecution of large frauds. The RBI has set up a fraud monitoring cell to coordinate the early reporting of fraud cases to the investigative agencies. And for those who have diverted money out of their companies, especially into highly visible assets abroad, a stern message sent by bankers sitting together with investigative agencies should help send the message that the alternatives to repayment can be harsh.

BANK RISK AVERSION

Bankers often argue that the easiest people to label in a fraud are the bankers themselves, who often could be victims rather than perpetrators. Similarly, they accuse the vigilance authorities of excessive zeal when loans go bad, of immediately suspecting bankers of malfeasance when the bad loan could be an unintended consequence of sensible risk taking. Unfortunately, all too often, such investigations also uncover sloppy due diligence or loan monitoring by bankers. After the fact, it is hard to distinguish sensible risk taking from carelessness or from corruption. While the vigilance authorities continuously attempt to reassure bankers that they are not vigilantes, the bankers themselves know that their own enthusiasm and deficiencies can expose them to unwarranted accusations of corruption.

Certainly, part of the solution is for bankers to pull up their socks. But another part of the solution is to not label a banker based on the outcome of a single loan but instead look for a pattern across loans. A banker who makes an excessive number of bad loans compared to his cohort deserves, at the very least, to be questioned. But the banker who makes the occasional bad loan amidst a lot of good ones probably needs to be rewarded. Such pattern-based monitoring by bank authorities, with serious punishment through vigilance action only if there is evidence of money changing hands, could control malfeasance while rewarding risk taking. This does require some changes in the current system, including de-emphasizing the committee-based approach to loan approval in banks, which appears to diffuse responsibility for loan decisions.

WHAT RESPONSIBILITY DOES THE RBI HAVE?

Bankers sometimes turn around and accuse regulators of creating the bad loan problem. The truth is bankers, promoters, and circumstances create the bad loan problem. The regulator cannot substitute for the banker's commercial decisions or micromanage them or even investigate them when they are being made. Instead, in most situations, the regulator can at best warn about poor lending practices when they are being undertaken, and demand banks hold adequate risk buffers. The important duty of the regulator is to force timely recognition of NPAs and their disclosure when they happen. Forbearance may be a reasonable but risky regulatory strategy when there is some hope that growth will pick up soon and the system will recover on its own. Everyone – banker, promoter, investors, and government officials – often urge such a strategy because it kicks the problem down the road, hopefully for someone else to deal with. The downside is that when growth does not pick up, the bad loan problem is bigger, and dealing with it is more difficult. It is when the bad loan problem is allowed to accumulate through forbearance or non-recognition that regulators have the difficult task of bringing the system back on track. That is the problem we have had to deal with at the RBI.

As I have shown you, the consequence since early 2014 of the past build-up of stressed loans was a slowdown in public sector bank lending in certain sectors. The cessation of RBI forbearance and the Asset Quality Review in mid 2015 were therefore not responsible for the slowdown. Instead, high distressed exposures in certain sectors were already occupying PSB management attention and holding them back. The only way for them to supply the economy's need for credit, which is essential for higher economic growth, was to clean up and recapitalize.

The silver lining message in the slower credit growth is that banks have not been lending indiscriminately in an attempt to reduce the size of stressed assets in an expanded overall balance sheet, and this bodes well for future slippages. In sum, to the question of what comes first, clean-up or growth, I think the answer is unambiguously 'Clean-up!' Indeed, this is the lesson from every other country that has faced financial stress. It is important, therefore, that the clean-up proceeds to its conclusion, without any resort to regulatory forbearance once again.

Sometimes, easier monetary policy is proposed as an answer to reducing the bad debt problem. For the heavily indebted promoter, however, easier monetary policy will typically bring no relief. Even with lower policy rates, the bank, which is typically not made whole even if it grabs all the borrower's cash flows, has no incentive to reduce the interest rate the borrower can pay. And few banks are competing for that borrower's business, so there is no competition to force down loan rates. The bottom line is that easier monetary policy is no answer to serious distress, contrary to widespread belief.

WHAT CAN THE GOVERNMENT DO?

The government is in the process of speeding up the debt recovery process, and creating a new bankruptcy system. These are important steps to improve the resolution process. In the near term, however, two actions will pay large dividends.

The first is to improve the governance of public sector banks so that we are not faced with this situation again. The government, through the Indradhanush initiative, has sent a clear signal that it wants to make sure that public sector banks, once healthy, stay healthy. Breaking up the post of Chairman and Managing Director, strengthening board and management appointments through the Banks Board Bureau, decentralizing more decisions to the professional board, finding ways to incentivize management, all these will help improve loan evaluation, monitoring and repayment.

The second is to infuse bank capital, with some of the infusion related to stronger performance, so that better banks have more room to grow. Capital infusion into weak banks should ideally accompany an improvement in governance, but given the need for absorbing the losses associated with balance sheet clean-up, better that government capital be infused quickly. Governments are sometimes reluctant to infuse bank capital because there are so many more pressing demands for funds. Yet, there are few higher return activities than capitalizing the public sector banks so that they can support credit growth. Finally, the Economic Survey has suggested the RBI should capitalize public sector banks. This seems a non-transparent way of proceeding, getting the banking regulator once again into the business of owning banks, with attendant conflicts of interest.

Better that the RBI pay the government the maximum dividend that it can, retaining just enough surplus buffers that are consistent with good central bank risk-management practice. Indeed, this is what we do, and in the last three years, we have paid all our surplus to the government. Separately, the government can infuse capital into the banks. The two decisions need not be linked. Alternatively, a less effective form of capital, if the government cannot buy bank equity directly with cash, is for it to issue the banks 'Government Capitalization Bonds' in exchange for equity. The banks would hold the bonds on their balance sheet. This would tie up part of their balance sheet, but would certainly be capital.

Postscript: I would not change anything in this speech today. The need for action on everyone's part is as urgent as ever, though the instruments to effect that action have grown. The NDA government amended the various acts governing debt recovery to make them less easy to game, and also enacted a new bankruptcy code. Further, it amended the working of debt recovery tribunals. These are important steps forward in rectifying the balance between borrower and lender in India. However, the operational effectiveness of these changes needs to be tracked, and further amendments enacted if necessary, until we have a resolution system that works in a rapid, fair and transparent way.

CHAPTER 7

THE ECONOMY AND OTHER ISSUES

I

The Governor of the Reserve Bank is much more than just a regulator or a central banker. Since the RBI is both the lender of last resort, as well as the custodian of the country's foreign exchange reserves, the Governor is the primary manager of macroeconomic risk in the country. If the Governor takes this role seriously, he (or she) has to warn when he fears the economy is in danger of going down the wrong path. As an apolitical technocrat, he can neither be a cheerleader for the government, nor can he be an unconstrained critic. This is a fine line to tread, and the Governor has to pick both the issues he speaks on, as well as the tone of his commentary, very carefully.

The mistake on all sides is to treat the RBI Governor as just another bureaucrat. If the Governor takes this mistaken view, he ends up being subservient to the central and state governments, and not offering an independent technocratic perspective that could keep the nation from straying into economic distress. The RBI Governor has to understand his role, and know it occasionally entails warning of macroeconomic risks from government actions or saying 'No!' firmly.

Every government tests what the RBI Governor will acquiesce to, and ideally, it will not push beyond a point, knowing that the RBI's cautions are worth heeding. If the government takes the mistaken view that the RBI Governor is just another bureaucrat, it will be displeased when it sees the Governor deviating from the usually deferential behaviour of bureaucrats, and it will strive to cut him down to size. This does not serve the country either.

I was determined not to neglect my responsibilities as national risk manager, even while trying to explain to the government of the day why this was a necessary role. Where I had direct responsibility, this meant saying no in private occasionally, even while offering safer alternatives for what the government intended. Where I had indirect responsibility, this meant advising or counselling in private, and occasionally, when the issue merited a national debate, speaking in public. Of course, my past experience as Chief Economist of the International Monetary Fund, where my job was to identify macroeconomic risks across a variety of countries, gave me a unique cross-country perspective, and heightened my sense of responsibility.

I also felt this responsibility from a different source. Because of the relentless press attention, I realized that many young people who were looking for a role model now saw the Governor of the Reserve Bank as one they wanted to learn from and imitate. I felt I had to display the highest professional integrity, over and above the obviously necessary personal integrity, if I were to discharge my responsibility to these youth.

While the Governor has to warn about risks where necessary, he is not an agent for the opposition. He continues to be an essential part of the country's administration, and his objectives have to be the broader government objectives of sustainable growth and development. The danger in a country that is unused to legitimate words of caution, and a press that is accustomed to deference from bureaucrats, is that it may misinterpret this role. A new narrative may form around the Governor. He can come to be seen by the press and social media as a critic, and every speech or comment of his is then scrutinized for evidence that supports the narrative. Should the Governor disappear from public view and not speak for fear of misinterpretation, or should he take the risk in order to discharge his responsibilities? I chose the latter, in part because I thought it was extremely important that our country should steer a stable path when surrounded by so much global risk, and in part because I thought young people (including my own younger staff at the RBI) should realize that it is important to speak up when one's responsibilities demand it. I did, however, meet regularly with the government to share my views and listen to its point of view, and always left feeling that there was mutual understanding.

Given my risk manager's perspective, and given that we were recovering from the currency turmoil, in my first speech on the economy I tried to talk up what was going on in India. However, I also had to respect the dharma of the central banker, and not indulge in excessive hype. Indeed, this swing from excessive euphoria to excessive pessimism and back was the subject of my speech at Harvard Business School in October 2013.

Filtering Out the Real India

Indian cricket fans are manic-depressive in their treatment of their favourite teams. They elevate players to god-like status when their team performs well, ignoring obvious weaknesses; but when it loses, as any team must, the fall is equally steep and every weakness is dissected. In fact, the team is never as good as fans make it out to be when it wins, nor as bad as it is made out to be when it loses. Its weaknesses existed in victory, too, but were overlooked.

Such bipolar behaviour seems to apply to assessments of India's economy as well, with foreign analysts joining Indians in similar swings between over-exuberance and self-flagellation. A few years ago, India could do no wrong. Commentators talked of 'Chindia', elevating India's performance to that of its northern neighbour. Today, India can do no right.

India does have its problems. Annual GDP growth slowed significantly in the last quarter to 4.4 per cent, inflation is high, and the current account and budget deficits last year were too large. Every commentator today highlights India's poor infrastructure, excessive regulation, small manufacturing sector, and a workforce with inadequate education and skills.

These are indeed deficiencies, and they must be fixed if India is to grow strongly and stably. But the same deficiencies existed when India was growing fast. To understand what needs to be done in the short run, we must understand what dampened the Indian success story.

In part, India's slowdown paradoxically reflects the substantial fiscal and monetary stimulus that its policy makers, like those in all major emerging markets, injected into its economy in the aftermath of the 2008 financial crisis. The resulting growth spurt led to inflation, especially because the world did not slide into a second Great Depression, as was originally feared. So monetary policy has had to be tight, with high interest rates contributing to slowing investment and consumption.

Moreover, India's institutions for acquiring land, allocating natural resources, and granting clearances were overwhelmed during the period of strong growth. Strong growth increased the scarcity and value of resources such as land or mineral wealth. To the extent that these were cheap in the past, there was little reward to misallocating them. Growth, however, increased the rents to corruption.

Similarly, industrial development led to growing encroachment on farmland and forests and the displacement of farmers and tribals. India is a developing country with a civil society possessed of first-world sensibilities. Protests organized by politicians and activists led to new environmental laws and land acquisition laws that aim to make development sustainable. Over time, India will learn to streamline the new laws to make them more functional, but in the short run a side effect has been more bureaucratic impediments to investment. So growth, as well as the reaction to that unbridled growth, created a greater possibility of corruption.

Fortunately, a vibrant democracy like India has its own checks and balances. India's investigative agencies, judiciary, and press started examining allegations of large-scale corruption. The unfortunate side effect as the clean-up proceeded was that bureaucratic decision making became more risk averse, and many large projects came to a grinding halt.

Only now, as the government creates new institutions to accelerate decision making and implement transparent processes, are these projects being cleared to proceed. Once restarted, it will take time for these projects to be completed, at which point output growth will increase significantly.

The combination of excessive (with the benefit of hindsight) post-crisis stimulus and stalling large projects had other consequences such as high internal and external deficits. The post-crisis fiscal-stimulus packages sent the government budget deficit soaring from what had been a very responsible level in 2007-08 of around 2.5 per cent to over 6 per cent. Similarly, as large mining projects stalled, India had to resort to higher imports of coal and scrap iron, while its exports of iron ore dwindled.

An increase in gold imports placed further pressure on the current account balance. Newly rich consumers in rural areas increasingly put their savings in gold, a familiar store of value, while wealthy urban consumers, worried about inflation, also turned to buying gold. Ironically, had they bought Apple shares, rather than a commodity (no matter how fungible, liquid, and investible it is), their purchases would have been treated as a foreign investment rather than as adding to the external deficit.

For the most part, India's current growth slowdown and its fiscal and current account deficits are not structural problems. They are all fixable by means of modest reforms. This is not to say that ambitious reform is not good, or is not warranted to sustain growth for the next decade. But India does not need to become a manufacturing giant overnight to fix its current problems.

The immediate tasks are more mundane, but also more feasible ones: clearing projects, reducing poorly targeted subsidies, and finding more ways to narrow the current account deficit and ease its financing. Over the last year, the government has been pursuing this agenda, which is already showing some early results. For example, the external deficit is narrowing sharply on the back of higher exports and lower imports. The government and the Reserve Bank said it would be $70 billion this fiscal year, down from $88 billion last fiscal year, but recent data suggests it could be lower still.

This leads me to another point. Because analysts keep looking for major structural reforms to fix the deeper economic challenges, they ignore smaller steps or dismiss them as 'band aids'. But strategically placed small steps – strategic incrementalism for want of a better term – taken together can deal with the immediate problems, thus buying time and economic and political space for the major structural reforms.

Put differently, when the Indian authorities said they would bring the fiscal deficit below 5.3 per cent last year, no one believed them. The final outturn was 4.9 per cent. Similarly, while we project the CAD to come down to 3.7 per cent this year, I think we could be pleasantly surprised. Not all the actions we have taken are pretty, and not all are sustainable, but they have done the job.

Indeed, despite its shortcomings, India's GDP will probably grow by 5-5.5 per cent this year – not great, but certainly not bad for what is likely to be a low point in economic performance. The monsoon has been good and will spur consumption, especially in rural areas, which are already growing strongly, owing to improvements in road transport and communications connectivity.

The banking sector has undoubtedly experienced an increase in bad loans, often owing to investment projects that are not unviable but only delayed. As these projects come onstream, they will generate the revenue needed to repay loans. India's banks have the capital to absorb losses in the meantime.

Likewise, India's finances are stronger than in the typical emerging-market country, let alone an emerging-market country in crisis. India's overall public debt/GDP ratio has been on a declining trend, from 73.2 per cent in 2006-07 to 66 per cent in 2012-13 (and the central government's debt/GDP ratio is only 46 per cent). Moreover, the debt is denominated in rupees and has an average maturity of more than nine years.

India's external debt burden is even more favourable, at only 21.2 per cent of GDP (much of it owed by the private sector), while short-term external debt is only 5.2 per cent of GDP. India's foreign-exchange reserves stand at $278 billion (about 15 per cent of GDP), enough to finance the entire current account deficit for several years. Even if you count all of trade credit as well as maturing deposits held by overseas Indians as short-term debt, India's reserves can pay them all down and still have money left over.

That said, India can do better – much better. The path to a more open, competitive, efficient, and humane economy will surely be bumpy in the years to come. But, in the short term, there is much low-hanging fruit to be plucked.

For instance, we are committed to developing our financial system, and carefully expanding access to finance can be a source of tremendous growth in the years to come. We are also embarked on large infrastructure projects. For example, the Delhi-Mumbai Industrial Corridor, a project with Japanese collaboration entailing over $90 billion in investment, will link Delhi to Mumbai's ports, covering an overall length of 1,483 km and passing through six states. This project will have nine mega industrial zones of about 200-250 sq. km., high speed freight lines, three ports, six airports, a six-lane intersection-free expressway connecting the country's political and financial capitals, and a 4,000 MW power plant. We have already seen a significant boost to economic activity as India built out the Golden Quadrilateral highway system, the boost from the Delhi-Mumbai Industrial Corridor can only be imagined. The best of India is yet to come.

Back to the cricketing analogy, India is an open argumentative society. But we are prone to mood swings, perhaps more so than other societies, perhaps in part driven by our excitable, competitive and very young press. Stripping out both the euphoria and the despair from what is said about India – and from what we Indians say about ourselves – will probably bring us closer to the truth.

II

We were impartial in advising all governments about the virtues of macroeconomic stability. In the Gadgil Lecture given on 13 February 2014, I gave the UPA government, which was going to present its last budget, the usual RBI caution on maintaining fiscal discipline, including urging it to address the vexing issue of oil subsidies. I offered similar advice to the NDA government also.

Macroeconomic Advice

Let me offer a quick recap of the macroeconomic situation. Growth is stabilizing on the back of a good harvest, strengthening exports, and some early signs of resumption of large stalled projects. However, growth is still very weak. We have to work to ensure macroeconomic stability, which means strengthening growth, especially through investment, maintaining a moderate current account deficit, achieving a fiscal deficit consistent with the government's fiscal roadmap, and reducing inflation. The government has to be commended for its efforts to revive growth, narrow the current account deficit, and meet fiscal targets. I have no doubt that the fiscal deficit for 2013-14 will be close to, or below, the finance minister's red line.

Going forward, however, we need to continue on the path of fiscal consolidation constantly improving the sustainability and quality of fiscal adjustment. It is very important that we spend money on needed public investment, even while reducing misdirected subsidies and entitlements.

Good fiscal control will help us in our fight against inflation. So will moderation in agricultural support price inflation, which will ensure that these prices only provide a baseline level of support when the farmer is in difficulty, without displacing market prices. Accurate market prices, together with good dissemination of data on sowing patterns, can do a far better job than support prices in directing agricultural production to where it is most valuable and needed.

Somewhat paradoxically, raising energy prices to market levels will also lead to lower inflation over the medium term, the horizon over which the RBI is trying to contain inflation. The reason is that higher prices will reduce excessive consumption, reduce subsidies and fiscal deficits, and incentivize investment and competition, even while allowing prices to be determined by an increasingly stable and plentifully supplied global market for energy. The consequences of inappropriate or inadequate price adjustments will be that the Reserve Bank will have to bear more of the burden in combating inflation.

I received numerous invitations to speak, the majority of which I turned down. But I could not turn down every request, and gave a speech on average once a month – later I realized this was not different from the frequency with which the Fed Chairman spoke in public. In India, however, the 24x7 channels, hungry for news, ensured that no speech went uncovered, no matter how minor the occasion or remote the location. Given press presence, I could not repeat speeches (the less there was a new message to report, the more likely the press might 'make' news by latching on to something peripheral), nor could I speak on monetary policy or financial sector reforms in every speech. What better way to speak on something different than to go back to my research on the political economy of reforms and growth, especially if it could contribute to the public debate as well as the RBI's mission? In the Lalit Doshi Memorial Lecture in August 2014, I linked the environment we lived in in India to the need for furthering our efforts on financial inclusion.

Finance and Opportunity in India

We are approaching the 67th anniversary of our Independence. Sixty-seven years is a long time in the life of man – indeed, it is about the average Indian's life expectancy today. Since life expectancy was shorter at the time of Independence, it is safe to say that most Indians born just after Independence are now no more. It is useful to take stock at such a time. Did we achieve the dreams of our founding fathers for freedom's first children? Or have we fallen woefully short? What more do we need to do?

Clearly, our founding fathers wanted political freedom for the people of India – freedom to determine who we would be governed by, as well as freedom of thought, expression, belief, faith, and worship. They wanted justice and equality, of status and opportunity. And they wanted us to be free from poverty.

We have made substantial progress in achieving political freedom. Our democracy has matured, with people confidently choosing to vote out governments that lose touch with their needs. Our institutions protecting the freedom to vote have grown stronger, with the Election Commission and the forces of law and order ensuring free and largely fair elections throughout the country. Political parties, NGOs, the press, and individuals exert checks and balances on public policy. And the judiciary has taken important steps to protect individual freedom.

Our economy is also far richer than it was at the time of independence and poverty has come down substantially. Of course, some countries like South Korea that were in a similar situation then are far better off today but many others have done far worse. Indeed, one of the advantages of a vibrant democracy is that it gives people an eject button which prevents governance from getting too bad. Democracy has probably ensured more stable and equitable economic growth than an authoritarian regime might have.

Yet a dispassionate view of both our democracy and our economy would suggest some concerns. Even as our democracy and our economy have become more vibrant, an important issue in the recent election was whether we had substituted the crony socialism of the past with crony capitalism, where the rich and the influential are alleged to have received land, natural resources and spectrum in return for payoffs to venal politicians. By killing transparency and competition, crony capitalism is harmful to free enterprise, opportunity, and economic growth. And by substituting special interests for the public interest, it is harmful to democratic expression. If there is some truth to these perceptions of crony capitalism, a natural question is why people tolerate it. Why do they vote for the venal politician who perpetuates it?

A HYPOTHESIS ON THE PERSISTENCE OF
CRONY CAPITALISM

One widely held hypothesis is that our country suffers from want of a 'few good men' in politics. This view is unfair to the many upstanding people in politics. But even assuming it is true, every so often we see the emergence of a group, usually upper-middle-class professionals, who want to clean up politics. But when these 'good' people stand for election, they tend to lose their deposits. Does the electorate really not want squeaky clean government?

Apart from the conceit that high morals lie only with the upper middle class, the error in this hypothesis may be in believing that problems stem from individual ethics rather than the system we have. In a speech I made before the Bombay Chamber of Commerce in 2008, I argued that the tolerance for the venal politician is because he is the crutch that helps the poor and underprivileged navigate a system that gives them so little access (this idea was inspired by Richard Hofstadter's seminal book *The Age of Reform*).

Let me explain. Our provision of public goods is unfortunately biased against access by the poor. In a number of states, ration shops do not supply what is due, even if one has a ration card – and too many amongst the poor do not have a ration card or a Below Poverty Line card; teachers do not show up at schools to teach; the police do not register crimes, or encroachments, especially if committed by the rich and powerful; public hospitals are not adequately staffed and ostensibly free medicines are not available at the dispensary; ... I can go on, but you know the all-too-familiar picture.

This is where the crooked but savvy politician fits in. While the poor do not have the money to 'purchase' public services that are their right, they have a vote that the politician wants. The politician does a little bit to make life a little more tolerable for his poor constituents – a government job here, an FIR registered there, a land right honoured somewhere else. For this, he gets the gratitude of his voters, and more important, their vote.

Of course, there are many politicians who are honest and

genuinely want to improve the lot of their voters. But perhaps the system tolerates corruption because the street-smart politician is better at making the wheels of the bureaucracy creak, however slowly, in favour of his constituents. And such a system is self-sustaining. An idealist who is unwilling to 'work' the system can promise to reform it, but the voters know there is little one person can do. Moreover, who will provide the patronage while the idealist is fighting the system? So why not stay with the fixer you know even if it means the reformist loses his deposit?

So the circle is complete. The poor and the underprivileged need the politician to help them get jobs and public services. The crooked politician needs the businessman to provide the funds that allow him to supply patronage to the poor and fight elections. The corrupt businessman needs the crooked politician to get public resources and contracts cheaply. And the politician needs the votes of the poor and the underprivileged. Every constituency is tied to the other in a cycle of dependence, which ensures that the status quo prevails.

Well-meaning political leaders and governments have tried, and are trying, to break this vicious cycle. How do we get more politicians to move from 'fixing' the system to reforming the system? The obvious answer is to either improve the quality of public services or reduce the public's dependence on them. Both approaches are necessary.

But then how does one improve the quality of public services? The typical answer has been to increase the resources devoted to the service, and to change how it is managed. A number of worthwhile efforts are under way to improve the quality of public education and health care. But if resources leak or public servants are not motivated, which is likely in the worst-governed states, these interventions are not very effective.

Some have argued that making a public service a right can change delivery. It is hard to imagine that simply legislating rights and creating a public expectation of delivery will, in fact, ensure delivery. After all, is there not an expectation that a ration card holder will get decent grain from the fair price shop, yet all too frequently grain is not available or is of poor quality.

Information decentralization can help. Knowing how many medicines the local public dispensary received, or how much money the local school is getting for mid-day meals, can help the public monitor delivery and alert higher-ups when the benefits are not delivered. But the public delivery system is usually most apathetic where the public is poorly educated, of low social status, and disorganized, so monitoring by the poor is also unlikely to be effective.

Some argue that this is why the middle class should enjoy public benefits along with the poor, so that the former can protest against poor delivery, which will ensure high quality for all. But making benefits universal is costly, and may still lead to indifferent delivery for the poor. The middle class may live in different areas from the poor. Indeed, even when located in the same area, the poor may not even patronize facilities frequented by the middle class because they feel out of place. And even when all patronize the same facility, providers may still be able to discriminate between the voluble middle class and the uncomplaining poor.

So if more resources or better management are inadequate answers, what might work? The answer may partly lie in reducing the public's dependence on government-provided jobs or public services. A good private sector job, for example, may give a household the money to get private health care, education, and supplies, and reduce their need for public services. Income could increase an individual's status and increase the respect they are accorded by the teacher, the policeman or the bureaucrat.

But how does a poor man get a good job if he has not benefited from good health care and education in the first place? In this modern world where good skills are critical to a good job, the unskilled have little recourse but to take a poorly paying job or to look for the patronage that will get them a good job. So do we not arrive at a contradiction: the good delivery of public services is essential to escape the dependence on bad public services?

MONEY LIBERATES AND EMPOWERS...

We need to go back to the drawing board. There is a way out of this contradiction, developing the idea that money liberates.

Could we not give poor households cash instead of promising them public services? A poor household with cash can patronize whomsoever it wants, and not just the monopolistic government provider. Because the poor can pay for their medicines or their food, they will command respect from the private provider. Not only will a corrupt fair price shop owner not be able to divert the grain he gets since he has to sell at market price, but because he has to compete with the shop across the street, he cannot afford to be surly or lazy. The government can add to the effects of empowering the poor by instilling a genuine cost to being uncompetitive – by shutting down parts of the public delivery systems that do not generate enough custom.

Much of what we need to do is already possible. The government intends to announce a scheme for full financial inclusion on Independence Day. It includes identifying the poor, creating unique biometric identifiers for them, opening linked bank accounts, and making government transfers into those accounts. When fully rolled out, I believe it will give the poor the choice and respect as well as the services they had to beg for in the past. It can break a link between poor public service, patronage, and corruption that is growing more worrisome over time.

Undoubtedly, cash transfers will not resolve every problem, nor are they uncontroversial. A constant refrain from paternalistic social workers is that the poor will simply drink away any transfers. In fact, studies by NGOs like Self Employed Women's Association indicate this is not true. Moreover, one could experiment with sending transfers to women, who may be better spenders. Some argue that attaching conditions to cash transfers – for example, they will be made provided the recipient's children attend school regularly – may improve the usage of the cash. The danger of attaching conditionality is that if the monitor is corrupt or inefficient, the whole process of direct benefits transfers can be vitiated. Nevertheless, it will be useful to monitor usage carefully where automation is possible, and automatically attach further benefits to responsible usage.

A related concern is whether cash transfers will become addictive – whether they become millstones keeping the poor in poverty rather than stepping stones out of it. This is an important concern. Cash transfers work best when they build capabilities through education and health care, thus expanding opportunity, rather than when they are used solely for inessential consumption. The vast majority amongst the poor will seize opportunities, especially for their children, with both hands. Nevertheless, if there is evidence that cash transfers are being misspent – and we should let data rather than preconceived notions drive policy – some portion could be given in the form of electronic coupons that can be spent by the specified recipient only on food, education or health care. Eventually, we will have to find a way to wean those who start earning significant amounts from receiving such transfers. How to do this without providing disincentives to working and earning is a future problem born of success which is best left for another day. The United States has dealt with the disincentive effects of getting off welfare with programmes like the earned income tax credit.

Another set of concerns has to do with whether private providers will bother to provide services in remote areas. Clearly, if people in remote areas have the cash to buy, private providers will find their way there. Indeed, a particularly desirable outcome will be if some of the poor find work providing services that hitherto used to be provided by public servants. Moreover, implementing cash transfers does not mean dismantling the system of public delivery wherever it is effective – it only means that the poor will pay when they use the public service.

The broader takeaway is that financial inclusion and direct benefits transfer can be a way of liberating the poor from dependency on indifferently delivered public services, and thus indirectly from the venal but effective politician. It is not a cure-all but will help the poor out of poverty and towards true political independence. But financial inclusion can do more; by liberating the poor and the marginalized from the clutches of the moneylender, by providing credit and advice to the entrepreneurial amongst the poor, and by giving households the ability to save and insure against accidents, it can set them on the road to economic independence, thus strengthening the political freedom that good public services will bring. This is why financial inclusion is so important.

FIVE PS OF FINANCIAL INCLUSION

Let me end with a vision of how the RBI can speed up and enhance financial inclusion of the kind I have just outlined. Financial inclusion in my view is about getting five things right: Product, Place, Price, Protection, and Profit.

If we are to draw in the poor, we need Products that address their needs; a safe place to save, a reliable way to send and receive money, a quick way to borrow in times of need or to escape the clutches of the moneylender, easy-to-understand accident, life and health insurance, and an avenue to engage in saving for old age. Simplicity and reliability are key – what one thinks one is paying for is what one should get, without hidden clauses or opt-outs to trip one up. The RBI is going to nudge banks to offer a basic suite of Products to address financial needs.

Two other attributes of Products are very important. They should be easy to access at low transactions cost. In the past, this meant that the Place of delivery, that is the bank branch, had to be close to the customer. So a key element of the inclusion programmes was to expand bank branching in unbanked areas. Today, with various other means of reaching the customer such as the mobile phone or the business correspondent, we can be more agnostic about the means by which the customer is reached. In other words, 'Place' today need not mean physical proximity, it can mean electronic proximity, or proximity via correspondents. Towards this end, we have liberalized the regulations on bank business correspondents, encouraged banks and mobile companies to form alliances, and started the process of licensing payment banks.

The transactions costs of obtaining the Product, including the Price the intermediary charges, should be low. Since every unbanked individual likely consumes low volumes of financial services to begin with, the provider should automate transactions as far as possible to reduce costs, and use employees that are local and are commensurately paid. Furthermore, any regulatory burden should be minimal. With these objectives in mind, the RBI has started the process of licensing small local banks, and is re-examining KYC norms with a view to simplifying them. Last month, we removed a major hurdle in the way of migrant workers and people living in makeshift structures obtaining a bank account, that of providing proof of current address.

New and inexperienced customers will require Protection. The RBI is beefing up the Consumer Protection Code, emphasizing the need for suitable products that are simple and easy to understand. We are also working with the government on expanding financial literacy. Teaching the poor the intricacies of finance has to move beyond literacy camps and into schools. Banks that lend to the entrepreneurial poor should find ways to advise them on business management too, or find ways to engage NGOs and organizations like NABARD in the process. We are also strengthening the customer grievance-redressal mechanism, while looking to expand supervision, market intelligence, and coordination with law and order to reduce the proliferation of fly-by-night operators.

Finally, while mandated targets are useful in indicating ambition (and allowing banks to anticipate a large enough scale so as to make investments), financial inclusion cannot be achieved without it being Profitable. So the last P is that there should be profits at the bottom of the pyramid. For instance, the government should be willing to pay reasonable commissions punctually for benefits transfers, and bankers should be able to charge reasonable and transparent fees or interest rates for offering services to the poor.

Let me conclude. One of the greatest dangers to the growth of developing countries is the middle income trap, where crony capitalism creates oligarchies that slow down growth. If the debate during the elections is any pointer, this is a very real concern of the public in India today. To avoid this trap, and to strengthen the independent democracy our leaders won for us sixty-seven years ago, we have to improve public services, especially those targeted at the poor. A key mechanism to improve these services is through financial inclusion, which is going to be an important part of the government and the RBI's plans in the coming years. I hope many of you in this audience will join in ensuring we are successful. Thank you.

IV

I was invited by the Chief Minister of Goa to speak at the D.D. Kosambi Ideas Festival in Goa on 20 February 2015. Since this was an 'Ideas' festival in honour of the great polymath, I reached into my research interests and a broader analysis of political economy to, once again, make the case for financial inclusion.

Democracy, Inclusion, and Prosperity

Thank you for inviting me to this Festival of Ideas. Since this festival is about ideas, I am not going to tax you with the Reserve Bank's views on monetary policy, which are, by now, well known. Instead, I want to talk about something I have been studying for many years, the development of a liberal market democracy. In doing this, I will wear my hat as a professor in the field known as political economy, and discard my RBI hat for the time being. If you came here expecting more insights on the path of interest rates, as I expect many of you did, let me apologize for disappointing you.

My starting point is the truism that people want to live in a safe prosperous country where they enjoy freedom of thought and action, and where they can exercise their democratic rights to choose their government. But how do countries ensure political freedom and economic prosperity? Why do the two seem to go together? And what more, if anything, does India have to do to ensure it has these necessary underpinnings for prosperity and continued political freedom? These are enormously important questions, but given their nature, they will not be settled in one speech. Think of my talk today, therefore, as a contribution to the debate.

FUKUYAMA'S THREE PILLARS OF A LIBERAL
DEMOCRATIC STATE

In his magisterial two-volume analysis of the emergence of political systems around the world (*The Origins of Political Order: From Pre-Human Times to the French Revolution*, 2011; and *Political Order and Political Decay: From the Industrial Revolution to the Globalization of Democracy*, 2014), political scientist Francis Fukuyama builds on the work of his mentor, Samuel Huntington (*Political Order in Changing Societies*, 1968), to argue that liberal democracies, which seem to be best at fostering political freedoms and economic success, tend to have three important pillars: a strong government, rule of law, and democratic accountability. I propose in this talk to start by summarizing my (necessarily imprecise) reading of Fukuyama's ideas to you. I would urge you to read the books to get their full richness. I will then go on to argue that he leaves out a fourth pillar, free markets, which are essential to make the liberal democracy prosperous. I will warn that these pillars are weakening in industrial countries because of rising inequality of opportunity, and end with lessons for India.

Consider Fukuyama's three pillars in greater detail. Strong government does not mean one that is only militarily powerful or uses its intelligence apparatus to sniff out enemies of the state. Instead, a strong government is also one that provides an effective and fair administration through clean, motivated, and competent administrators who can deliver good governance.

Rule of law means that government's actions are constrained by what we Indians would term dharma – by a historical and widely understood code of moral and righteous behaviour, enforced by religious, cultural, or judicial authority.

And democratic accountability means that the government has to be popularly accepted, with the people having the right to throw unpopular, corrupt, or incompetent rulers out.

Fukuyama makes a more insightful point than simply that all three traditional aspects of the state – executive, judiciary, and legislature – are needed to balance one another. In sharp contrast to the radical libertarian view that the best government is the minimal 'night watchman', which primarily protects life and property rights while enforcing contracts, or the radical Marxist view that the need for the government disappears as class conflict ends, Fukuyama, as did Huntington, emphasizes the importance of a strong government in even a developed country.

No matter how thuggish or arbitrary the government in a tin-pot dictatorship, these are weak governments, not strong ones. Their military or police can terrorize the unarmed citizenry but cannot provide decent law and order or stand up to a determined armed opposition. Their administration cannot provide sensible economic policy, good schools or clean drinking water. Strong governments need to be peopled by those who can provide needed public goods – they require expertise, motivation, and integrity. Realizing the importance of strong government, developing countries constantly request multilateral institutions for help in enhancing their governance capacity.

Strong governments may not, however, move in the right direction. Hitler provided Germany with extremely effective administration – the trains ran on time, as did the trains during our own Emergency in 1975-77. His was a strong government, but Hitler took Germany efficiently and determinedly on a path to ruin, overriding the rule of law and dispensing with elections. It is not sufficient that the trains run on time, they have to go in the right direction at the desired time. The physical rail network guiding the trains could be thought of as analogous to rule of law, while the process by which consensus is built around the train schedule could be thought of as democratic accountability.

But why do we need both rule of law and democratic accountability to keep strong government on the right path? Would democratic accountability not be enough to constrain a dictatorial government? Perhaps not! Hitler was elected to power, and until Germany started suffering shortages and reversals in World War II, enjoyed the support of the majority of the people. The rule of law is needed to prevent the tyranny of the majority that can arise in a democracy, as well as to ensure that basic 'rules of the game' are preserved over time so that the environment is predictable, no matter which government comes to power. By ensuring that all citizens have inalienable rights and protections, the rule of law constrains the majority's behaviour towards the minorities. And by maintaining a predictable economic environment against populist democratic instincts, the rule of law ensures that businesses can invest securely today for the future.

What about asking the question the other way? Would rule of law not be enough? Probably not, especially in a vibrant developing society! Rule of law provides a basic slow-changing code of conduct that cannot be violated by either government or the citizenry. But that, by itself, may not be sufficient to accommodate the aspirations of new emerging groups or the consequences of new technologies or ideas. Democratic accountability ensures the government responds to the wishes of the mass of the citizenry, allowing emerging groups to gain influence through political negotiation and competition with others. Even if groups cannot see their programmes translated into policy, democracy allows them to blow off steam non-violently. So both rule of law and democratic accountability check and balance strong government in complementary ways.

WHERE DO THESE THREE PILLARS COME FROM?

Much of Fukuyama's work is focused on tracing the development of each pillar in different societies. He suggests that the nature of states we see today is largely explained by their historical experience. For instance, China had long periods of chaos, most recently before the Communists came to power; groups engaged in total war against one another. Such unbridled military competition meant groups had to organize themselves as hierarchical military units, with rulers having unlimited powers. When eventually a group was victorious over the others, it was natural for it to impose centralized autocratic rule to ensure that chaos did not re-emerge. To rule over the large geographic area of the country, China needed a well-developed elite bureaucracy – hence the mandarins, chosen by exam based on their learning. So China had strong unconstrained effective government whenever it was united, and Fukuyama argues, unlike Western Europe or India, did not have strong alternative sources of power founded in religion or culture to impose rule of law.

In Western Europe, by contrast, the Christian church imposed constraints on what the ruler could do. So military competition, coupled with constraints on the ruler imposed by canon law, led to the emergence of both strong government and rule of law.

In India, he argues, the caste system led to division of labour, which ensured that entire populations could never be devoted totally to the war effort. So through much of history, war was never as harsh, or military competition between states as fierce, as in China. As a result, the historical pressure for Indian states to develop strong governments that intruded into every facet of society was muted. At the same time, however, the codes of just behaviour for rulers emanating from ancient Indian scriptures served to constrain any arbitrary exercise of power by Indian rulers. India, therefore, had weaker government, constrained further by rule of law. And, according to Fukuyama, these differing histories explain why government in China today is seen as effective but unrestrained, while government capacity in India is seen as weak, but Indian governments are rarely autocratic.

Any of these grand generalizations can, and should, be debated. Fukuyama does not claim history is destiny, but does suggest a very strong influence. Of course, the long influence of history and culture is less perceptible when it comes to democracy where some countries like India have taken to it like a duck to water. A vibrant, accountable democracy does not only imply that people cast their vote freely every five years. It requires the full mix of a raucous investigative press, public debate uninhibited by political correctness, many political parties representing varied constituencies, and a variety of non-governmental organizations organizing and representing interests. It will continue to be a source of academic debate why a country like India has taken to democracy, while some of its neighbours with similar historical and cultural pasts have not.

I will not dwell on this. Instead, I turn to a different question that Fukuyama does not address. Clearly, strong governments are needed for countries to have the governance to prosper. Equally, free markets underpin prosperity. But why is it that every rich country is also a liberal democracy subject to rule of law?

I will make two points in what follows: First, free enterprise and the political freedom emanating from democratic accountability and rule of law can be mutually reinforcing so a free enterprise system should be thought of as the fourth pillar underpinning liberal market democracies. Second, the bedrock on which all four pillars stand is a broadly equitable distribution of economic capabilities among the citizenry. That bedrock is fissuring in industrial countries, while it has to be strengthened in emerging markets like India.

FREE ENTERPRISE AND POLITICAL FREEDOM

Why are political freedoms in a country, of which representative democracy is a central component, and free enterprise mutually supportive?

There is, of course, one key similarity: both a vibrant democracy and a vibrant free enterprise system seek to create a level playing field which enhances competition. In the democratic arena, the political entrepreneur competes with other politicians for the citizen's vote, based on his past record and future policy agenda. In the economic sphere, the promoter competes with other entrepreneurs for the consumer's rupee, based on the quality of the product he sells.

But there is also at least one key difference. Democracy treats individuals equally, with every adult getting one vote. The free enterprise system, by contrast, empowers consumers based on how much income they get and property they own. What then prevents the median voter in a democracy from voting to dispossess the rich and successful? And why do the latter not erode the political rights of the ordinary voter. This fundamental tension between democracy and free enterprise appeared to be accentuated in the recent U.S. presidential elections as President Barack Obama appealed to middle-class anger about its stagnant economic prospects, while former Massachusetts governor Mitt Romney appealed to business people, disgruntled about higher taxes and expanding health care subsidies.

One reason that the median voter rationally agrees to protect the property of the rich and to tax them moderately may be that she sees the rich as more efficient managers of that property, and therefore as creators of jobs and prosperity that everyone will benefit from. So, to the extent that the rich are self-made, and have come out winners in a competitive, fair, and transparent market, society may be better off allowing them to own and manage their wealth, settling in return for a reasonable share of their produce as taxes. The more, however, that the rich are seen as idle or crooked – as having simply inherited or, worse, gained their wealth nefariously – the more the median voter should be willing to vote for tough regulations and punitive taxes on them.

In some emerging markets today, for example, property rights of the rich do not enjoy widespread popular support because so many of a country's fabulously wealthy oligarchs are seen as having acquired their wealth through dubious means. They grew rich because they managed the system, not because they managed their businesses well. When the government goes after rich tycoons, few voices are raised in protest. And, as the rich kowtow to the authorities to protect their wealth, a strong check on official arbitrariness disappears. The government is free to become more autocratic.

Consider, in contrast, a competitive free-enterprise system with a level playing field for all. Such a system generally tends to permit the most efficient to acquire wealth. The fairness of the competition improves perceptions of legitimacy. Moreover, under conditions of fair competition, the process of creative destruction tends to pull down badly managed inherited wealth, replacing it with new and dynamic wealth. Great inequality, built up over generations, does not become a source of great popular resentment.

On the contrary, everyone can dream that they, too, will become a Bill Gates or a Nandan Nilekani. When such universal aspirations seem plausible, the system gains added democratic support. The rich, confident of popular legitimacy, can then use the independence that accompanies wealth to limit arbitrary government, support rule of law, and protect democratic rights. Free enterprise and democracy sustain each other.

There are, therefore, deeper reasons for why democratic systems support property rights and free enterprise than the cynical argument that votes and legislators can be bought, and the capitalists have the money. The cynics can only be right for a while. Without popular support, wealth is protected only by increasingly coercive measures. Ultimately, such a system loses any vestige of either democracy or free enterprise.

THE BEDROCK: EQUITABLE DISTRIBUTION OF ECONOMIC CAPABILITIES

There is, however, a growing concern across the industrial world. The free enterprise system works well when participants enter the competitive arena with fundamentally equal chances of success. Given the subsequent level playing field, the winner's road to riches depends on greater effort, innovation, and occasionally luck. But success is not pre-determined because no class of participants has had a fundamentally different and superior preparation for the competition. If, however, some group's economic capabilities are sufficiently differentiated by preparation, the level playing field is no longer sufficient to equalize a priori chances of success. Instead, the free enterprise system will be seen as disproportionately favouring the better prepared. Democracy is unlikely to support it, nor are the rich and successful as likely to support democracy.

Such a scenario is no longer unthinkable in a number of Western democracies. Prosperity seems increasingly unreachable for many, because a good education, which seems to be today's passport to riches, is unaffordable for many in the middle class. Quality higher educational institutions are dominated by the children of the rich, not because they have unfairly bought their way in, but because they simply have been taught and supported better by expensive schools and private tutors. Because middle class parents do not have the ability to give their children similar capabilities, they do not see the system as fair. Support for the free enterprise system is eroding, as witnessed by the popularity of books like Thomas Pikkety's *Capital in the 21st Century* while the influence of illiberal parties on both the Left and Right who promise to suppress competition, finance, and trade is increasing. The mutual support between free enterprise and democracy is giving way to antagonism.

Moreover, as class differences create differentiated capabilities among the public, governments can either continue choosing the most capable applicants for positions but risk becoming unrepresentative of the classes, or they can choose representativeness over ability, and risk eroding effectiveness. Neither biased nor ineffective government can administer well. So government capacity may also be threatened.

Thus, as the bedrock of equitable distribution of capabilities has started developing cracks in industrial countries, all four pillars supporting the liberal free market democracy have also started swaying. This is, to my mind, an enormously important concern that will occupy states across the world in the years to come.

LESSONS FOR INDIA

Let me conclude with lessons for India. India inherited a kind of democracy during British rule and has made it thoroughly and vibrantly her own. Of the three pillars that Fukuyama emphasizes, the strongest in India is therefore democratic accountability. India also adheres broadly to the rule of law. Where arguably we may have a long way to go, as Fukuyama has emphasized, is in the capacity of the government (and by this I mean regulators like the RBI also) to deliver governance and public services.

This is not to say that we do not have areas of excellence strewn throughout central and state governments – whether it is the building of the New Delhi Metro, the reach of the public distribution system in Tamil Nadu, or the speed of the roll-out of the Pradhan Mantri Jan Dhan Yojana – but that such capabilities have to permeate every tehsil in every state. Moreover, in many areas of government and regulation, as the economy develops, we need more specialists, with the domain knowledge and experience. For instance, well-trained economists are at a premium throughout the government, and there are far too few Indian Economic Service officers to go around.

An important difference from the historical experience of other countries is that elsewhere strong government has typically emerged there first, and it is then restrained by rule of law and democratic accountability. In India, we have the opposite situation today, with strong institutions like the judiciary, opposition parties, the free press, and NGOs, whose aim is to check government excess. However, necessary government function is sometimes hard to distinguish from excess. We will have to strengthen government (and regulatory) capability resisting the temptation to implant layers and layers of checks and balances even before capacity has taken root. We must choose a happy medium between giving the administration unchecked power and creating complete paralysis, recognizing that our task is different from the one that confronted the West when it developed, or even the task faced by other Asian economies.

For instance, a business-approval process that mandates numerous government surveys in remote areas should also consider our administrative capacity to do those surveys well and on time. If it does not provide for that capacity, it ensures there will be no movement forward. Similarly, if we create a multiple appellate process against government or regulatory action that is slow and undiscriminating, we contain government excess but also risk halting necessary government actions. If the government or regulator is less effective in preparing its case than private parties, we ensure that the appellate process largely biases justice towards those who have the resources to use it, rather than rectifying a miscarriage of justice. So in thinking through reforms, we may want to move from the theoretical ideal of how a system might work in a country with enormous administrative capacity, to how it would work in the actual Indian situation. Let me emphasize, we need 'checks and balance', but we should ensure a balance of checks. We cannot have escaped from the Licence Permit Raj only to end up in the Appellate Raj!

Finally, a heartening recent development is that more people across the country are becoming well-educated and equipped to compete. One of the most enjoyable experiences at the RBI is meeting the children of our Class IV employees, many of whom hold jobs as business executives in private sector firms. As, across the country, education makes our youth upwardly mobile, public support for free enterprise has expanded. Increasingly, therefore, the political dialogue has also moved, from giving handouts to creating jobs. So long as we modulate the pace of liberalization to the pace at which we broaden economic capabilities, it is likely that the public will be supportive of reform. This also means that if we are to embed the four pillars supporting prosperity and political freedom firmly in our society, we have to continue to nurture the broadly equitable distribution of economic capabilities among our people. Economic inclusion, by which I mean easing access to quality education, nutrition, health care, finance, and markets to all our citizens, is therefore a necessity for sustainable growth. It is also, obviously, a moral imperative.

Postscript: One name in this entire speech proved controversial: 'Hitler'. If I had known the connections that would be made on social media, I would not have used it. The speech was about the need to remedy the weakness of government capacity in general in India – with no specific administration in mind. It was instead construed as a warning against strong government, specifically the current administration. I could not, however, bulletproof my speeches against any and all imagined interpretations.

V

Perhaps the most important proposal for the reshaping of India's future path during my tenure was the NDA government's proposal to 'Make in India'. I thought this was an excellent idea, for it would mean the government would focus on improving India's capacity to produce, whether it be goods or services, either for the domestic economy through import substitution, or for the global economy through exports. I thought it important to clarify that making in India did not necessarily mean selling primarily to the export markets. Given both slow global growth, as well as increasing protectionism, we should not rule out making for the large and vibrant Indian market. Indeed, for a while, this could well be the primary growth market for Indian products. In the short run, we would probably make in India, largely for India. The longer run could be different, depending on how circumstances developed. This is what I laid out in my Dr Bharat Ram Lecture, delivered in Delhi in December 2014, which was primarily a speech about how we should manage risks if we catered primarily to domestic demand.

Make in India, Largely for India

The global economy is still weak, despite a strengthening recovery in the United States. The Euro area is veering close to recession, Japan has already experienced two quarters of negative growth after a tax hike, and many emerging markets are rethinking their export-led growth models as the industrial world stagnates. In the last couple of years, the IMF has repeatedly reduced its growth forecasts. After six years of a tepid post-crisis recovery, the IMF titled its most recent World Economic Outlook 'Legacies, Clouds, Uncertainties'.

WHAT ABOUT EMERGING MARKETS?

Slow industrial country growth has made more difficult a traditional development path for emerging markets – export-led growth. Indeed, in the last decade, even as China developed on the back of its exports to industrial countries, other emerging markets flourished as they exported to China. Emerging markets now have to rely once again on domestic demand, always a difficult task because of the temptation to overstimulate. That task has become more difficult because of the abundance of liquidity sloshing around the world as a result of ultra-accommodative monetary policies in industrial countries. Any signs of growth can attract foreign capital, and if not properly managed, these flows can precipitate a credit and asset price boom and exchange rate overvaluation. When industrial country monetary policies are eventually tightened, some of the capital is likely to depart emerging market shores. Emerging markets have to take extreme care to ensure they are not vulnerable at that point.

What implications should an emerging economy like India, which has weathered the initial squalls of the 'Taper Tantrums' of the summer of 2013, take away for its policies over the medium term? I would focus on four: 1) Make in India; 2) Make for India; 3) Ensure transparency and stability of the economy; 4) Work towards a more open and fair global system.

LESSONS FOR INDIA

I. MAKE IN INDIA

The government has the commendable aim of making more in India. This means improving the efficiency of producing in India, whether of agricultural commodities, mining, manufacturing, or services.

To achieve this goal, it has to implement its ambitious plans for building out infrastructure. This includes

- Physically linking every corner of the country to domestic and international markets through roads, railways, ports and airports. The kind of economic activity that is generated when a pukka all-weather road is built into a village – the explosion of horticulture, poultry, and dairy farming, the opening of clothing and assorted goods shops, the increasing use of powered vehicles – is extraordinary, as is the kind of activity that emerges around national highways.
- Ensuring the availability of inputs such as power, minerals, and water at competitive prices.
- Linking everyone electronically and financially to the broader system through mobiles, broadband, and intermediaries such as business correspondents.
- Encouraging the development of public institutions such as markets, warehouses, regulators, information aggregators and disseminators, etc.
- Making possible affordable and safe homes and workplaces.

A second necessity for increasing productivity in India is to improve human capital. This requires enhancing the quality and spread of health care, nutrition, and sanitation to start with so that people are healthy and able. People also need better and more appropriate education, skills that are valued in the labour markets, and jobs where firms have the incentive to invest more in their learning.

The government is examining the cost of doing business in India with a view to bring it down. The woes of the small entrepreneur, as she confronts the myriad mysterious regulations that govern her, and the numerous inspectors who have the power of closing her down, are well known. The petty bureaucrat, empowered by these regulations, can become a tyrant. It is appropriate that the government intends to make him help business rather than hinder it. As regulators, we too have to continuously examine the costs and benefits of the regulations we impose.

Finally, we need make access to finance easier. I have spoken about that in other contexts, and will not dwell on it here. Before I move on, let me add some caveats.

There is a danger when we discuss 'Make in India' of assuming it means a focus on manufacturing, an attempt to follow the export-led growth path that China followed. I don't think such a specific focus is intended.

First, as I have just argued, slow-growing industrial countries will be much less likely to be able to absorb a substantial additional amount of imports in the foreseeable future. Other emerging markets certainly could absorb more, and a regional focus for exports will pay off. But the world as a whole is unlikely to be able to accommodate another export-led China.

Second, industrial countries themselves have been improving capital-intensive flexible manufacturing, so much so that some manufacturing activity is being 're-shored'. Any emerging market wanting to export manufacturing goods will have to contend with this new phenomenon. Third, when India pushes into manufacturing exports, it will have China, which still has some surplus agricultural labour to draw on, to contend with. Export-led growth will not be as easy as it was for the Asian economies who took that path before us.

I am not advocating export pessimism here – India has been extremely successful at carving out its own areas of comparative advantage, and will continue to do so. Instead, I am counselling against an export-led strategy that involves subsidizing exporters with cheap inputs as well as an undervalued exchange rate, simply because it is unlikely to be as effective at this juncture. I am also cautioning against picking a particular sector such as manufacturing for encouragement, simply because it has worked well for China. India is different, and developing at a different time, and we should be agnostic about what will work.

More broadly, such agnosticism means creating an environment where all sorts of enterprise can flourish, and then leaving entrepreneurs, of whom we have plenty, to choose what they want to do. Instead of subsidizing inputs to specific industries because they are deemed important or labour intensive, a strategy that has not really paid off for us over the years, let us figure out the public goods each sector needs, and strive to provide them. For instance, SMEs might benefit much more from an agency that can certify product quality, or a platform to help them sell receivables, or a state portal that will create marketing websites for them, than from subsidized credit. The tourist industry will probably benefit more from visa on arrival and a strong transportation network than from the tax sops they usually demand.

A second possible misunderstanding is to see 'Make in India' as a strategy of import substitution through tariff barriers. This strategy has been tried and it has not worked because it ended up reducing domestic competition, making producers inefficient, and increasing costs to consumers. Instead, 'Make in India' will typically mean more openness, as we create an environment that makes our firms able to compete with the rest of the world, and encourages foreign producers to come take advantage of our environment to create jobs in India.

2. MAKE FOR INDIA

If external demand growth is likely to be muted, we have to produce for the internal market. This means we have to work on creating the strongest sustainable unified market we can, which requires a reduction in the transactions costs of buying and selling throughout the country. Improvements in the physical transportation network I discussed earlier will help, but so will fewer but more efficient and competitive intermediaries in the supply chain from producer to the consumer. A well-designed GST bill, by reducing state border taxes, will have the important consequence of creating a truly national market for goods and services, which will be critical for our growth in years to come.

Domestic demand has to be financed responsibly, as far as possible through domestic savings. Our banking system is undergoing some stress. Our banks have to learn from past mistakes in project evaluation and structuring as they finance the immense needs of the economy. They will also have to improve their efficiency as they compete with new players such as the recently licenced universal banks as well as the soon-to-be licensed payment banks and small finance banks. At the same time, we should not make their task harder by creating impediments in the process of turning around, or recovering, stressed assets. The RBI, the government, as well as the courts have considerable work to do here.

We also have to work on spreading financial services to the excluded, for once they learn how to manage finances and save they can be relied on to borrow responsibly. New institutions and new products to seek out financial savings in every corner of the country will also help halt the erosion in household savings rates, as will a low and stable inflation rate. The income tax benefits for an individual to save have been largely fixed in nominal terms till the recent budget, which means the real value of the benefits have eroded. Some budgetary incentives for household savings could help ensure that the country's investment is largely financed from domestic savings.

3. ENSURE TRANSPARENCY AND STABILITY OF THE ECONOMY

As I argued earlier in the speech, even developed countries like Portugal and Spain have been singularly unable to manage domestic demand. Countries tend to overstimulate, with large fiscal deficits, large current account deficits, high credit and asset price growth, only to see growth collapse as money gets tight. The few countries that have avoided such booms and busts typically have done so with sound policy frameworks.

As a country that does not belong to any power blocs, we do not ever want to be in a position where we need multilateral support. It will be all the more important to get our policy frameworks right.

Clearly, a sound fiscal framework around a clear fiscal consolidation path is critical. The Dr Bimal Jalan Committee's report will provide a gameplan for the former, while the government has clearly indicated its intent to stick to the fiscal consolidation path that has been laid out. Whether we need more

institutions to ensure deficits stay within control and the quality
of budgets is high, is something worth debating. A number of
countries have independent budget offices/committees that opine
on budgets. These offices are especially important in scoring
budgetary estimates, including unfunded long-term liabilities that
the industrial countries have shown are so easy to contract in
times of growth and so hard to actually deliver.

On the monetary side, a central bank focused primarily on
keeping inflation low and stable will ensure the best conditions
for growth. In reacting to developments, however, the central
bank has to recognize that emerging markets are not as resilient
as industrial economies. So the path of disinflation cannot be as
steep as in an industrial economy because an emerging market is
more fragile, and people's buffers and safety nets are thinner. A
'Volcker' like disinflation was never on the cards in India, but an
Urjit Patel glide path fits us very well, ensuring moderate growth
even while we disinflate. Going forward, we will discuss an
appropriate timeline with the government in which the economy
should move to the centre of the medium-term inflation band of
2 to 6 per cent.

In addition to inflation, however, a central bank has to pay
attention to financial stability. This is a secondary objective,
but it may become central if the economy enters a low-inflation
credit and asset price boom. Financial stability sometimes means
regulators, including the central bank, have to go against popular
sentiment. The role of regulators is not to boost the Sensex but to
ensure that the underlying fundamentals of the economy and its
financial system are sound enough for sustainable growth. Any
positive consequences to the Sensex are welcome but are only a
collateral benefit, not the objective.

Finally, India will, for the foreseeable future, run a current
account deficit, which means we will need net foreign financing.
The best form of financing is long-term equity, that is, Foreign
Direct Investment (FDI), which has the additional benefit of
bringing in new technologies and methods. While we should not
be railroaded into compromising India's interest to attract FDI
– for example, the requirements to patent a medicine in India

are perfectly reasonable, no matter what the international drug companies say – we should ensure policies are transparent and redress quick. If we make it easier for young Indian companies to do business, we will also make it easier for foreign companies to invest, for after all both are outsiders to the system. This means a transparent and quick legal process to deal with contractual disputes, and a proper system of bankruptcy to deal with distress. Both are issues the government has taken on.

Let me turn finally to the international framework.

4. WORK TOWARDS A MORE OPEN AND FAIR GLOBAL SYSTEM

As a country that does not belong to any power bloc, and that does not export vital natural resources but is dependent on substantial commodity imports, India needs an open, competitive and vibrant system of international trade and finance. Our energy security, for example, lies not in owning oil assets in remote fragile countries but in ensuring the global oil market works well and is not disrupted. We need strong independent multilateral institutions that can play the role of impartial arbiter in facilitating international economic transactions.

Unfortunately, the international monetary system is still dominated by the frameworks put in place in the past by industrial countries, and its governance is still dominated by their citizens. To be fair, it is changing, albeit slowly. But there is a more immediate reason for faster change. With slow growth, as well as the need to finance large debt loads, the interest of industrial countries in an open global system cannot be taken for granted. For instance, regulations that have the appearance of shoring up the safety and soundness of the industrial country financial system may have the collateral effect of discouraging investment in emerging market assets. We have to recognize that slow growth may direct industrial economy policy makers' attention inwards, even while politics turns protectionist. The multilateral governance system, still dominated by industrial countries, may not provide a sufficient defence of openness.

Emerging markets may therefore have the responsibility of keeping the global economy open. For this, not only do emerging markets have to work on quota and management reforms in the multilateral institutions, but they also have to work on injecting new agendas, new ideas, and new thinking into the global arena. No longer will it suffice for India to simply object to industrial country proposals, it will have to put some of its own on the table. And this means that our research departments, universities, and think tanks have to develop ideas that they can feed to India's representatives in international meetings.

CONCLUSION

Let me conclude. We are more dependent on the global economy than we think. That it is growing more slowly, and is more inward looking, than in the past means that we have to look to regional and domestic demand for our growth – to make in India primarily for India. Domestic-demand-led growth is notoriously difficult to manage, and typically leads to excess. This is why we need to strengthen domestic macroeconomic institutions, so that we can foster sustainable and stable growth. At the same time, we cannot let foreign markets shrink further, and we have to take up the fight for an open global system. Rather than being reactive, we have to be active in setting the agenda. That requires investment in our idea-producing institutions – research departments of official bodies, think tanks, as well as universities. In sum, the diminished expectations in the world at large should not be a reason for us to lower our sights.

Postscript: This speech was ultimately one on national risk management – what we needed to do in the environment of falling trade and rising protectionism that faced us. It became mildly controversial, I believe, because it was misunderstood. Critics said it was an attack on 'Make in India', and I was proposing an alternative, 'Make for India'. This was completely incorrect. No sensible economist could be against making in India if that came from an improvement in the business and infrastructure environment rather than our old, discredited policy of raising import barriers to encourage import substitution. Equally clearly, my critics had not read the title 'Make in India, Largely for India', let alone the content of the speech, which elaborated on, and extended, the government proposal. I did not disagree with where one should encourage production – we should 'Make in India'. Where I felt some of the narrow votaries were being overly optimistic is in expecting strong global demand at this time, given global weakness. I was not advocating export pessimism, but realism, borne out by the subsequent significant weakness in exports that we have experienced. We had to make in India, but initially largely for India, and so we have done at the time of writing.

I was invited to give the convocation address at my alma mater, the Indian Institute of Technology, Delhi. As I pondered over what I would say, I realized that the graduating students were young enough to be my children. What message would I give my children at this time, a message that would challenge as well as inspire them, as convocation speeches are meant to do? It could not be another speech on economics – that might educate but not inspire. The moment made the choice of topic clear. There was a raging debate in India in late 2015 on the issue of tolerance, and this is what I decided to speak on. I explained to the young graduating scholars that India's strength is her enduring tradition of tolerance and debate, and that it will be our source of comparative economic advantage as we approach the frontiers of innovation. This is the speech I delivered on 31 October 2015.

Tolerance and Respect: Essentials for Economic Progress

Thank you very much for inviting me back to the Institute to deliver the convocation address. I graduated with a degree in Electrical Engineering thirty years ago. I was overly anxious then about what the future held for me, because I did not realize that the Institute had prepared me so well for what lay ahead. Our professors – and I will not single out any to avoid a disservice to those I do not name – were dedicated professionals. They asked a lot of us, knowing that in challenging us they allowed us to learn what we were capable of. Equally important, our Electrical

Engineering class – in those days, Computer Science was part of Electrical Engineering in IIT Delhi – had some of the smartest people it has been my privilege to know. After working with them as colleagues, and competing with them for grades, I learned what it took to succeed in the fiercest environments; very hard work, friendship, and boatloads of luck. Those lessons have stayed with me since.

IIT Delhi then, as I am sure it is now, was not only about studies – it was about growing up. We were, with a few notable exceptions, the proverbial school nerds who had been excluded from all school sports by the macho sports cases. With almost everyone in the same boat at IIT, for the first time in our lives we got a chance to bat and bowl at the nets, instead of being posted at deep long on to retrieve the odd six by the stars. Everyone did something, ranging from photography to publishing. Of course, we all aspired to join dramatics, where you got to spend long hours with members of the opposite sex. Unfortunately, I was no good at acting, so I had to look for self-actualization elsewhere. But there were enough places to look.

Student politics was vibrant, with plenty of scheming, strategizing, and back-stabbing. It was an intellectual pastime, however, without the violence and corruption that plagues student politics elsewhere in our country. You had to convince the small intelligent electorate to vote for you, and in figuring out how to get that vote, we all learnt the art of persuasion.

So we grew up in the classrooms, in the squash courts at the RCA, in the civilizing SPIC-Macay overnight classical music concerts and in the overcrowded rock concerts at the OAT. Some of us spent long hours waiting hopefully outside Kailash Hostel, and when occasionally our wait was rewarded, beautiful autumn nights with our friends, chatting and gazing at the stars while sitting on the roof of Convocation Hall. The Institute replaced our naivety with a more confident maturity. We came in as smart boys and girls and left as wiser young men and women. I am confident that the Institute has done to you what it did to us. You will thank it in the years to come for that.

In speaking here today, I am aware that most convocation

addresses are soon forgotten. That creates a form of moral hazard for the speaker. If you are not going to remember what I say, I don't have the incentive to work hard at crafting my words. The net effect is what economists refer to as a bad equilibrium; my speech is forgettable, and you therefore forget it soon. If so, we are probably better off with me skipping the rest of the speech, and all of us going on to other pressing duties.

Nevertheless, I am going to look beyond my personal incentives and fulfil my dharma as chief guest. I will speak on why India's tradition of debate and an open spirit of enquiry is critical for its economic progress. Let me explain.

Robert Solow won the Nobel Prize in Economics for work that showed that the bulk of economic growth did not come from putting more factors of production such as labour and capital to work. Instead, it came from putting those factors of production together more cleverly, that is, from what he called total factor productivity growth. Put differently, new ideas, new methods of production, better logistics – these are what lead to sustained economic growth. Of course, a poor country like ours can grow for some time by putting more people to work, by moving them from low productivity agriculture to higher value-added industry or services, and by giving them better tools to do their jobs. As many of you who have taken economics will recognize, we in India are usually far from the production possibility frontier, so we can grow for a long while just by catching up with the methods of industrial countries.

But more intelligent ways of working will enable us to leapfrog old methods and come more quickly to the production possibility frontier – as for example, we have done in parts of the software industry. And, of course, once you are at the frontier and using the best methods in the world, the only way to grow is to innovate and be even better than others in the world. This is what our software firms are now trying to do.

Our alums, whom you students will shortly join, are leading India's charge to the frontier and beyond. Take the fantastic developments in e-commerce, ranging from the creation of electronic marketplaces to new logistics networks and payments systems. Today, a consumer in a small town can have the same choice of clothing fashions that anyone from the large metros enjoys, simply because the Internet has brought all the shops in India to her doorstep. And while her local shop no longer can sell shoddy apparel, it now focuses on the perishable items she needs in a hurry, even while sub-contracting to provide the last leg of the logistic network that reaches her. Economic growth through new ideas and production methods is what our professors and alums contribute to the nation.

So what does an educational institution or a nation need to do to keep the idea factory open? The first essential is to foster *competition* in the marketplace for ideas. This means encouraging challenge to all authority and tradition, even while acknowledging that the only way of dismissing any view is through empirical tests. What this rules out is anyone imposing a particular view or ideology because of their power. Instead, all ideas should be scrutinized critically, no matter whether they originate domestically or abroad, whether they have matured over thousands of years or a few minutes, whether they come from an untutored student or a world-famous professor.

I am sure many of you have come across Richard Feynman's *Lectures on Physics*, a must-read when we were at IIT. The Nobel prize-winning physicist was one of the giants of the twentieth century. In his autobiography, though, he writes how he found the atmosphere at the Institute of Advanced Studies at Princeton stultifying. Now, as you know, the Institute of Advanced Studies brings together some of the finest scholars in the world to ponder problems in a multi-disciplinary environment. But he found the atmosphere sterile because there were no students to ask him questions, questions that would force him to rethink his beliefs and perhaps discover new theories. Ideas start with questioning and alternative viewpoints, sometimes seemingly silly ones. After all, Einstein built his Theory of Relativity pondering the somewhat wacky question of what someone travelling in a train at the speed of light would experience. So nothing should be excluded but everything should be subject to debate and constant testing. No one should be allowed to offer unquestioned pronouncements. Without this competition for ideas, we have stagnation.

This then leads to a second essential: *protection*, not of specific ideas and traditions, but the right to question and challenge, the right to behave differently so long as it does not hurt others seriously. In this protection lies societal self-interest, for it is by encouraging the challenge of innovative rebels that society develops, that it gets the ideas that propel Solow's total factor productivity growth. Fortunately, India has always protected debate and the right to have different views. Some have even embedded these views in permanent structures. Raja Raja Chola, in building the magnificent Brihadeeswara Shaivite temple at Thanjavur, also incorporated sculptures of Vishnu as well as the meditating Buddha, thus admitting to alternative viewpoints. When Shahenshah Jalaluddin Muhammad Akbar invited scholars of all manner of persuasion to debate the eternal verities at his court, he was only following older traditions of our Hindu and Buddhist kings, who encouraged and protected the spirit of enquiry.

What then of group sentiment? Should ideas or behaviour that hurt a particular intellectual position or group not be banned? Possibly, but a quick resort to bans will chill all debate as everyone will be anguished by ideas they dislike. It is far better to improve the environment for ideas through tolerance and mutual respect.

Let me explain. Actions that physically harm anyone, or show verbal contempt for a particular group so that they damage the group's participation in the marketplace for ideas, should certainly not be allowed. For example, sexual harassment, whether physical or verbal, has no place in society. At the same time, groups should not be looking for slights any and everywhere, so that too much is seen as offensive; the theory of confirmation bias in psychology suggests that once one starts looking for insults, one can find them everywhere, even in the most innocuous statements. Indeed, if what you do offends me but does not harm me otherwise, there should be a very high bar for prohibiting your act. After all, any ban, and certainly any vigilante acts to enforce it, may offend you as much, or more, than the offence to me. Excessive political correctness stifles progress as much as excessive licence and disrespect.

Put differently, while you should avoid pressing the buttons that upset me to the extent possible, when you do push them you should explain carefully why that is necessary so as to move the debate forward, and how it should not be interpreted as a personal attack on me. You have to tread *respectfully*, assuring me that a challenge to the ideas I hold is necessary for progress. At the same time, I should endeavour to hold few ideas so closely intertwined with my personality that any attack on them is deemed an intolerable personal affront. *Tolerance* means not being so insecure about one's ideas that one cannot subject them to challenge – it implies a degree of detachment that is absolutely necessary for mature debate. Finally, respect requires that in the rare case when an idea is tightly associated with a group's core personality, we are extra careful about challenging it.

Tolerance can take the offence out of debate, and indeed instil respect. If I go berserk every time a particular button is pressed, rebels are tempted to press the button, while mischief-makers indeed do so. But if I do not react predictably, and instead ask button pressers to explain their concerns, rebels are forced to do the hard work of marshalling arguments. So, rebels do not press the button frivolously, while the thuggish mischief-makers who abound in every group are left without an easy trigger. Tolerance and respect then lead to a good equilibrium where they reinforce each other.

For example, rebellious youth in the United States used to burn the American flag. It was calculated to upset the older generation that had fought in America's wars, for the flag was a symbol of all they had fought for. And the police, many of whom were veterans, used to react with violence, which was precisely the reaction the rebels sought to further their cause. Over time, though, U.S. society has become more tolerant of flag-burning. Because it no longer triggers a reaction, it is no longer used as an instrument to shock. In sum, if group sentiment becomes more tolerant and less easily hurt, the actions that try to hurt it will diminish. As Mahatma Gandhi said, 'The golden rule of conduct is mutual toleration, seeing that we will never all think alike and we shall always see Truth in fragments and from different points of vision.'

Let me conclude. IITans like you will lead India's race for ideas. The India that you will graduate into is much more capable of using your technological prowess than the India we graduated into. I wish you unlimited ambition, and forecast great success for those of you who continue thinking and challenging. But as you go out in the world, remember our tradition of debate in an environment of respect and tolerance. By upholding it, by fighting for it, you will be repaying your teachers in this great institution, and your parents who worked so hard to send you here. And you will be doing our country a great patriotic service. Thank you and good luck.

Postscript: I knew this speech would be misinterpreted by the usual critics, but I had decided to look beyond them. Once again, many who did not read, criticized nevertheless. They felt I was complaining about India's intolerance when in fact the speech is about maintaining our tradition for tolerance. Some of the commentary bordered on the hilarious, essentially saying 'we are a tolerant nation, he accuses us of intolerance, so fire him' or words to that effect. What mattered most to me, however, was a one-liner from one of my staunchest young critics, my teenage son. From far away, he read my speech closely, and satisfied it met his exacting standards, he wrote, 'I am proud of you.'

VII

Social media does take a life of its own. In its world of alternative truths, the reality can get grossly distorted. Occasionally, in a game resembling Chinese Whispers, each commentator opined on what they thought I had said, based on a previous commentator's garbled version, without many bothering to find out what I actually said.

Speaking of being misunderstood, perhaps the greatest flak I got was for some comments I made at the end of a tiring day at the IMF meetings. I was being interviewed for MarketWatch by Greg Robb, whom I knew well. In the middle of a long interview, the question I was posed was:

> MarketWatch: The Indian economy is the bright spot in the global economy. When other central bankers and finance ministers ask you for your secret sauce, what do you tell them?

My natural caution as a central banker as well as my concern that our recovery was work in progress suggested I should not boast. So here is what I said.

> Rajan: Well, I think we've still to get to a place where we feel satisfied. We have this saying, 'in the land of the blind, the one-eyed man is king.' We're a little bit that way. We feel things are turning to the point where we could achieve what we believe is our medium-run growth potential. Because things are falling into place. Investment is starting to pick up strongly. We have a fair degree of macro-stability. Of course, not immune to every shock, but immune to a fair number of shocks. The current account deficit is around 1 per cent. The fiscal deficit has come down and continues to come down and

the government is firm on a consolidation path. Inflation has come down from 11 per cent to less than 5 per cent now. And interest rates therefore can also come down. We have an inflation targeting framework in place. So a bunch of good things have happened.

There are still some things to do. Of course, structural reforms are ongoing. The government is engaged in bringing out a new bankruptcy code. There is goods and services tax on the anvil. But there is a lot of exciting stuff which is already happening. For example, just last week, I was fortunate to inaugurate a platform which allows mobile-to-mobile transfers from any bank account to any other bank account in the country. It is a public platform, so anybody can participate. It is not owned by any one company, unlike Apple Pay or Android Pay or whatever. I think it is the first of its kind. So technological developments are happening and making for a more, hopefully, reasonable life for a lot of people. Let's see how it goes.

On any fair read of my entire answer, one would conclude that I was optimistic about India, not downplaying what was going on, even while recognizing we had work to do. But social media went to town after plucking just the following words out of the answer: 'We have this saying, "in the land of the blind, the one-eyed man is king." We're a little bit that way.' A couple of ministers, fed this quote, commented adversely on what I said. I was finally fed up of the perhaps motivated search for controversy. So I picked the National Institute of Bank Management Convocation on 20 April 2016 to say the following, cautioning on euphoria and ending by emphasizing once again the need for mutual respect and tolerance.

Words Matter but So Does Intent

As I reflected on what I should speak on, I thought I would speak on a recent experience that offers what the Americans call 'a teachable moment'. To get to the experience, start first with where India is. India is the fastest growing large country in the world, though with manufacturing capacity utilization low at 70 per cent and agricultural growth slow following two bad monsoons, our potential is undoubtedly higher.

Growth, however, is just one measure of performance. The level of per capita GDP is also important. We are still one of the poorest large countries in the world on a per capita basis, and have a long way to go before we reasonably address the concerns of each one of our citizens. We are often compared with China. But the Chinese economy, which was smaller than ours in the 1960s, is now five times our size at market exchange rates. The average Chinese citizen is over four times richer than the average Indian. The sobering thought is we have a long way to go before we can claim we have arrived.

As a central banker who has to be pragmatic, I cannot get euphoric if India is the fastest growing large economy. Our current growth certainly reflects the hard work of the government and the people of the country, but we have to repeat this performance for the next twenty years before we can give every Indian a decent livelihood. This is not to disparage what has been and is being done. The central and state governments have been creating a platform for strong and sustainable growth, and I am confident the payoffs are on their way, but until we have stayed on this path for some time, I remain cautious.

We must remember that our international reputation is of a country with great promise, which has under-delivered in the past. This is why we are still the poorest country on a per capita basis among the BRICS. We need to change perceptions by delivering steadily on our promise for a long time – by implementing, implementing, and implementing. We cannot get carried away by our current superiority in growth, for as soon as we believe in our own superiority and start distributing future wealth as if we already have it, we stop doing all that is required to continue growing. This movie has played too many times in India's past for us to not know how it ends.

So in speaking to a foreign journalist the other day, who asked what it felt like to be the bright spot in the world economy, I used the phrase 'Andhon mein kana raja' or 'In the land of the blind, the one-eyed man is king'. The proverb has a long multinational history. The Dutch philosopher, Erasmus, used it in Latin when he wrote 'In regione caecorum rex est luscus', but he probably was inspired by earlier work.

My intent was to signal that our outperformance was accentuated because world growth was weak, but we in India were still hungry for more growth. I then explained that we were not yet at our potential, though we were at a cusp of a substantial pick-up in growth given all the reforms that were under way.

In our news-hungry country, however, our domestic papers headlined the phrase I used. To be fair, they also offered the surrounding context, but few read beyond the headline. So the interview became moderately controversial, with the implication that I was denigrating our success rather than emphasizing the need to do more.

More generally, every word or phrase a public figure speaks is intensely wrung for meaning. When words are hung to dry out of context, as in a newspaper headline, it then becomes fair game for anyone who wants to fill in meaning to create mischief. Worst, of course, are words or proverbs that have common usage elsewhere, because those can be most easily and deliberately misinterpreted. If we are to have a reasonable public dialogue, everyone should read words in their context, not stripped of it. That may be a forlorn hope!

I do, however, want to apologize to a section of the population that I did hurt, the blind. After all, the proverb suggests that a one-eyed man is better than a blind one. A moment's thought suggests this is not true. For the blind can develop capabilities that more than make up for their disability. Indeed, the sheer willpower and hunger to succeed of the disabled can help them become over-achievers in a seeing man's world. Moreover, because their other faculties, such as touch, smell, and hearing, are more finely honed, the blind may add new perspectives and new variety to our world, making it richer and more vibrant. So I am indeed sorry for implying the blind were otherwise than capable.

But this leads to an important question. How much of our language is tinged with meaning that is liable to misinterpretation? How forgiving should we be of a bad choice of words when the intent is clearly different?

Let me give you two examples. Gandhiji used to say, 'An eye for an eye will only make the whole world go blind'. Clearly, what is implied is that the whole world going blind is not a desirable state of affairs. One might take umbrage since it suggests blindness is an inferior state to that of being able to see, and the saying could be seen as discriminatory. Yet Gandhiji's focus was on the absurdity of a policy of revenge, not on blindness, and his intent was not to disparage the blind.

My second example comes from a faculty meeting I once attended where a male professor used the phrase 'As a rule of thumb' to make his point. A female history professor became visibly agitated and angry. She explained that 'the rule of thumb' referred historically to the maximum width of the stick with which a man could beat his wife without breaking the law. She was angry the male professor used the phrase so lightly, seemingly condoning domestic violence. He, of course, had no clue of the historical origins of the phrase, and apologized profusely. Clearly, his ignorance suggested he had no intent to offend, yet the female professor was offended.

There are two important issues here. First, if we spend all our time watching our words and using inoffensive language or hedging everything with caveats, we will be dull and will not be able to communicate because no one will listen.

For instance, 'An eye for an eye will only make the world go blind' could be replaced by 'Revenge reduces collective welfare'. The latter is short, inoffensive, and pithy, but meaningless for most listeners. Alternatively, we could say 'The taking of any body part for another will temporarily reduce the collective capabilities of the population thus affected, until they develop the faculties that will allow them to compensate for the missing body parts.' This restatement is more correct than the original, but lacks zing and therefore the ability to persuade.

At the same time, not paying attention to words or phrases that give offence risks perpetuating debilitating stereotypes that prevent advancement. When referring to bankers, scientists, engineers, or surgeons in the abstract, we often refer to them as 'he', thus perpetuating the unfortunate stereotype that these are not jobs for women. Clearly, in doing so we ignore the increasing presence, and even dominance, of women in these fields. What should we do to remedy matters?

I think we all have work to do to improve public dialogue. Speakers have to be more careful with words and not be gratuitously offensive. At the same time, listeners should not look for insults everywhere, and should place words in context so as to understand intent. In other words, for effective communication and debate, rather than the angry exchanges that we see on some TV shows, we need both respect and tolerance. The greatest danger of all is that we do not communicate or debate, for then we will allow distorted stereotypes to flourish unchallenged, and divisiveness to increase. In a country like ours, conceived and flourishing in diversity, that will truly be a disaster.

Interestingly, some of the reports of this speech were also confused. Was I contrite and apologizing for my words, was I apologizing to the blind, or was I defiant. I thought there was no need to clarify further. Those who did not wish to understand could not be forced to do so.

CHAPTER 8

INTERNATIONAL ISSUES

I

Through much of my term, I worried about the flood of liquidity unleashed by the central banks of industrial countries. In my previous role as Chief Economic Advisor, and co-chair of the Framework Working Group of the G-20, I, together with my very capable advisors, including Dr Prachi Mishra, had pushed the G-20 to finally recognize the possible adverse spillover effects (through capital flows) caused by industrial country monetary policies. When the U.S. Federal Reserve embarked on its process of tightening, I spoke publicly of the need for it to take the consequences of its actions around the world into account – I was committing the cardinal central banker sin of commenting on another central bank's policy, but I thought it was important for India. While I was not naïve enough to believe this would alter Fed policy, it contributed to an attitudinal change. Perhaps as a result of such commentary from a variety of sources, the Fed did say in a number of its subsequent statements that it was sensitive to conditions outside the United States, and in one policy meeting, may have held its hand because of unsettled conditions abroad. At any rate, I was invited to give a speech at the Brookings Institution on 10 April 2014 on my concerns.* Ben Bernanke, the recently retired Fed Chairman, was in the audience.

---

*A list of references I used for this piece can be found at https://www.rbi.org.in/scripts/BS_SpeechesView.aspx?Id=886.

Competitive Monetary Easing:
Is It Yesterday Once More?

As the world seems to be struggling back to its feet after the great financial crisis, I want to draw attention to an area we need to be concerned about: the conduct of monetary policy in this integrated world. A good way to describe the current environment is one of extreme monetary easing through unconventional policies. In a world where debt overhangs and the need for structural change constrain domestic demand, a sizeable portion of the effects of such policies spill over across borders, sometimes through a weaker exchange rate. More worryingly, it prompts a reaction. Such competitive easing occurs both simultaneously and sequentially, as I will argue, and both advanced economies and emerging economies engage in it. Aggregate world demand may be weaker and more distorted than it should be, and financial risks higher. To ensure stable and sustainable growth, the international rules of the game need to be revisited. Both advanced economies and emerging economies need to adapt, else I fear we are about to embark on the next leg of a wearisome cycle.

Central bankers are usually reluctant to air their concerns in public. But because the needed change has political elements to it, I take my cue from speeches by two central bankers whom I respect greatly, Ben Bernanke in his 2005 'Global Savings Glut' speech, and Jaime Caruana in his 2012 speech at Jackson Hole, both of whom have raised similar concerns to mine, although from different perspectives.

Before starting, I should disclose my interests in this era of transparency. For the last few months India has experienced large inflows of capital, not outflows, and is seen by the markets as an emerging economy that has made some of the necessary policy adjustments. We are well buffered with substantial reserves, though no country can be de-coupled from the international system. My remarks are motivated by the desire for a more stable international system, a system that works equally for rich and poor, large and small, and not the specifics of our situation.

UNCONVENTIONAL POLICY

I want to focus on unconventional monetary policies (UMP), by which I mean both policies that hold interest rates at near zero for long, as well as balance sheet policies such as quantitative easing or exchange intervention that involve altering central bank balance sheets in order to affect certain market prices. The key point that I will emphasize throughout this talk is that quantitative easing and sustained exchange intervention are in an economic equivalence class, though the channels they work through may be somewhat different. Our attitudes towards them should be conditioned by the size of their spillover effects rather than by any innate legitimacy of either form of intervention.

Let me also add there is a role for unconventional policies – when markets are broken or grossly dysfunctional, central bankers do have to think innovatively. Fortunately for the world, much of what they did immediately after the fall of Lehman was exactly right, though they were making it up as they went in the face of extreme uncertainty. They eased access to liquidity through innovative programmes such as Term Asset-Backed Securities Loan Facility (TALF), Term Auction Facility (TAF), Troubled Asset Relief Programme (TARP), Securities Market Programme (SMP), and Long-Term Refinancing Operation (LTRO). By lending long term without asking too many questions of the collateral they received, by buying assets beyond usual limits, and by focusing on repairing markets, they restored liquidity to a world financial system that would otherwise have been insolvent based on prevailing market asset prices. In this matter, central bankers are deservedly heroes. (I was not a member of the fraternity at that time, so I do not feel a conflict in doling out praise!)

The key question is what happens when these policies are prolonged long beyond repairing markets – and there the benefits are much less clear. Let me list four concerns:

1) Is unconventional monetary policy the right tool once the immediate crisis is over? Does it distort behaviour and activity so as to stand in the way of recovery? Is

accommodative monetary policy the way to fix a crisis
that was partly caused by excessively lax policy?

2) Do such policies buy time or does the belief that the
central bank is taking responsibility prevent other, more
appropriate, policies from being implemented? Put
differently, when central bankers say, however reluctantly,
that they are the only game in town, do they become the
only game in town?

3) Will exit from unconventional policies be easy?

4) What are the spillovers from such policies to other
countries?

Since I have dwelt at length on the first two concerns in an earlier
speech, let me focus on the last two.

EXIT

The macroeconomic argument for prolonged unconventional
policy in industrial countries is that it has low costs, provided
inflation stays quiescent. Hence it is worth pursuing, even if the
benefits are uncertain. A number of economists have, however,
raised concerns about financial sector risks that may build with
prolonged use of unconventional policy. Asset prices may not just
revert to earlier levels on exit, but they may overshoot on the
downside, and exit can cause significant collateral damage.

One reason is that leverage may increase both in the financial
sector and amongst borrowers as policy stays accommodative.
One channel seems to be that a boost to asset liquidity leads
lenders to believe that asset sales will backstop loan recovery,
leading them to increase loan to value ratios. When liquidity
tightens, though, too many lenders rely on asset sales, causing
asset prices and loan recovery to plummet. Because lenders do not
account for the effects of their lending on the 'fire sale' price, and
subsequently on lending by others, they may have an excessive
incentive to build leverage. These effects are exacerbated if, over
time, lenders become reliant on asset sales for recovery, rather
than on upfront project evaluation and due diligence. Another

possible channel is that banks themselves become more levered, or equivalently, acquire more illiquid balance sheets, if the central bank signals it will intervene in a sustained way when times are tough because unemployment is high.

Leverage need not be the sole reason why exit may be volatile after prolonged unconventional policy. Investment managers may fear underperforming relative to others. This means they will hold a risky asset only if it promises a risk premium (over safe assets) that makes them confident they will not underperform holding it. A lower path of expected returns on the safe asset makes it easier for the risky asset to meet the required risk premium, and indeed draws more investment managers to buy it – the more credible the forward guidance on 'low for long', the more the risk taking. However, as investment managers crowd into the risky asset, the risky asset is more finely priced so that the likelihood of possible fire sales increases if the interest rate environment turns. Every manager dumps the risky asset at that point in order to avoid being the last one holding it.

Leverage and investor crowding may therefore exacerbate the consequences of exit. When monetary policy is ultra-accommodative, prudential regulation, either of the macro or micro kind, is probably not a sufficient defence. In part, this is because, as Fed Governor Stein so succinctly put it, monetary policy 'gets into every crack', including the unregulated part of the financial system. In part, ultra accommodative monetary policy creates enormously powerful incentive distortions whose consequences are typically understood only after the fact. The consequences of exit, however, are not just felt domestically, they could be experienced internationally.

SPILLOVERS

Perhaps most vulnerable to the increased risk taking in this integrated world are countries across the border. When monetary policy in large countries is extremely and unconventionally accommodative, capital flows into recipient countries tend to increase local leverage; this is not just due to the direct effect of cross-border banking flows but also the indirect effect, as the appreciating exchange rate and rising asset prices, especially of real estate, make it seem that borrowers have more equity than they really have.

Exchange rate flexibility in recipient countries in these circumstances sometimes exacerbates booms rather than equilibrates. Indeed, in the recent episode of emerging market volatility after the Fed started discussing taper in May 2013, countries that allowed the real exchange rate to appreciate the most during the prior period of quantitative easing suffered the greatest adverse impact to financial conditions. Countries that undertake textbook policies of financial sector liberalization are not immune to the inflows – indeed, their deeper markets may draw more flows in, and these liquid markets may be where selling takes place when conditions in advanced economies turn.

Macro-prudential measures have little traction against the deluge of inflows – Spain had a housing boom despite its countercyclical provisioning. Recipient countries should adjust, of course, but credit and flows mask the magnitude and timing of needed adjustment. For instance, higher collections from property taxes on new houses, sales taxes on new sales, capital gains taxes on financial asset sales, and income taxes on a more prosperous financial sector may misleadingly suggest a country's fiscal house is in order, even while low-risk premia on sovereign debt add to the sense of calm. At the same time, an appreciating nominal exchange rate may also keep down inflation.

The difficulty of distinguishing the cyclical from the structural is exacerbated in some emerging markets where policy commitment is weaker, and the willingness to succumb to the siren calls of populist policy greater. But it would be a mistake to think that pro-cyclical policy in the face of capital inflows is primarily a disease of the poor; Even rich recipient countries with strong institutions, such as Ireland and Spain, have not been immune to capital-flow-induced fragility.

Ideally, recipient countries would wish for stable capital inflows, and not flows pushed in by unconventional policy. Once unconventional policies are in place, however, they do recognize the problems stemming from prolonged easy money, and thus the need for source countries to exit. But when source countries move to exit unconventional policies, some recipient countries are leveraged, imbalanced, and vulnerable to capital outflows. Given that investment managers anticipate the consequences of the future policy path, even a measured pace of exit may cause severe market turbulence and collateral damage. Indeed, the more transparent and well-communicated the exit is, the more certain the foreign investment managers may be of changed conditions, and the more rapid their exit from risky positions.

Recipient countries are not being irrational when they protest both the initiation of unconventional policy as well as an exit whose pace is driven solely by conditions in the source country. Having become more vulnerable because of leverage and crowding, recipient countries may call for an exit whose pace and timing is responsive, at least in part, to conditions they face.

THE CASE FOR INTERNATIONAL MONETARY POLICY COORDINATION

Hence, my call is for more coordination in monetary policy because I think it would be an immense improvement over the current international non-system. International monetary policy coordination, of course, is unpopular among central bankers, and I therefore have to say why I reiterate the call and what I mean by it.

I do not mean that central bankers sit around a table and make policy collectively, nor do I mean that they call each other regularly and coordinate actions. In its strong form, I propose that large country central banks, both in advanced countries and emerging markets, internalize more of the spillovers from their policies in their mandate, and are forced by new conventions on the 'rules of the game' to avoid unconventional policies with large adverse spillovers and questionable domestic benefits. Given the difficulties of operationalizing the strong form, I suggest that, at the very least, central banks reinterpret their domestic mandate to take into account other country reactions over time (and not just the immediate feedback effects), and thus become more sensitive to spillovers. This weak 'coordination' could be supplemented with a re-examination of global safety nets.

THE GAINS FROM COORDINATION

Economists generally converged on the view that the gains to policy coordination were small provided each country optimized its own policies keeping in mind the policies of others. The 'Nash equilibrium' was not that far from the global optimum, hence the 'own house in order' doctrine was dominant in the international monetary field. National macroeconomic stability was seen as sufficient for international macroeconomic stability. The domestic and international aspects were essentially regarded as two sides of the same coin.

Two factors have led to a rethinking of the doctrine. First, domestic constraints including political imperatives of bringing unemployment down and the economic constraint of the zero lower bound may lead monetary policy to be set at levels different from the unconstrained domestic optimal. Dysfunctional domestic politics could also contribute in moving monetary policy further from the unconstrained optimal. In other words, the central bank, responding to a variety of political pressures and weaknesses, may stray away from even the constrained optimal – towards third best policies rather than second best policies. Second, cross-border capital flows can lead to a more dramatic transmission of policies, driven by agency (and other) considerations that do not necessarily relate to economic conditions in the recipient countries.

One argument along these lines is that if some large country adopts unconventional and highly accommodative sub-optimal policies, other countries may follow suit to avoid exchange rate appreciation in a world with weak demand. As a result, the policy equilibrium may establish at rates that are too low compared to that warranted by the global optimal. Another argument is that when the sending country is at the zero lower bound, and the receiving country responds to capital inflows with aggressive reserve accumulation, both may be better off with more moderate policies. Indeed, it may well be that coordination may allow policy makers political room to move away from sub-optimal policies. If political paralysis and consequent fiscal tightening forces a source country to a sub-optimal reliance on monetary stimulus, policy coordination that allows for expanded demand elsewhere could allow the source country to cut back on its dependence on monetary stimulus.

DOMESTIC OPTIMAL IS CLOSE TO THE GLOBAL OPTIMAL

Despite these arguments, official statements by multilateral institutions such as the IMF continue to endorse unconventional monetary policies while downplaying the adverse spillover effects to other countries. Indeed, in an excellent analysis of the obstacles to international policy coordination, the IMF's own Jonathan Ostry and Atish Ghosh argue that 'impartial' international policy assessments by multilateral entities could be suspected of bias

> '...if there were a systematic tendency of the assessor to identify a change in policy (tighter fiscal policy; looser monetary policy; structural reform) as always yielding welfare gains at the national and global levels. This would breed suspicion because the base case should be that countries do not fail to exploit available welfare gains...it is implausible that welfare gains at the national and global levels should always be positively correlated...'

By downplaying the adverse effects of cross-border monetary transmission of unconventional policies, we are overlooking the elephant in the post-crisis room. I see two dangers here. One is that any remaining rules of the game are breaking down. Our collective endorsement of unconventional monetary policies essentially says it is okay to distort asset prices if there are other domestic constraints to reviving growth, such as the zero lower bound. But net spillovers, rather than fancy acronyms, should determine internationally acceptable policy.

Otherwise, countries could legitimately practice what they

might call quantitative external easing or QEE, whereby they intervene to keep their exchange rate down and build huge reserves. The reason we frowned on QEE in the past is because we believed the adverse spillover effects for the rest of the world were significant. If we are unwilling, however, to evaluate all policies based on their spillover effects, there is no legitimate way multilateral institutions can declare that QEE contravenes the rules of the game. Indeed, some advanced economy central bankers have privately expressed their worry to me that QE 'works' primarily by altering exchange rates, which makes it different from QEE only in degree rather than in kind.

The second danger is a mismanaged exit will prompt fresh distortionary behaviour. Even as source country central banks go to great pains to communicate how their removal of accommodation will be contingent on domestic activity, they have been silent on how they will respond to foreign turmoil. Market participants conclude that recipient countries, especially those that do not belong to large reserve currency blocks, are on their own, and crowd devastatingly through the exit.

Indeed, the lesson some emerging markets will take away from the recent episode of turmoil is (i) don't expand domestic demand and run large deficits (ii) maintain a competitive exchange rate (iii) build large reserves, because when trouble comes, you are on your own. In a world with deficient aggregate demand, is this the message the international community wants to send?

For this is not the first episode in which capital has been pushed first in one direction and then in another, each time with devastating effect. In the early 1990s, rates were held low in the United States, and capital flowed to emerging markets. The wave of emerging market crises starting with Mexico in 1994 and ending with Argentina in 2001, sweeping through East Asia and Russia in between, was partially caused by a reversal of these flows as interest rates rose in industrial countries. The subsequent reserve build-up in emerging markets, including China, contributed to weak global demand and excess spending by some industrial countries, culminating in the global financial crisis of 2007-09. Once again, though, post-crisis unconventional monetary policy has pushed capital to emerging markets, with the associated build-up in fragility. Are we setting the stage for a resumption of the 'global savings glut' as emerging markets build reserves once again?

Two obvious remedies suggest themselves; less extreme monetary policies on all sides with some thought given to adverse spillover effects when setting policy, and better global safety nets to mitigate the need for countries to self-insure through reserve buffers.

MORE MODERATE POLICY

Even though we live in a world where monetary transmission is global, policy focus is local. Central banks mount a number of defences as to why they should not take full account of spillovers. One way to demonstrate the weaknesses in the usual arguments that are put forward to defend the status quo is to see how they would sound if they were used to defend QEE, that is, sustained intervention in the exchange market to keep the exchange rate competitive.

Defence 1: We are a developing country and we are mandated to support growth. Institutional constraints in enhancing productivity, and our vulnerability to sudden stops, means that a competitive exchange rate, and thus QEE, is essential to fulfilling our mandate.

Defence 2: Would the world not be better off if we grew strongly? QEE is essential to our growth.

Defence 3: We take into account feedback effects to our economy from the rest of the world while setting policy. Therefore, we are not oblivious to the consequences of QEE on other countries.

Defence 4: Monetary policy with a domestic focus is already very complicated and hard to communicate. It would be impossibly complex if we were additionally burdened with having to think about the effects of QEE on other countries.

There are many problems with these defences that those who have complained about currency manipulation will recognize. Currency manipulation may help growth in the short run (even this is debatable) but creates long-run distortions that hurt the manipulating country. There are more sensible policies to foster growth. And even if a central bank has a purely domestic mandate, the country's international responsibilities do not allow it to arbitrarily impose costs on the rest of the world. The net spillover effects need to be estimated, and it cannot be taken for granted that the positive spillovers from the initiating country's growth (say through greater trade) more than offset the adverse spillovers to other countries. Feedback effects to the source country represent only a small part of the spillover effects experienced by the world, and a central bank will be far from implementing the globally optimal policy if it is solely domestically oriented, even if it takes these feedback effects into account. Countries are required to pay attention to the effects of their policies on others, no matter how much the added complication, because we all have international responsibilities.

Of course, the reader will recognize that each one of these arguments has been made defending unconventional monetary policy. Yet multilateral institutions treat sustained currency intervention with great opprobrium while giving unconventional monetary policy a clean chit. Should the cleanliness of the chit not depend on the size of the net spillovers and the competitive response it engenders? Without estimating them carefully, how can we tell?

OPERATIONALIZING COORDINATION: SOME SUGGESTIONS

We need to break away from this cycle of unconventional policies and competitive monetary easing. Already, the events of recent months have set the stage for renewed reserve accumulation by the emerging markets. And this time, it will be harder for advanced economies to complain if they downplay their own spillover effects while they are pushing for recovery.

AN INDEPENDENT ASSESSOR

In an ideal world, unconventional monetary policies such as QE or QEE should be vetted by an independent assessor for their spillover effects. The assessment procedure is easy to visualize; Perhaps following a complaint by an impacted country (as in the WTO), the independent assessor could analyse the effects of such policies and come to a judgment on whether they follow the rules of the game. Policies where the benefits are largely domestic, while the costs fall largely abroad, would be especially carefully scrutinized. And if the assessor deems the policy reduces global welfare, international pressure should be applied to stop such policies.

The problems with such an idealistic process are easy to see. Where is such an impartial assessor to be found? The staff at multilateral institutions is excellent, and well capable of independent judgment. But political pressure subsequent to the initial assessment operates unevenly. Initial assessments typically remain unaltered when a small country complains (no country likes independent assessments), but are often toned down when a large economy protests. There are many exceptions to this, but more work is needed to build trust in the impartiality of assessments of multilateral institutions.

Even if multilateral organizations become immune to power politics, they are not immune to cognitive capture. Their staff has been persuaded by the same models and frameworks as the staff of industrial country central banks – models where monetary policy is an extremely powerful tool to elevate activity, and exchange rate flexibility does wonders in insulating countries from the most debilitating spillovers. 'Decoupling' is always possible in such models, even though the evidence is that the models typically underestimate the extent of 'coupling'. Indeed, many of these models do not have realistic models of credit, or of monetary transmission in an economy with debt overhang, which reduces their value considerably. Progress is being made but it will take time.

And, of course, even if a truly independent assessment came to the conclusion that certain policies were in violation, how would such a judgment be enforced?

The reality is that the rules of the game were framed in a different era to deter competitive devaluations and currency manipulation. They have not been updated for today's world of more varied competitive easing. But it is unclear that even if they were updated, they could be assessed and enforced in the current environment.

A MORE MODEST PROPOSAL

Perhaps, then, it would be better to settle for a more modest proposal. Central banks should assess spillover effects from their own actions, not just in terms of immediate feedback, but also in terms of medium-term feedback as other countries alter their policies. In other words, the source country should not just worry about the immediate flows of capital to other countries from its policies, but the longer run reaction such as sustained exchange intervention that this would bring about. This would allow central banks to pay more attention to spillovers even while staying within their domestic mandate.

For example, this would mean that while exiting from unconventional policies, central banks would pay attention to conditions in emerging markets also while deciding the timing of moves, while keeping the overall direction of moves tied to domestic conditions. Their policy statements should acknowledge such concerns. To be concrete in a specific case, the Fed postponing tapering in September 2013 allowed emerging economies more time to adjust after the initial warning in May 2013. Whatever the underlying rationale for postponement, it helped set the stage for tapering start smoothly in December 2013, without disrupting markets. In contrast, with volatility hitting emerging markets after the Argentinian problems in January 2014, the Fed policy statement in January 2014, with no mention of concern about the emerging market situation, and with no indication Fed policy would be sensitive to conditions in those markets in the future, sent the probably unintended message that those markets were on their own. Speeches by regional Fed presidents emphasizing the Fed's domestic mandate did not help. Since then, Fed communication has been more nuanced, though the real challenge in communication lies ahead when policy rates have to move up.

INTERNATIONAL SAFETY NETS

Emerging economies have to work to reduce vulnerabilities in their economies, to get to the point where, like Australia, they can allow exchange rate flexibility to do much of the adjustment for them to capital inflows. But the needed institutions take time to develop. In the meantime, the difficulty for emerging markets in absorbing large amounts of capital quickly and in a stable way should be seen as a constraint, much like the zero lower bound, rather than something that can be altered quickly. Even while resisting the temptation of absorbing flows, they will look to safety nets.

So another way to prevent a repeat of substantial reserve accumulation is to build stronger international safety nets. As the financial crisis suggested, this is not just an emerging economy concern. In a world where international liquidity can dry up quickly, the world needs bilateral, regional, and multilateral arrangements for liquidity. Multilateral arrangements are tried and tested, and are available more widely, and without some of the possible political pressures that could arise from bilateral and regional arrangements. Indeed swap arrangements can be channelled through multilateral institutions like the IMF instead of being conducted on a bilateral basis, so that the multilateral institution bears any (small) credit risk, and the source central bank does not have to justify the arrangements to its political authorities.

Perhaps equally valuable would be a liquidity line from the IMF, where countries are pre-qualified by the IMF and told (perhaps privately) how much of a line they would qualify for under current policy – with the size of the available line revised annually after the IMF's assessment and any curtailment becoming effective six months later so as to give a country time to adjust policies to qualify for higher limits, or to find alternative arrangements. Access to the line would get activated by the IMF Board in a situation of generalized liquidity shortage (as, for example, when policy tightening in source countries after an extended period of low rates causes investment managers to become risk averse). The IMF has suggested such arrangements in a discussion paper, and they should be explored because they allow countries access to liquidity without the stigma of approaching the Fund, and without the conditionality that accompanies most Fund arrangements.

Clearly, the Fund's resources will be safe only if the situation is one of genuine temporary illiquidity rather than one where countries need significant reforms to regain market access. Equally clearly, access will vary across countries, and prolonged use after the liquidity emergency is declared over will necessitate an IMF programme. Nevertheless, the twin proposals of the Global Stability Mechanism and Short-term Liquidity Line that the IMF Board has examined in the past deserve close examination for they come closest to genuinely helping offset reserve build-up.

Finally, it would be a useful exercise for the Fund, in a period of growing vulnerability to capital flow reversals, to identify those countries that do not have own, bilateral, regional, or multilateral liquidity arrangements to fall back on, and to work to improve their access to some safety net. The role of honest ex-ante marriage broker may be one that could prove to be immensely important when the interest rate environment changes.

CONCLUSION

The current non-system in international monetary policy is, in my view, a source of substantial risk, both to sustainable growth as well as to the financial sector. It is not an industrial country problem, nor an emerging market problem, it is a problem of collective action. We are being pushed towards competitive monetary easing.

If I use terminology reminiscent of the Depression era non-system, it is because I fear that in a world with weak aggregate demand, we may be engaged in a futile competition for a greater share of it. In the process, unlike Depression-era policies, we are also creating financial sector and cross-border risks that exhibit themselves when unconventional policies come to an end. There is no use saying that everyone should have anticipated the consequences. As the former Bank of International Settlements (BIS) General Manager Andrew Crockett put it, 'financial intermediaries are better at assessing relative risks at a point in time, than projecting the evolution of risk over the financial cycle.'

A first step to prescribing the right medicine is to recognize the cause of the sickness. Extreme monetary easing, in my view, is more cause than medicine. The sooner we recognize that, the more sustainable world growth we will have.

CHAPTER 9

RBI MATTERS

I

Perhaps the most energizing aspect of my term at the Reserve Bank was the opportunity to work with some of the most dedicated professionals I have met in my life, the staff of the Reserve Bank. The average quality of people was high by even international standards, let alone public sector standards, the organization took pride in its work, and it had a great tradition of comradery and community. The younger staff of the RBI were from a broad variety of schools and backgrounds, truly representative of Indian diversity. They were enthusiastic, and eager to work and learn. I soon realized that when I set a group a task, they would invariably rise to the occasion and produce high quality work. On the 80 anniversary of the RBI on 1 April 2015, this is the message I sent my colleagues.

Remarks on RBI's 80th Anniversary

The Reserve Bank of India is eighty years old today. Eighty years is a long time in the life of a human, one which people in the south celebrate with a Sathabhishekham, but it is not a long time in the life of an institution. Nevertheless much has happened since the year 1935 when the Reserve Bank was set up to 'regulate the issue of Bank notes and the keeping of reserves with the view to securing monetary stability in India and generally to operate the currency and credit system of the country to its advantage'.

India was then under British rule, and the first Governor, Sir Osborne Smith, was an Australian. But the RBI was certainly not a British institution, and has been working right from the outset for Indian economic interests. It has also nurtured Indian talent. In 1943, Chintaman Dwarkanath Deshmukh, one of our finest financial minds, was appointed as the first Indian governor of the Reserve Bank. Not only did he represent India at the Bretton Woods conference, he also went on to become one of its longest serving finance ministers. Amongst the problems he had to confront was how to deal respectfully but firmly with the debts the colonial power had accumulated to India during World War II.

Over the years, the Reserve Bank has been blessed with a number of such fine leaders, a reflection also of the importance the government places in having a strong central bank. The list of past governors and deputy governors reads like a who's who of the Indian economic establishment, with governors like Benegal Rama Rau, M. Narasimham, Dr I.G. Patel, Dr Manmohan Singh, Dr C. Rangarajan, Dr Bimal Jalan, Dr Y.V. Reddy, and Dr D. Subbarao, ably assisted by Deputy Governors such as S.S. Tarapore, Vepa Kamesan, Dr Rakesh Mohan, Shyamala Gopinath, Usha Thorat, and Dr Subir Gokarn. The RBI's board has also been superb, with people like Sir Purshottamdas Thakurdas and Yezdi Malegam guiding it.

Interestingly, many of the governors were from the administrative services, with only one, M. Narasimham, from the RBI itself. Nevertheless, all understood that the Reserve Bank's role is to safeguard the monetary and financial stability of the country even while working towards its financial development. There has always been a healthy dialogue between the government and the Bank, informed by their respective time horizons and attitudes towards risk. And invariably, as history records, successive governments have appreciated the wisdom of the Reserve Bank's counsel.

No institution is bigger than the people who work for it. If the

Reserve Bank is respected today, it is because of the many thousands who have worked over the years for the Bank, with capability and dedication. Let me recognize two as representative of the many. Rani Durve, a DGM in the Bhopal office, has created numerous films, books, and street plays on themes such as fictitious emails and excessive interest rates so as to educate and alert the public. Nirmal Pattnayak, an AGM in the Department of Information Technology, enabled the pan-India electronic transfer of funds for government departments through the national electronic payment systems, thus overnight making the government a significant user of these systems. Both have gone beyond the ordinary call of duty, but so do many others in the Bank.

Equally commendable is the general integrity of the staff. It is a matter of great pride for me today that when someone enters our building to persuade us to change a regulation, they come armed not with money but with arguments about what is right.

Strong national institutions are difficult to build. Therefore existing ones should be nurtured from the outside, and constantly rejuvenated from the inside, for there are precious few of them. Rejuvenation means constantly thinking about how we can do better in serving the people of this country. Whether we contribute by speeding up files we are sitting on, curtailing expenses, simplifying paperwork and regulations, doing innovative research, or working cooperatively with colleagues, there are many ways we all can do our bit. I ask you to join me in rededicating ourselves in the 81st year of this great institution to ensure that the Reserve Bank of India continues to help the nation secure prosperity and economic opportunity for all.

While I was very proud of the Bank, there was room for improvement. We embarked on a serious internal reorganization, intended to streamline the organization. We also revamped the performance-evaluation system, and worked to improve the skill-assessment and skill-building processes. All these changes were designed by senior management, without the involvement of outside consultants, so that the organization would own the changes. There were no public speeches on all this, but some of this did become public: Every year-end, I wrote a letter to our staff. While this was meant to be an internal communication, the following letter was leaked piecemeal to the press (reflecting the adage that nothing the RBI Governor says or writes is secret). Unfortunately, what leaked out were primarily my reflections on the scope for improvement (suggesting that was newsworthy) and not my sense of what was working well. I reproduce it in its entirety because it is already in the public domain.

Year-end Letter to RBI Staff, 31 December 2015

Dear Colleagues:
   I wish all of you and your loved ones a very happy, healthy, and fulfilling New Year. I hope you spent some time with your families and friends in the last week of the year.
   The last year has been full of actions and accomplishments by our colleagues. I will not catalogue them here – I trust you have followed the developments in the newspapers, and will read an

overall detailed view in our annual report. I am confident that based on the compliments I hear from the public about our staff's professionalism and integrity, our ability to continue recruiting the highest quality talent into our staff will be maintained. I continue to be impressed by the dedication and capabilities of many of our staff – most recently, a team of regulators and supervisors that has worked tirelessly over the last few months, foregoing numerous holidays, on the very important task of cleaning up bank balance sheets.

Nevertheless, a strong organization relies on continuous self-examination in order to stay at high levels of excellence. In the coming months, we will have the occasion to have a dialogue through town hall meetings. Let me, however, flag some areas of strength as well as those of concern.

EFFECTIVE SERVICE

We are a service organization. We have customers, whether they are the regulated organizations, the public, or the government. We need to serve them effectively and efficiently. By and large, our staff members perform well, with a few committed extraordinary individuals going way beyond the call of duty. Nevertheless, if I press the stakeholders I meet, I do hear criticisms. Our regulations are not always very clear, our staff sometimes is neither well informed about our own regulations nor willing to help the customer, our responses are occasionally extraordinarily slow and bureaucratic (in the sense of hiding behind opaque rules or avoiding a decision rather than taking a sensible course of action). The imagery that comes to mind for critics is of a traditional, unimaginative organization rather than a dynamic, intelligent one.

We are working on streamlining our regulations in the new master documents, and trying to weed out old historical ones. We need to continue to improve the language in them so that every concerned person can understand without much effort the letter and spirit of what we want to say. Simple-to-understand regulations will be a benefit to our staff also, especially those who are new to a department, because they can come up to speed quickly. We also need to build a library of cases that will help us understand how similar questions were dealt with in the past, that is, we need to build institutional memory rather than let crucial experiences get carried away into retirement in individual memories. This requires experts in departments to document their knowledge, especially as they get ready to leave. Indeed, one could visualize a process of documentation and debriefing as an essential part of the transfer process. We also need to streamline all our forms and put the bulk of filing online, with unique customer ids so that repetitive filling of common details is eliminated. Finally, we need to adhere to timelines. We are in the process of tracking response times. We hope to see concrete measures during the coming year on bringing them down where necessary.

CULTURE OF COMPLIANCE

It has often been said that India is a weak state. Not only are we accused of not having the administrative capacity of ferreting out wrongdoing, we do not punish the wrongdoer – unless he is small and weak. This belief feeds on itself. No one wants to go after the rich and well-connected wrongdoer, which means they get away with even more. If we are to have strong sustainable growth, this culture of impunity should stop. Importantly, this does not mean being against riches or business, as some would like to portray, but being against wrongdoing.

As the premier and most respected regulator in the country, we should take the lead. We have motivated staff with the highest integrity at every level. Yet there is a sense that we do not enforce compliance. Are we allowing regulated entities to get away year after year with poor practices even though these are noted during inspections/scrutinies? Should we become more intolerant of sloppy practices at regulated entities, so that these do not result in massive scams years later? Should we haul up accountants who do not flag issues they should detect? My sense is that we need a continuing conversation about tightening both detection as well as penalties for non-compliance throughout the hierarchy. We cannot be seen as a paper tiger. We are changing our attitude towards compliance, but this is work in progress.

SELF-EXAMINATION AND MUTUAL SUPPORT

If we demand more of the regulated, we should not be found wanting ourselves. As with all organizations, we are reliant on a few stalwarts who carry the organization on their broad shoulders. These are the best performers. There is a second tier that exceeds the needs of the job through their effort or their capabilities, but they fall a little short of being truly excellent. A third tier consists of time-servers, for whom the job is a source of livelihood but who have lost the desire to excel. They put in a reasonable day's work, but not an ounce more than what is demanded of them. And then there are those who are overwhelmed by the work or who have lost any desire to perform. I have encountered all these types at the Bank.

Unfortunately, our performance-evaluation system did not help us identify who needed motivation and improvement, and how they could be helped to do so. Almost everyone was deemed excellent, ranging from those who gave their heart and soul for the Bank to those who shirked all responsibility or duty.

We need to change this, to reward those who perform and to help those who do not. The new performance-evaluation system is meant to aid in this. We do realize there were shortcomings in the initial round, as there will be with every new system. We are working to fix them. But please do not attribute a lower than normal rating for yourself to a shortcoming in the process. There may be information in the rating that you should take seriously. As an organization, if we do not subject ourselves to serious self-examination and continue to pretend everyone is working fine, let me assure you that the organization cannot become better than what it is now. We need to continuously review and renew ourselves if we have to compete with the best in the world.

In the coming year, much will be demanded of reporting officers. They need to let their subordinates know, perhaps even as frequently as every quarter, how their performance has been, and even informally document this discussion. The final performance appraisal should differentiate good from bad performance, and should not come as a surprise to the person being evaluated – they should have picked up cues during the year. Subordinates who are not getting regular feedback should ask their reporting officers. This means more work for all, but it will be critical in helping us improve.

Let me highlight an issue that especially concerns me. As I sit through promotion interviews, I am worried that people are losing curiosity, the desire to learn and improve themselves. I am concerned that some people do not read outside the papers that come across their desk, that they have no idea of other branches of the Bank and their work, let alone the wider world. We emphasize specialization, but that does not mean there is no need to read the newspapers, let alone magazines and books. This has to change if the organization is to remain vibrant. In complacency and self-satisfaction lies a slow descent into mediocrity.

We do want to revamp the support we give our staff to learn. We intend to invest in our staff on a continuing basis, as evidenced by the expansion in Golden Jubilee fellowships. The coming year will be focused on revamping the Human Resource Department's efforts to assess individual needs and career plans and provide the necessary skill building. We want more of one's career in the Bank to be self-driven rather than driven by the needs of the Bank – though a mix of the two will always be inevitable, it is best when the two coincide. Senior management would appreciate any suggestions and ideas that you may have in this regard.

COMMUNICATION AND COOPERATION

I have made this point before, and will make it again. We need to improve channels of communication within the Bank, both horizontally and vertically. The Bank cannot afford to be divided into silos – too much of our work cuts across departmental boundaries. For managers, better communication means more willingness to meet in person or by video conference/phone/email than by interdepartmental memos and file pushing. It means fast responses to the queries that come to your desk, recognizing that cooperation will be amply repaid. It means regular meetings with staff to address their questions.

For staff, it means being willing to ask questions and resolve anxieties when you have face-to-face meetings with managers, rather than be silent at that time and then succumbing to unfounded rumours floated by vested interests who want to prey on your anxieties. It is always fun to concoct conspiracy theories, and we Indians often prefer them to more mundane explanations. However, management in the Bank is open, and one only needs to ask to get the facts.

We also need to communicate better with the outside. This means that we should get ahead of the press, rather than be reactive. If we want to highlight achievements or regulations, we should prepare a press release to focus the press on what is important – with the release getting to the point quickly rather than starting with pages of irrelevant history. Press releases are best done at or before 5.30 pm if you want it to show up in the papers. Beyond that, reporters do not have the time to write copy for the next day, and the news is too old for the day after.

Some in the Bank disdain communication. 'Why not let our achievements speak for themselves?' they might say. Unfortunately, in this world where the press is more attentive and the public more hungry for news, we either should shape news or we will be shaped by it. The latter is infinitely more unpleasant – some may recall the way we were termed anti-technology for some actions we took against a taxi company.

FLEXIBILITY

Successful organizations are usually vibrant and flexible. They adapt to circumstances. As we confront the challenges ahead, we need to be flexible. At one level, this means seizing opportunities that are thrown up by the expanding Indian economy. For example, the new function of gathering market intelligence, which feeds into State-level Coordination Committees, was a dynamic response to our inability to regulate all the operators who attempted to take advantage of regulatory vacuums. Going forward, we need to create regulatory capacity to monitor new entities like the internet market places that are also getting into lending.

While we should be wary of regulatory overreach, we must also recognize that if we do not expand our responsibilities, others will fill them. That is not always a bad thing, but if new regulators lead to a Balkanization of regulation and many regulatory gaps, the system will be worse off. So let us be prepared to step up where necessary instead of assuming others will take responsibility.

But this also means we should be prepared to hire new capabilities into the organization. While we will look for home grown talent where possible, we need lateral entry in some areas. We will minimize these areas, but if we are as good as we think we are, we should be prepared to see some lateral entry wherever necessary – provided internal people have a fair chance to compete for the jobs. This is one area where I feel protectionist attitudes in the organization are strong and require to be debated.

EMBEDDED IN THE COMMUNITY

Finally, we are embedded in a changing community. What was okay in the past is no longer all right when the public demands transparency and better governance from public organizations. I am glad to report that henceforth our budget will be approved by our Central Board. Our dividend policy is currently being debated with the government, but we intend to make it rule-based using cutting edge principles, so that the stability of the Bank is protected, even while the government gets all possible dividends from ownership. We also intend to improve the Board's oversight of wage and perquisite negotiations. Transparency and good governance are ways to protect ourselves from roving enquiries – everyone should recognize that an effective regulator has enemies, and like Caesar's wife, should be above all suspicion.

We also need to pay attention to the demands of the community. While it would be hard to argue that our profits net of reserves belong to anybody other than the government, which is already in the business of public and community service, we can conduct CSR out of our own personal funds. I am proud that our employees have agreed to donate significant amounts to the various tragedies that have hit the country, most recently in Chennai, by giving up a day's leave encashment. I am even prouder of our regional offices that have risen to the occasion when faced with calamity, and ensured banking services keep functioning, even while their own families were facing difficulties. I am told that our medical officers in Chennai provided vital public services in the days after the floods. This is truly commendable, but only consistent with the community spirit that courses through our organization.

We have also committed to working for a cleaner India. Let us set an example by cleaning up our environment, whether it is at the office or in our colonies, or even outside, in our communities. We need to revitalize our Swachh Bharat efforts in the Bank to meet the challenge set out by our Prime Minister.

Let me end by saying we are all privileged to be working for such a fine institution, an institution that compensates well and gives us challenging work even while giving us the fulfilment of doing public service. If I have pointed out areas where we can improve, it is because I believe to do otherwise would be to do this great organization a disservice. In a similar vein, I would like you to point out where we in senior management can improve. Ideas and suggestions, as well as constructive criticism, should flow both up and down if we are to stay dynamic.

Let me wish everyone a Happy New Year once again.

III

The quality and integrity of the RBI's staff is a national treasure that we should do everything to preserve. On the internal front, my biggest regret is that I could not solve a long-pending matter that I inherited from my predecessors: securing for retired RBI staff the same pension benefits that government employees enjoy, despite repeated assurances from the government that the matter would be addressed. I hope the government will do the right thing here.

The Reserve Bank, perhaps because of its competence and integrity, is called upon to do a lot. Moreover, because it is the primary institution safeguarding our monetary and financial security, it has to say no to a lot of powerful people with significant interests. All this means there are perpetual battles with those who disagree with RBI policy, and who believe the easiest way to change policy is not to persuade the RBI but to take away its powers. I did not think the RBI needed all the powers it had, nor did it have all the powers it needed, but I was wary of suggestions for change that were not accompanied by sound rationale. I feared that without such rationales, we might be giving in to motivated interests (who wanted a less competent regulator) or power grabs (from those in government who wanted to expand turf) or the RBI might become a scapegoat (as we were entrusted with tasks that could not possibly be accomplished).

I mentioned earlier that committee reports are the way to initiate change in government. The legitimacy of committee reports, of course, varies, especially if they are driven by a specific agenda or by interested parties. A vast quantity of underlying research can mask the fact that many policy recommendations are ultimately just opinions, unsupported by research. The Financial Sector Legislative Reforms Committee (FSLRC) report, commissioned by the finance ministry in the UPA government, recommended enormous changes to the financial system. Some recommendations were very useful and well-thought-out, but my fellow regulators and I had serious concerns about the practicality of, and rationale for, other recommendations, and whether they were really connected to the research that underlay the report. Here, the biases of some of those who commissioned the report or the drafters, rather than a reasoned consensus among all members, seemed to be coming through. Few realized that the report was submitted with a large number of recorded dissents to its final draft. With pressure building to implement it without a consensus being reached with regulators – as if it was the law of the land rather than simply another report – I thought it was important to air some of our concerns and I did so in a speech in June 2014. I had to be diplomatic, but also raise the right questions.

Financial Sector Legislative Reforms Committee Report (FSLRC): What to Do and When?

The Financial Sector Legislative Reforms Committee (FSLRC) Report is one of the most important, well-researched, as well as well-publicized reports in Indian financial history. It not only lays out the functions of the financial sector and how it should be structured, but also how legislation and regulation governing it ought to look like. The authors of this report truly have to be commended for their national service.

There is much to like and agree with in the report. In laying out the need for consumer protection, raising the issue of whether products sold are suitable for the target customer, and putting the onus on the financial institution to determine suitability, the report has forced regulators to review their consumer protection frameworks. We at the RBI are indeed engaged in such an exercise, informed by the valuable guidelines in the FSLRC report.

There is more of great value. The FSLRC wants law not to micromanage, and prefers to give regulators more leeway. This is indeed important as the world we regulate changes faster than the pace at which legislation can change. The FSLRC's emphasis on the need for a clear monetary framework culminated in the Dr Urjit Patel Committee report, which will guide our thinking in the years to come. Similarly, its focus on creating new institutions like the Financial Resolution Authority to fill gaps in our institutional structure is much needed.

I could go on. But I come here not to praise the FSLRC Report, but to argue that it would be a mistake to implement some proposals in the report today. For some proposals, the underlying logic is questionable, and seems to go against the very rationale of regulation. In other cases, the proposals make more sense for an economy where the regulatory framework is more developed and the judiciary more seasoned in matters financial. To implement the proposals now would be to tie the system up in knots. Let me explain.

THE LOGIC FOR REGULATION

The logic for regulation according to the FSLRC is to deal with market failure or, more colloquially, bad behaviour. The committee talks about incomplete information or poor incentives as a reason for bad behaviour, but one of the most important reasons for bad behaviour necessitating regulation is what economists call incomplete contracts; that the behaviour of the regulated entity (vis-à-vis customers, the public at large, the taxpayer, or the market) cannot be completely specified in contracts because it is too difficult to observe or verify in real time, or it can only be gauged across many contracts.

While courts can enforce specific contracts, the regulator

can sometimes do better. For instance, a bank may attract a lot
of complaints from its credit card customers. While no single
customer may think the case worth taking to court, and while
no customer may be able to prove the bank was in the wrong,
the large number of complaints will suggest to the regulator
that the bank needs to shape up. By comparing the nature of the
complaints it gets from this bank's customers with the complaints
it gets from other banks, the regulator can gauge what is wrong
and act. Similarly, if a particular product attracts a lot more
complaints than other products, the regulator can ask the industry
to modify the product appropriately, or even ban it.

A regulator may also have to prevent certain forms of
contracting – such as the exotic securities that emerged before the
financial crisis. If the regulator thinks a certain kind of security
will impose undue systemic risks on the system, he can ban it,
even though the security would have traded amongst consenting
adults. While he has no proof that the security will behave as he
thinks it will, he cannot wait till the risks occur, for it may be too
late.

The broader point is that a lot of regulatory action is about
the sound exercise of judgment by the regulator based on years of
experience. In doing so, he fills in the gaps in laws, contracts, and
even regulations. Not everything the regulator does can be proven
in a court of law. Courts do not interfere in the specific decisions
of a corporate board – using the business judgment rule, they do
not second guess business decisions, and only pull up boards when
there is a violation of the legal process of arriving at a decision.
In the same way, there are a range of regulatory decisions where
regulatory judgment should not be second guessed.

THE DANGER OF EXCESSIVE LEGAL OVERSIGHT

Yet the FSLRC wants almost everything the regulator does, not
just the framing of regulation but also the exercise of regulatory
judgment, to be subject to legal appeal. For that, it wants to
create a Financial Sector Appellate Tribunal. The intent is to
place more checks and balances on regulatory actions (note that

most regulatory actions can already be appealed in high court). But how much checking and balancing is enough, and can legal oversight become excessive?

There are three dangers we have to guard against. The first is to ask courts to make judgments that they simply do not have the capability, experience, or information to make, and where precise evidence may be lacking. If we attempt to do this, we will undermine the very purpose of a regulator. Of course, one could trust the good sense of the tribunal to follow a 'regulatory judgment' rule and not intervene in a broad array of matters, but does this not imply a double standard – we trust the tribunal's judgment but not the regulator. More likely, though, past experience suggests that entities like to justify their existence, and if set up, a tribunal will intervene more than necessary.

A second danger is that easing the appellate process will invite appeal. In a developed country with well-established regulations, a case history of judgments, and speedy courts, this would not be a problem. In India, where the financial system is developing and many new regulations have to be framed (more so if we move to a principles-based approach for legislation), while the judiciary will have a significant amount of learning to do even while judicial processes have been slow, the encouragement to appeal could paralyse the system and create distortions, as needed regulations are held up and participants exploit loopholes.

Finally, in every country, a healthy respect for the regulator serves to keep participants on the straight and narrow. In a developing country, where private behaviour is less constrained by norms or institutions, this is especially important. But to the extent that private parties with their high-priced lawyers can check the regulator, that healthy respect dissipates. So the final danger is that the regulator could become a paper tiger, and lose his power of influencing good behaviour, even in areas that are not subject to judicial review.

Am I arguing that no checks and balances are needed? Certainly not! But there are already checks and balances in place, including the fact that high courts can review regulatory decisions and that the regulator is appointed, and can be removed, by democratically elected representatives of the people. The FSLRC recommends an annual report to parliament, as well as regular discussions with parliamentarians. These are good suggestions, which would add to oversight. But I would strongly urge the government not to draw parallels to other regulated sectors and tie the financial regulator with further judicial oversight under a misplaced sense that this is the path to financial development.

REGULATORY ARCHITECTURE

Another area where the FSLRC has strong views is on regulatory architecture. As I said earlier, some of its suggestions here are much needed, including the Financial Resolution Authority. But the logic for some of the suggested changes is weak, and sometimes inconsistent.

Let us take the suggestion to merge all regulation of trading under a new Unified Financial Agency. So the Forward Markets Commission as well as the bond regulation activities currently undertaken by the RBI would move, as would SEBI. But this assumes that the central regulatory synergy is the fact that the instrument is traded. But could other synergies exist? And how important are they?

For instance, in forward trading where a real commodity is delivered, regulatory oversight over real markets for the commodity where price is discovered, as well as over warehouses where the commodity is delivered, may be an important source of regulatory synergy. Should the FMC be subsumed under the Unified Financial Agency or be better off having stronger links to the ministries overseeing the real commodities? I think the answer needs more investigation.

Similarly, is the regulation of bond trading more synergistic with the regulation of other debt products such as bank loans and with the operation of monetary policy (where bonds are traded) or with other forms of trading? Once again, I am not sure we have a compelling answer in the FSLRC report. My personal view is that moving the regulation of bond trading at this time would severely hamper the development of the government bond market, including the process of making bonds more liquid across the spectrum, a process which the RBI is engaged in.

The FSLRC also seems to be inconsistent in its emphasis on synergies and regulatory uniformity. All regulation of trading should move under one roof, all regulation of consumer protection should move under another roof, but the regulation of credit should be balkanized – banks should continue to be regulated by the RBI but the regulation of the quasi-bank NBFCs should move to the Unified Financial Agency, a regulatory behemoth that would combine supervision of trading as well as credit. This balkanization makes little sense and would hamper regulatory uniformity, the supervision of credit growth, and the conduct of monetary policy.

More broadly, the FSLRC seems to have an idealistic view of the benefits of reorganization. It seems to believe that once activities are combined in an organization, synergies can be fully exploited, while if they exist in separate organizations, synergies will not be exploited. I too shared such a view, but I now believe it is too extreme. Silos within a large bureaucratic regulator may prevent synergies from being exploited, while frequent inter-regulatory meetings can allow regulators to capture many of available synergies between their activities. Indeed, one particularly useful proposal by the FSLRC is to put the Financial Sector Development Council on a firmer footing. It is a good venue for inter-regulatory cooperation, and its benefits are further augmented by personal interactions. For instance, Chairman SEBI and I try to get together once every month to note and resolve issues.

At the same time, while negotiations and cooperation between regulators can overcome organizational barriers, it is not wise to give a regulator a responsibility and leave the tools for exercising that responsibility in other hands. The RBI has responsibility for managing the internal and external value of the rupee, and more broadly, working towards macroeconomic stability. As a number of multilateral agencies and academics have recognized, the ability to shape capital inflows is now a recognized part of the macro-prudential tool kit. But by taking away control over internal capital inflows from the RBI, isn't the FSLRC taking away an important tool from the RBI?

IF IT AIN'T BROKE...

Lest all this sound like an unthinking defence of regulatory turf, let me add that there are places where the RBI could give up powers. For instance, if the government wants to manage its own debt, there is no reason for the RBI to stand in the way. I don't believe the government suffers any less from conflicts of interest in debt management (unlike the views of the FSLRC), but the RBI could well carry out the government's instructions without any loss in welfare. I imagine, however, that the government will depend on deputations from the RBI for a while to help it manage its debt.

Instead, think of my remarks as an attempt to distil what is useful from the FSLRC report, while eschewing grand schemes with dubious chances of success. Undoubtedly our laws need reform, but that is no reason to try entirely new approaches to legislation, overlaid on entirely new regulatory structures, overlaid on entirely new oversight over regulation. Undoubtedly, we have had, and will have, periods when regulators have not gotten along with each other. But is that a reason to merge some organizations and break up others, perhaps ensuring dysfunctionality along many other dimensions. After all, there is no single regulatory architecture that has emerged with distinction from the crisis. Instead, different regulatory architectures have succeeded or failed based on the circumstances of the country failed and the quality of the regulator.

Undoubtedly, we have also had occasions when regulators have exceeded their remit or been high-handed. But is that a reason to subject their every action to judicial second-guessing? Is there a reason we need more checks and balances, or are we trying to solve a problem that does not exist. As the Chinese would say, let us recognize the value of crossing the river by feeling each stone before we put our weight on it. Let us not take a blind jump hoping that a stone will be there to support us when we land.

IV

As I entered my last few days in office, I wanted to leave explaining why an independent central bank was necessary in India. An invitation from St Stephen's College, which has produced so many good economists in India, was the ideal venue. There was one specific issue I wanted to clarify, the RBI dividend. Despite paying the largest amounts the RBI had ever paid to the government as dividend during my term as Governor, there was still constant suggestions that we could pay more. Some of these suggestions reflected an inadequate understanding of the economics at work in a central bank's balance sheet. On my last day in office, 3 September 2016, I addressed both issues.

The Independence of the Central Bank

Good morning. It is great to be invited to speak at St Stephen's College. In 1980, I toyed with the idea of joining my best friends in applying for admission to the BA in Economics here. Because I had worked so hard for the IIT exam, however, I succumbed to the sunk cost fallacy and studied Electrical Engineering. I don't regret a moment of that misspent youth but I hope you will grant me temporary membership of your club today!

Over the last few weeks, I have outlined the RBI's approach to inflation, distressed debt, financial inclusion, banking sector reform, and market reform. Today, I want to explain why all this means India needs a strong and independent RBI to ensure macroeconomic stability. Then I will discuss what I think is needed to ensure such independence going forward.

THE NEED FOR MACROECONOMIC STABILITY

Growth is good, but growth with stability is better, especially in a poor country where so many people live at the margin. For the RBI, it means ensuring growth does not exceed our potential, adopting prudential policies that reduce our risk, and building sufficient buffers that the country is protected against shocks.

HAVING YOUR CAKE AND EATING IT TOO: INTEREST RATES AND THE EXCHANGE RATE

This mission, however, exposes the central bank to criticism. If we try and bring down inflation, interest rates will remain higher than borrowers desire. If inflation comes down, the currency will depreciate less than some exporters desire. If we push the banks to clean up, banks may be less tolerant towards habitual non-payers. Whatever we do, someone will object. The RBI then becomes the favourite scapegoat for underperformance – if exports are not picking up, it is because interest rates are too high and because the exchange rate is too strong.

Unlike the complainants, the RBI does not have the luxury of economic inconsistency. If we start buying dollars in a big way to depreciate the exchange rate, we will be able to buy fewer government bonds if we are to maintain control over liquidity. The consequence will be higher interest rates in the bond market. Moreover, the depreciated exchange rate will mean higher inflation, which in turn will mean higher policy interest rates given the inflation objective the government has set for us. Once again, this means higher interest rates. Just look at Brazil or Russia to understand you cannot have a significantly depreciated exchange rate and lower interest rates at the same time if you want stable growth!

FIRST YEAR ECONOMICS: THERE IS NO FREE LUNCH. RBI DIVIDEND POLICY

A fundamental lesson in economics is there is no free lunch. This can be seen in the matter of the RBI dividend: Some commentators seem to suggest that public sector banks could be recapitalized entirely if only the RBI paid a larger dividend to the government. Let me explain why matters are not so simple. If what follows is complicated, trust me, it is. But pay attention, students, especially because it is about your money. I am sure you will understand.

How does the RBI generate surplus profits? We, of course, print the currency held by the public, as well as issue deposits (that is, reserves) to commercial banks. Those are our fixed liabilities. As we issue these liabilities, we buy financial assets from the market. We do not pay interest on our liabilities. However, the financial assets we hold, typically domestic and foreign government bonds, do pay interest. So we generate a large net interest income simply because we pay nothing on virtually all our liabilities.

Our total costs, largely for currency printing and banker commissions, amount to only about 1/7th of our total net interest income. So we earn a large surplus profit, more than almost the entire public sector put together, because of the RBI's role as the manager of the country's currency. This belongs entirely to the country's citizens. Therefore, after setting aside what is needed to be retained as equity capital to maintain the creditworthiness of the RBI, the RBI Board pays out the remaining surplus to the RBI's owner, the government.

The RBI Board has decided it wants the RBI to have an international AAA rating so that RBI can undertake international transactions easily, even when the Government is in perceived difficulty – in the midst of the Taper Tantrum, no bank questioned our ability to deliver on the FCNR(B) swaps, even though the liability could have been tens of thousands of crores. Based on sophisticated risk analysis by the RBI's staff, the Board has decided in the last three years that the RBI's equity position, currently around 10 lakh crores, is enough for the purpose. It therefore has paid out the entire surplus generated to the government, amounting to about Rs 66,000 crores each in the last two years, without holding anything back. This is of the order of magnitude of the dividends paid by the entire public sector to the government. In my three years at the RBI, we have paid almost as much dividend to the government as in the entire previous decade. Yet some suggest we should pay more, a special dividend over and above the surplus we generate.

Even if it were legally possible to pay unrealized surplus (it is not), and even if the Board were convinced a higher dividend would not compromise the creditworthiness of the RBI, there is a more fundamental economic reason why a special dividend would not help the government with its budgetary constraints.

Here's why: Much of the surplus we make comes from the interest we get on government assets or from the capital gains we make off other market participants. When we pay this to the government as dividends, we are putting back into the system the money we made from it – there is no additional money printing or reserve creation involved. (This is not strictly true. Our earnings on foreign exchange assets come from outside the system, so when we pay this to the government as dividend, we are printing additional money. We do account for this.) But when we pay a special dividend to the government, we have to create additional permanent reserves, or more colloquially, print money. Every year, we have in mind a growth rate of permanent reserves consistent with the economy's cash needs and our inflation goals. Given that budgeted growth rate, to accommodate the special dividend we will have to withdraw an equivalent amount of money from the public by selling government bonds in our portfolio (or alternatively, doing fewer open market purchases than we budgeted).

Of course, the government can use the special dividend to spend, reducing its public borrowing by that amount. But the RBI will have to sell bonds of exactly that amount to the public in order to stick to its target for money creation. The overall net sale of government bonds by the government and the RBI combined to the public (that is, the effective public sector borrowing requirement) will not change. But the entire objective of financing government spending with a special RBI dividend is to reduce overall government bond sales to the public. That objective is not achieved!

The bottom line is that the RBI should transfer to the government the entire surplus, retaining just enough buffers that are consistent with good central bank risk management practice. Indeed, this year the Board paid out an extra 8,000 crores than was promised to the government around budget time. Separately, the government can infuse capital into the banks. The two decisions need not be linked. There are no creative ways of extracting more money from the RBI – there is no free lunch! Instead, the government should acknowledge its substantial equity position in the RBI and subtract it from its outstanding debt when it announces its net debt position. That would satisfy all concerned without monetary damage.

If what I have said just now seems complicated, it is, but it is also the correct economic reasoning. Similar detailed rationales lead us to turn down demands to cut interest rates in the face of high inflation, to depreciate or appreciate the exchange rate depending on the whim of the moment, to use foreign exchange reserves to fund projects, to display forbearance in classifying bad loans or waived farmer loans as NPAs, and so on...

We have been tasked with a job of maintaining macroeconomic stability, and often that task requires us to refuse seemingly obvious and attractive proposals. The reason why we have to do what we have to do may not be easy for every unspecialized person, even ones with substantial economics training, to grasp quickly. Of course, we still must explain to the best of our ability but we also need to create a structure where the public trusts the central bank to do the right thing. This then is why we need a trusted independent central bank.

CENTRAL BANK INDEPENDENCE

In this environment, where the central bank has to occasionally stand firm against the highest echelons of central and state government, recall the words of my predecessor, Dr Subbarao, when he said 'I do hope the Finance Minister will one day say, "I am often frustrated by the Reserve Bank, so frustrated that I want to go for a walk, even if I have to walk alone. But thank God, the Reserve Bank exists."' I would go a little further. The Reserve Bank cannot just exist, its ability to say 'No!' has to be protected. At the same time, the central bank cannot become free of all constraints, it has to work under a framework set by the government. This requires a number of actions.

OUTLINE RESPONSIBILITIES OF THE RBI

When the responsibilities of the RBI are fuzzy, its actions can continuously be questioned. Instead, if the constitutional authorities outline a framework for the responsibilities of the RBI, it can take actions consistent with those responsibilities and be held to outcomes. The inflation objectives recently set for the RBI by the government are an example of what is needed. Critics can lambast the RBI if it fails continuously to meet the objectives, but if they want it to lower interest rates even when the RBI barely meets its objectives, they should instead petition the government to change the objectives.

Similarly, the RBI Board has adopted a risk-management framework which indicates the level of equity the RBI needs, given the risks it faces. The dividend policy of the RBI then becomes a technical matter of how much residual surplus is available each year after bolstering equity. Frameworks thus reduce the space for differences.

The RBI's role in macroeconomic stability is, however, still fuzzy. While RBI clearly has responsibility for the safety and soundness of credit institutions and the stability of the external account, there are some areas that are hazier. For example, with an inflation-focused framework, the RBI's ability to be accommodative depends on fiscal prudence from the centre and states. How much should the RBI warn on fiscal profligacy, including the building up of contingent liabilities, and when should such warning be seen as interfering in the legitimate decisions of the elected representatives of the people? This is an area where clarity would be useful.

STRENGTHEN OVERSIGHT

The freedom the RBI has to take operational decisions such as the FCNR (B) swap arrangement, albeit invariably in consultation with the finance ministry, is important. However, there are always government entities that are seeking oversight over various aspects of the RBI's activities. Multiple layers of scrutiny, especially by entities that do not have the technical understanding, will only hamper decision making. Instead, the government-appointed RBI Board, which includes ex-officio government officials as well as government appointees, should continue to play its key oversight role. In this regard, all important RBI decisions including budgets, licences, regulation, and supervision are now either approved by the Board or one of its sub-committees. Vacancies in the RBI Board, which have remained unfilled for many months now, should be filled quickly so that the full expertise and oversight of the Board can be utilized.

It is also important that Parliament understand what the central bank is doing. The Governor and deputy governors interact regularly with various parliamentary committees, but we have also initiated a six-monthly interaction with the Parliamentary Standing Committee on Finance, where the Governor reports on the activities of the Bank, and the Committee offers its views and concerns.

RANK OF RBI GOVERNOR

There is a reason why central bank governors sit at the table along with the finance ministers in G-20 meetings. It is that the central bank Governor, unlike other regulators or government secretaries, has command over significant policy levers and has to occasionally disagree with the most powerful people in the country.

It is dangerous to have a *de facto* powerful position with low *de jure* status. Today, the RBI Governor has the salary of the Cabinet Secretary. He or she is appointed by the Prime Minister in consultation with the Finance Minister. The Governor's rank in the government hierarchy is not defined but it is generally agreed that decisions will be explained only to the Prime Minister and the Finance Minister. There is an informal understanding in India that the Governor has the room to make needed decisions. In the interests of macroeconomic stability, none of this should be changed, though if these issues are ever revisited, there may be some virtue in explicitly setting the Governor's rank commensurate with her position as the most important technocrat in charge of economic policy in the country.

COMMUNICATION

I do not fool myself into thinking that reporters and TV cameras follow me around everywhere because I am a magnetic speaker. They follow RBI governors around because they may offer market-moving information on policy. Fortunately, I have escaped unintentionally saying anything that moves markets.

At the same time, while different RBI governors have different approaches to communication, no one can dispense with it. Unlike a developed country, where the central bank chairman can offer periodic Delphic pronouncements about the course of monetary policy, and occasionally remonstrate with Parliament or the government about the course of fiscal policy, in our developing democracy the RBI Governor has to continuously make the case for the actions the central bank is taking, including the many structural reforms that are under way.

Indeed, communication is as much about educating as it is about informing. For instance, even as I explained to entrepreneurs and retail borrowers why interest rates were not falling faster, I had to use the price of dosas to explain to pensioners why they were actually better off earning lower nominal but higher real interest rates. Public understanding can help ease the way for reforms, as well as increase support for policies. The RBI Governor therefore has to explain again and again.

Occasionally, of course, the Governor has to warn about the dangers of certain courses of action or certain tendencies in the economy for growth and macroeconomic stability. Finally, the Governor is also a role model for the youth in this country, and should therefore not duck the responsibility to urge them to follow the highest standards of citizenship when he or she is invited to speak directly to them.

CONCLUSION

This is the last public speech I will give in India for a while – my successor has to take over the RBI's communication and I want to get out of his way. It has been an honour to work for the country and especially to talk to people like you, its future. Thanks for listening to me.

> Postscript: I am not the RBI Governor any more. But the point in my speech is worth reiterating: there is a danger in keeping the position ill-defined, because the constant effort of the bureaucracy is to whittle down its power. This is not a recent phenomenon, as observers like T.C.A. Srinivasa-Raghavan have noted, but the RBI risks becoming dangerously weakened as successive governments and finance ministers misunderstand its role. The RBI Governor, as the technocrat with responsibility for the nation's economic risk management, is not simply another bureaucrat or regulator, and efforts to belittle the position by bringing it into the bureaucratic hierarchy are misguided and do not serve the national interest. More clarity about the RBI's role, and a clearer assertion of its independence, would be in the nation's interest.

V

Perhaps the hardest letter to write to my colleagues at the RBI was a letter informing them that I would be leaving at the end of my term. It is probably fitting to end the pieces on my term at the RBI with that letter, written on 18 June 2016. I wanted to reflect on how much we had accomplished together, even while promising a flurry of activity to tie up loose ends in the few months I had left.

Message to RBI Staff

Dear Colleagues,
I took office in September 2013 as the 23rd Governor of the Reserve Bank of India. At that time, the currency was plunging daily, inflation was high, and growth was weak. India was then deemed one of the 'Fragile Five'. In my opening statement as Governor, I laid out an agenda for action that I had discussed with you. By implementing these measures, I said we would 'build a bridge to the future, over the stormy waves produced by global financial markets'.

Today, I feel proud that we at the Reserve Bank have delivered on all these proposals. A new inflation-focused framework is in place that has helped halve inflation and allowed savers to earn positive real interest rates on deposits after a long time. We have also been able to cut interest rates by 150 basis points after raising them initially. This has reduced the nominal interest rate the government has to pay even while lengthening maturities it can issue – the government has been able to issue a forty-year bond for the first time. Finally, the currency stabilized after our actions, and our foreign exchange reserves are at a record high, even after we have fully provided for the outflow of foreign currency deposits we secured in 2013. Today, we are the fastest growing large economy in the world, having long exited the ranks of the Fragile Five.

We have done far more than was laid out in that initial statement, including helping the government reform the process of appointing public sector bank management through the creation of the Bank Board Bureau (based on the recommendation of the RBI-appointed Nayak Committee), creating a whole set of new structures to allow banks to recover payments from failing projects, and forcing timely bank recognition of their unacknowledged bad debts and provisioning under the Asset Quality Review (AQR). We have worked on an enabling framework for National Payments Corporation of India to roll out the Universal Payment Interface, which will soon revolutionize mobile-to-mobile payments in the country. Internally, the RBI has gone through a restructuring and streamlining, designed and driven by our own senior staff. We are strengthening the specialization and skills of our employees so that they are second to none in the world. In everything we have done, we have been guided by the eminent public citizens on our Board such as Padma Vibhushan Dr Anil Kakodkar, former Chairman of the Atomic Energy Commission and Padma Bhushan and Magsaysay award winner Ela Bhatt of the Self Employed Women's Association. The integrity and capability of our people, and the transparency of our actions, is unparalleled, and I am proud to be a part of such a fine organization.

I am an academic and I have always made it clear that my ultimate home is in the realm of ideas. The approaching end of my three-year term, and of my leave at the University of Chicago, was therefore a good time to reflect on how much we had accomplished. While all of what we laid out on that first day is done, two subsequent developments are yet to be completed. Inflation is in the target zone, but the monetary policy committee that will set policy has yet to be formed. Moreover, the bank clean-up initiated under the Asset Quality Review, having already brought more credibility to bank balance sheets, is still ongoing. International developments also pose some risks in the short term.

While I was open to seeing these developments through, on due reflection, and after consultation with the government, I want to share with you that I will be returning to academia when my term as Governor ends on 4 September 2016. I will, of course, always be available to serve my country when needed.

Colleagues, we have worked with the government over the last three years to create a platform of macroeconomic and institutional stability. I am sure the work we have done will enable us to ride out imminent sources of market volatility like the threat of Brexit. We have made adequate preparations for the repayment of Foreign Currency Non-Resident (B) deposits and their outflow, managed properly, should largely be a non-event. Morale at the Bank is high because of your accomplishments. I am sure the reforms the government is undertaking, together with what will be done by you and other regulators, will build on this platform and reflect in greater job growth and prosperity for our people in the years to come. I am confident my successor will take us to new heights with your help. I will still be working with you for the next couple of months, but let me thank all of you in the RBI family in advance for your dedicated work and unflinching support. It has been a fantastic journey together!

With gratitude

Yours sincerely
Raghuram G. Rajan

Section II

THE GLOBAL FINANCIAL CRISIS

|

The 2005 Jackson Hole Conference was to be the then Federal Reserve Board Chairman Alan Greenspan's last, and the theme, therefore, was the legacy of the Greenspan Era. I was the Chief Economist of the International Monetary Fund at that time, on leave from the University of Chicago. I was asked to present a paper to the world's central banking fraternity on how the financial sector had evolved during Greenspan's term at the helm. I started to write a paper extolling the developments in finance, but as I analysed the data, I became worried about what was going on. I shifted tack and wrote the paper on the risks posed by the financial system.

I remember telling my wife as I left home for the conference that this speech, so far out of line with what I knew would be congratulatory speeches at the conference, would either be seen as singularly prescient, or unwarranted scaremongering. The global financial crisis in 2007-08 ensured opinion largely switched from the latter to the former. The following piece is based on that paper, and was published in the IMF's monthly *Straight Talk* in September 2005.

Risky Business: Skewed Incentives for Investment Managers May Be Adding to Global Financial Risk

In the past thirty years, financial systems around the world have undergone revolutionary change. People can borrow greater amounts at cheaper rates, invest in a multitude of instruments catering to every possible profile of risk and return, and share risks with strangers across the globe. Financial markets have expanded and deepened, and the typical transaction involves more players and is carried out at greater arm's length.

At least three forces are behind these changes. Technical change has reduced the cost of communication and computation, as well as the cost of acquiring, processing, and storing information. For example, techniques ranging from financial engineering to portfolio optimization, and from securitization to credit scoring, are now widely used. Deregulation has removed artificial barriers preventing entry of new firms, and has encouraged competition between products, institutions, markets, and jurisdictions. And institutional change has created new entities within the financial sector – such as private equity firms and hedge funds – as well as new political, legal, and regulatory arrangements (for example, the emergence over the past two decades of the entire institutional apparatus behind the practice of inflation targeting, ranging from central bank independence to the publication of regular inflation reports).

While these changes in the financial landscape have been termed 'disintermediation' because they involve moving away from traditional bank-centred ties, the term is a misnomer. Although in a number of industrialized countries, individuals don't deposit a significant portion of their savings directly in banks any more, they invest indirectly in the market via mutual funds, insurance companies, and pension funds, and in firms via venture capital funds, hedge funds, and other forms of private equity. The managers of these financial institutions, whom I shall call 'investment managers', have displaced banks and 'reintermediated' themselves between individuals and markets.

What about banks themselves? While banks can now sell much of the risk associated with the 'commodity' transactions they originate, such as mortgages, by packaging them and getting them off their balance sheets, they have to retain a portion. This is typically the first loss, that is, the loss from the first few mortgages in the package that stop paying. Moreover, they now focus far more on transactions where they have a comparative advantage, typically transactions where explicit contracts are hard to specify or where the consequences need to be hedged by trading in the market. For example, banks offer back-up lines of credit to commercial paper issuances by corporations. This means that when the corporation is in trouble and commercial paper markets dry up, the bank will step in and lend. Clearly, these are risky and illiquid loans. And they reflect a larger pattern: as traditional transactions become more liquid and amenable to being transacted in the market, banks are moving on to more illiquid transactions. Competition forces them to flirt continuously with the limits of illiquidity.

No doubt, the expansion in the variety of intermediaries and financial transactions has major benefits, including reducing the transaction costs of investing, expanding access to capital, allowing more diverse opinions to be expressed in the marketplace, and permitting better risk sharing. But it also has potential downsides, raising the question of whether we have unwittingly accepted a Faustian bargain, trading greater welfare most of the time for a small probability of a catastrophic meltdown. My view is that the world may be riskier because of skewed incentives among investment managers, which I will now describe, but it's unlikely we will know for sure. Thus, the message for central bankers and financial system regulators is simple: best to be prepared.

GETTING THE INCENTIVES RIGHT

In the past, bank managers were paid a largely fixed salary. Given that regulation kept competition muted, there was no need for shareholders to offer managers strong performance incentives (such incentives might even have been detrimental as it would have tempted bank managers to reach out for risk). The main check on bank managers making bad investment decisions was the bank's fragile capital structure (and possibly regulators). If bank management displayed incompetence or knavery, depositors would get jittery and possibly run. The threat of this extreme penalty, coupled with the limited upside from salaries that were not buoyed by stock or options compensation, combined to make bankers extremely conservative. This served depositors well since their capital was safe. Shareholders, who enjoyed a steady rent because of the limited competition, were also happy.

In the new, deregulated, competitive environment, investment managers can't be provided the same staid incentives as bank managers of yore. Because they need the incentive to search for good investments, their compensation has to be sensitive to investment returns, especially returns relative to their competitors. Furthermore, new investors are attracted by high returns. And current investors, if dissatisfied, do take their money elsewhere (although they often suffer from inertia in doing so). Since compensation also varies with assets under management, overall, investment managers face a compensation structure that moves up very strongly with good performance, and falls, albeit more mildly, with poor performance.

Therefore, the incentive structure for investment managers today differs from the incentive structure for bank managers of the past in two important ways. First, there is typically less downside and more upside from generating investment returns, implying that these managers have the incentive to take more risk. Second, their performance relative to other peer managers matters, either because it's directly embedded in their compensation, or because investors exit or enter funds on that basis. The knowledge that managers are being evaluated against others can induce superior performance, but also perverse behaviour of various kinds.

PERVERSE BEHAVIOURS

Performance-based pay can induce risky behaviour among investment managers. One type is to take risk that is concealed from investors. Since risk and return are related, the manager then looks as if he outperforms peers given the risk he takes. Typically, the kinds of risks that can most easily be concealed, given the requirement of periodic reporting, are 'tail' risks – that is, risks that have a small probability of generating severe adverse consequences and offer generous compensation the rest of the time. A second type is to herd with other investment managers on investment choices, because herding provides insurance the manager will not underperform his peers. However, herd behaviour can move asset prices away from fundamentals.

Both behaviours can reinforce each other during an asset price boom, when investment managers are willing to bear the low probability 'tail' risk that asset prices will revert to fundamentals abruptly, and the knowledge that many of their peers are herding on this risk gives them comfort that they will not underperform significantly if boom turns to bust. These behaviours can be compounded in an environment of low interest rates, where the incentives of some participants to 'search for yield' not only increase, but where asset prices also spiral upwards, creating the conditions for a sharp and messy realignment.

Do banks add to this behaviour or restrain it? The compensation of bank managers, while not so tightly tied to returns, has not been left completely untouched by competitive pressures. Banks make returns both by originating risks and by bearing them. As traditional risks such as mortgages or loans can be moved off bank balance sheets into the balance sheets of investment managers, banks have an incentive to originate more of them. Thus they will tend to feed rather than restrain the appetite for risk. As I argued earlier, however, banks cannot sell all risk. In fact, they often have to bear the most complicated and volatile portion of the risks they originate, so even though some risk has been moved off their balance sheets, balance sheets are being reloaded with fresh, more complicated risks. The data support this assessment – despite a deepening of financial markets, banks may not be any safer than in the past. Moreover, even though the risks banks now bear are seemingly smaller, such risks are only the tip of an iceberg.

But perhaps the most important concern is whether banks will be able to provide liquidity to financial markets so that if the 'tail' risk does materialize, financial positions can be unwound and losses allocated so as to minimize the consequences to the real economy. Past episodes indicate that banks have played this role successfully. However, there is no assurance they will continue to be able to do so. Banks have in the past been able to provide liquidity in part because their sound balance sheets allowed them to attract available spare liquidity in the market. However, banks today require more liquid markets to hedge some of the risks associated with the complicated products they have created or guarantees they have offered. Their greater reliance on market liquidity can make their balance sheets more suspect in times of crisis, making them less able to provide the liquidity assurance that they have provided in the past.

Taken together, these trends suggest that even though there are far more participants who are able to absorb risk today, the financial risks that are being created by the system are indeed greater. And even though there should theoretically be a diversity of opinion and actions by market participants, and a greater capacity to absorb risk, competition and compensation may induce more correlation in behaviour than is desirable. While it is hard to be categorical about anything as complex as the modern financial system, it's possible that these developments are creating more financial-sector-induced procyclicality than in the past. They may also create a greater (albeit still small) probability of a catastrophic meltdown.

Unfortunately, we won't know whether these are, in fact, serious worries until the system has been tested. The best hope is that the system faces shocks of increasing size, figures out what is lacking each time, and becomes more resilient. To paraphrase St Augustine, we should therefore pray: 'Lord, if there be shocks, let them first be small ones.' The danger is that the economy will be hit unexpectedly by a perfect storm before it has been stress-tested.

If indeed risk taking is excessive, why don't investors offer their managers compensation contracts that restrain the short-term emphasis on returns and associated risk taking? The answer is that there may be too little private incentive to do so. For one, there is very little systematic evidence that past performance in financial investment is an indicator of future performance, Warren Buffet or Peter Lynch notwithstanding. This implies that the constant movement by investors between funds has little social value. But investors in an individual fund benefit when new investments pour in because the fund's average costs go down. As a result, the private gains from attracting investors through a fund's superior short-term performance exceed the social value, and investors have too little incentive to restrain managers from focusing on the short term.

Of course, if in addition investors don't have complete control over managers – because of weaknesses in corporate governance, for example – and managers have private incentives to generate returns in the short term (to preserve their jobs or for the public adulation that success brings), the private equilibrium may again generate excessive risk taking. It's also hard for a private actor to fully capture the benefits of providing liquidity – if prices are higher and more closely reflect fundamentals, all those who trade will benefit, not just the actor who injected liquidity into the market. Therefore, the private sector has too little incentive to provision for it also.

LIMITING THE FALLOUT

So what can policy makers do? While too much regulation can stifle the competition that drives financial sector innovation, not doing anything at all doesn't seem like a good option either. While we still know little about the complex workings of financial markets, two main tools come to mind.

Monetary policy. Monetary policy must be informed by its effects on incentives. As already pointed out, both a low level as well as an unanticipated sharp fall in interest rates can have perverse effects on incentives. This implies that rapid, large, changes in monetary policy have significant costs, not just in the domestic economy but in all interconnected markets. One implication is that policy changes ought to happen at a measured (though not necessarily predictable) pace rather than abruptly. Second, while deflation can be immensely harmful for the real economy, an unanticipated but persistent low interest rate can be a source of significant distortions for the financial sector, and thence for asset prices. Not only does this mean staying further away from deflation so that extremely low policy rates don't have to be used as a tool, it also implies exercising greater supervisory vigilance when those rates are in place to contain asset price bubbles. Third, and somewhat obviously, one can no longer just examine the state of the banking system and its exposure to credit to reach conclusions about aggregate credit creation, let alone the stability of the financial system. Finally, the financial sector may experience greater liquidity and solvency problems in some situations, so central banks have to be vigilant for any possible shortfalls in aggregate liquidity.

PRUDENTIAL SUPERVISION

The prudential net may have to be cast wider than simply around commercial or investment banks to include institutions such as hedge funds. What instruments might be used? Certainly, greater transparency and disclosure, along with capital regulation, have a role to play. But policymakers might also need to consider using the managerial compensation system to align the behaviour of investment managers with the public interest. Rather than limiting or constraining compensation, compensation regulation might simply require long-term investment of a portion of top investment managers' compensation in the claims issued by the investment that is being managed. Given that some investors already require this of their investment managers, such a requirement may not be excessively intrusive. Of course, one has to be careful about making investment managers overly conservative, and thus losing the benefits their risk-taking behaviour brings to the economy. This is why the optimal probability of a financial sector meltdown will never be zero.

Postscript: As the *Wall Street Journal* reported on 2 January 2009 in an article by Justin Lahart on my Jackson Hole presentation:

'Incentives were horribly skewed in the financial sector with workers reaping rich rewards for making money but being only lightly penalized for losses, Mr Rajan argued. That encouraged financial firms to invest in complex products, with potentially big payoffs, which could on occasion fail spectacularly.

He pointed to "credit default swaps" which act as insurance against bond defaults. He said insurers and others were generating big returns selling these swaps with the appearance of taking on little risk, even though the pain could be immense if defaults actually occurred.

Mr Rajan also argued that because banks were holding a portion of the credit securities they created on their books, if those securities ran into trouble, the banking system itself would be at risk. Banks would lose confidence in one another, he said. "The interbank market could freeze up, and one could well have a full-blown financial crisis."

Two years later, that's essentially what happened.'

II

I returned to academia in January 2007 after a three and a half year stint at the IMF. What follows are a sampling of the pieces, including public speeches. The following elaborates on the risk-taking incentives in the system, and was delivered in February 2007, just before the crisis.

Financial Conditions, Asset Management, and Political Risks: Trying to Make Sense of Our Times

Despite widespread strong productivity growth, nominal investment, especially corporate investment, has remained relatively weak for the world as a whole, while desired savings is strong. Call this a 'savings glut' as did Chairman Bernanke or 'investment restraint' as did the IMF, the net effect is an imbalance between desired savings and realized investment. Consequently, real long-term interest rates have been low for some time. Interestingly, even as the Federal Reserve raised policy rates during 2006, long-term interest rates fell further – in slowing domestic demand in the United States, markets may believe the Fed is aggravating the worldwide excess of desired savings over realized investment further.

Current conditions are unlikely to be permanent. Given aging populations in developed countries though, one would presume that the rebalancing of worldwide investment to desired savings will have to take place primarily in non-industrial countries. Investment will increase partly through foreign direct investment, but partly mediated by the financial systems in emerging markets, which will have to develop further. Increases in consumption as safety nets improve and retail finance becomes widely available will also help reduce desired savings. Certainly, the seemingly perverse pattern of net capital flows, from poor to rich countries, will have to change, if for no other reason than to accommodate demographics.

I now want to turn to the increasing institutionalization of, and competition within, advanced financial markets. The link between the issues will soon be clear. The break-up of oligopolistic banking systems and the rise of financial markets has expanded individual financial investment choices tremendously. While individuals don't deposit a significant portion of their savings directly in banks any more, they don't invest directly in the market either. They invest indirectly via mutual funds, insurance companies, pension funds, venture capital funds, hedge funds, and other forms of private equity. The managers of these financial institutions, whom I shall call 'investment managers,' have largely displaced banks and 'reintermediated' themselves between individuals and markets.

As competition between these various institutional forms for the public's investment dollar increases, each one attempts to assure the public that they will offer superior performance. But what does superior performance mean?

PERFORMANCE MANAGEMENT

The typical manager of financial assets generates returns based on the systematic risk he takes – the so-called beta risk – and the value his abilities contribute to the investment process – his so-called alpha. Shareholders in any asset management firm are unlikely to pay the manager much for returns from beta risk – for example, if the shareholder wants exposure to large traded U.S. stocks, she can get the returns associated with that risk simply by investing in the Vanguard S&P 500 index fund, for which she pays a fraction of a per cent in fees. What the shareholder will really pay for is if the manager beats the S&P 500 index regularly, that is, generates excess returns while not taking more risk. Indeed, hedge fund managers often claim to produce returns that are uncorrelated with the traditional market (the so-called market neutral strategies) so that all the returns they generate are excess returns or alpha, which deserve to be well compensated.

In reality, there are only a few sources of alpha for investment managers. One comes from having truly special abilities in identifying undervalued financial assets – Warren Buffet, the U.S. billionaire investor, certainly has these, but study after academic study shows that very few investment managers do, and certainly not in a way that can be predicted before the fact by ordinary investors.

A second source of alpha is from what one might call activism. This means using financial resources to create, or obtain control over, real assets and to use that control to change the payout obtained on the financial investment. A venture capitalist who transforms an inventor, a garage, and an idea into a full-fledged profitable and professionally managed corporation is creating alpha. A private equity fund that undertakes a hostile corporate takeover, cuts inefficiency, and improves profits is also creating alpha. So is a vulture investor who buys up defaulted emerging market debt and presses authorities through various legal devices to press the country to pay more.

A third source of alpha is financial entrepreneurship or engineering – investing in exotic financial securities that are not easily available to the ordinary investor, or creating securities or cash flow streams that appeal to particular investors or tastes. Of course, if enough of these securities or streams are created, they cease to have scarcity or diversification value, and are valued like everything else. Thus this source of alpha depends on the manager constantly innovating and staying ahead of the competition.

Finally, alpha can also stem from liquidity provision. For instance, investment managers, having relatively easy access to finance, can hold illiquid or arbitrage positions to maturity: if a closed end fund is trading at a significant premium to the underlying market, the manager can short the fund, buy the underlying market, and hold the position till the premium eventually dissipates. What is important here is that the investment managers have the liquidity to hold till the arbitrage closes.

ILLIQUIDITY SEEKING

This discussion should suggest that alpha is quite hard to generate since most ways of doing so depend on the investment manager possessing unique abilities – to pick stock, identify weaknesses in management and remedy them, or undertake financial innovation. Unique ability is rare. How then do the masses of investment managers justify the faith reposed in them by masses of ordinary investors? The answer is probably liquidity provision, which is the activity that depends least on special managerial ability and could be termed the poor manager's source of alpha.

The problem when the world has excess desired savings relative to investment, and when central banks are accommodative, is that it is awash in liquidity. Many investment managers can enter the business of liquidity provision, and even as they take ever more illiquid positions, they compete away the returns from doing so. The point is that current benign conditions engender 'illiquidity-seeking' behaviour. But they could have worse effects.

TAIL RISK AND HERDING

For what is the manager with relatively limited ability to do when central banks flood the market with liquidity and the rents from liquidity provision are competed away? He could hide risk – that is, pass off returns generated through taking on beta risk as alpha by hiding the extent of beta risk. Since additional risks will generally imply higher returns, managers may take risks that are typically not in their comparison benchmark (and hidden from investors) so as to generate the higher returns to distinguish themselves.

For example, a number of hedge funds, insurance companies, and pension funds have entered the credit-derivative market to sell guarantees against a company defaulting. Essentially, these investment managers collect premia in ordinary times from people buying the guarantees. With very small probability, however, the company will default, forcing the guarantor to pay out a large amount. The investment managers are thus selling disaster insurance or, equivalently, taking on 'peso' or 'tail' risks, which produce a positive return most of the time as compensation for a rare very negative return. These strategies have the appearance of producing very high alphas (high returns for low risk), so managers have an incentive to load up on them, especially when times are good and disaster looks remote. Every once in a while, however, they will blow up. Since true performance can only be estimated over a long period, far exceeding the horizon set by the average manager's incentives, managers will take these risks if they can.

One example of this behaviour was observed in 1994, when a number of money market mutual funds in the United States came close to 'breaking the buck' (going below a net asset value of $1 per share, which is virtually unthinkable for an ostensibly riskless fund). Some money market funds had to be bailed out by their parent companies. The reason they came so close to disaster was because they had been employing risky derivatives strategies in order to goose up returns, and these strategies came unstuck in the tail event caused by the Federal Reserve's abrupt rate hike.

While some managers may load up on hidden 'tail' risk to look as if they are generating alpha, others know that for the more observable investments or strategies for their portfolio, there is safety in mimicking the investment strategies of competitors – after all, who can be fired when everybody underperforms? In other words, even if they suspect financial assets are overvalued, they know their likely underperformance will be excused if they herd with everyone else.

Such herd behaviour – a desire to not underperform the observable strategies of peers – may have motivated a number of European insurers, who moved into equities in the late 1990s just before the crash. It could be motivating the move by pension funds and insurance companies today into investing in commodities or hedge funds.

Both the phenomenon of taking on 'tail' risk and that of herding can reinforce each other during an asset-price boom, when investment managers are willing to bear the low probability 'tail' risk that asset prices will revert to fundamentals abruptly, and the knowledge that many of their peers are herding on this risk gives them comfort that they will not underperform significantly if boom turns to bust.

RISK SEEKING

Times of plentiful liquidity not only induce investment managers to seek illiquidity, 'tail' risk, as well as herd, since they are also times of low interest rates, they may induce more familiar risk-seeking behaviour. For example, when an insurance company has promised premium holders returns of 6 per cent, while the typical matching long-term bond rate is 4 per cent, it has no option if it thinks low interest rates are likely to persist, or if it worries about quarterly earnings, but to take on risk, either directly or through investments in alternative assets like hedge funds. Similarly, a pension fund that has well-defined long-dated obligations will have a greater incentive to boost returns through extra risk when risk-free returns are low. All manner of risk premia are driven down by this search for yield and thus risk.

So let me summarize. We are experiencing a widespread phenomenon of high productivity growth, but low investment relative to desired savings, which has pushed down interest rates and pushed up asset prices. With plentiful liquidity, investment managers have reduced the premia for risk as they search for yield. In an attempt to generate alpha, many managers may be taking on beta risk, and even underpricing it. Of course, low interest rates and plentiful access to credit will, for a time, result in low default rates, which will appear to justify the low risk premia. The search for yield and for illiquidity knows no borders as oceans of capital spread across the globe, and asset prices across the globe are being pumped up. As the French say, 'Pourvu que ça dure!'

CONSEQUENCES

What could go wrong? The hope is of a 'soft' landing in the real sector where the factors that led to the current real sector imbalances reverse gently – for instance, domestic demand picks up in the non-industrial world, and growth recovers in Europe and Japan, even while tighter financial conditions slow consumption in the United States. As a better balance between desired savings and investment is achieved, interest rates move up slowly, credit becomes less easy (aided by central bank tightening), and illiquidity seeking and risk seeking reverse gently without major blow-ups.

Of course, if any of this happens more abruptly, the consequences could be uglier. The problems would be most acute if the banking sector is infected. Banks make returns both by originating risks and by bearing them. Since risks that do not need management or are relatively easy to assess can be moved off bank balance sheets into the balance sheets of investment managers, banks have an incentive to originate more of them. Thus they will tend to feed rather than restrain the appetite for risk. Banks cannot, however, sell all risks. They often have to bear the most complicated, hard-to-manage, and volatile portion of the risks they originate. So even though some risk has been moved off bank balance sheets, balance sheets have been reloaded with fresh, more complicated, risks. In fact, the data suggest that despite a deepening of financial markets, banks may not be any safer than in the past. Moreover, the risk they now bear is a small (though perhaps the most volatile) tip of an iceberg of risk they have created.

Perhaps a more important concern is whether banks will be able to provide liquidity to financial markets so that if 'tail' risks do materialize, financial positions can be unwound and losses allocated so that the consequences to the real economy are minimized. Past episodes indicate that banks have played this role successfully. However, there is no assurance they will continue to be able to play the role. In particular, banks have been able to provide liquidity in the past, in part because their sound balance sheets have allowed them to attract the available spare liquidity in the market. But banks today also require liquid markets to hedge some of the risks associated with the complicated products they have created, or guarantees they have offered. Their greater reliance on market liquidity can make their balance sheets more suspect in times of crisis, making them less able to provide the liquidity assurance that they have provided in the past.

Even if the banking system is safe, supervisors and regulators have to be concerned about the rest of the financial system – in the United States, 80 per cent of value is added by the financial sector that is outside the banking system. The non-bank sector is increasingly central to economic activity and is not just a passive holder of assets. Moreover, some non-banks such as insurance companies and some hedge funds are subject to runs. But most important, risks to financial stability are invariably compounded by political risk.

Let me explain this last concern. First, the general public's money is being invested in some of the more risky ventures, a fact highlighted by the revelation that a number of state pension funds in the United States were invested in a risky hedge fund like Amaranth. Diversification into such alternative investments can be a valuable component of an overall investment strategy if it is carefully thought out. The problem is that all too often, it takes place as a form of herding and late in the game – after lagging pension managers see the wonderful returns in energy or from writing credit derivatives made by their more competent or lucky competitors, there is pressure on them to enter the field. They do so late, when the good hedge or commodity funds are closed to investment, and when the cycle is nearer peak than trough. Myriad new unseasoned hedge or commodity funds are started precisely to exploit the distorted incentives of the pension or insurance fund managers who queue like lemmings to dutifully place the public's money. Thus far losses from isolated failures have been washed away in diversified portfolios and the public has not noticed. Will this always continue?

In Europe, we have already had a taste of the potential fallout as pensioners, who were inappropriately advised to invest in Argentinian Bonds or Parmalat, just before these entities defaulted, pressed for compensation. The defaults were isolated, so the fallout was manageable. Could a more generalized downturn lead to more widespread revulsion against financial markets? What of emerging markets where the investors who have been drawn into the financial markets over the last few years have never experienced a downturn?

Second, the fees charged by investment managers like hedge funds and private equity cannot but arouse envy. It is surprising that despite the furor over CEO pay, very little angst has been expressed over investment manager pay, even though Steve Kaplan and Joshua Rauh of the University of Chicago suggest in a 2006 working paper titled 'Wall Street and Main Street: What Contributes to the Rise in the Highest Incomes?' that investment manager pay growth has probably exceeded CEO pay growth. My sense is that there is a belief amongst the public that many investment managers are following sophisticated investment strategies – in other words, that the managers are generating alphas and earning returns for their talents – hence their pay is not questioned.

Yet investigations of collapsed funds such as LTCM don't seem to indicate terribly sophisticated strategies – indeed more beta than alpha. While there is a selection bias in examining failed funds – they are likely to have more beta – it is also likely that large funds with unsophisticated strategies got to that size through a series of lucky bets that paid off. So their managers will have taken home enormous sums of money before it is realized that they had simply been gambling with other people's money. Large losses, 'greedy' managers, and an angry public – this is a perfect scenario for a muck-raking politician to build a career on. The regulatory impediments that could be imposed on the investment managers who add value, and on the financial sector as a whole, could be debilitating.

Third, and accentuating the political problem, is that while it is clear to the public how a bank making a loan benefits the real economy or 'Main Street', it is less clear to it how an investment manager who spreads and allocates risk, improves governance, or reveals information through his trading, helps. We economists know these are very important functions in the economy but they are not so easily sold politically.

And finally, since capital has spread across borders, any sudden future retrenchment could not only inflict pain on recipient countries but also generate foreign political pressure seeking to impede the free flow of capital.

Let me conclude. The last few years have been, in many ways, the best of times for the world economy. The financial sector has contributed immensely. However, the current conjuncture has led to some practices that deserve examination. In particular, I worry whether compensation structures give too much incentive to take risk and, relatedly, whether pay is sufficiently linked to performance. While claims are made that the financial sector is becoming more and more efficient, and that it is adding more and more value, the amount of true value added by the sector is hard to observe. With high pay, questionable practices, and hard-to-observe value addition, the financial sector is politically vulnerable. In a downturn, even if there are no systemic risks in the financial system – for instance, if all the losses are run by stable passive holders of assets such as pension funds – the political system may react in a way that has systemic consequences. To avoid the risk of possibly excessive political reaction, it is important that the issues that I have just alluded to be discussed by the financial sector itself, and where necessary, and possible, adjustments made. It would be a shame if sparks from the red-hot financial sector set off a conflagration that destroyed the very real gains finance has made in the last few decades. Indeed, history suggests abundant caution.

In 2009, as regulators started figuring out what needed to be done to make sure the financial system was made more secure after the financial crisis, I delivered the Homer Jones Lecture organized by the Federal Reserve Bank of St Louis in St Louis on 15 April. This is what I said. (I thank Luigi Zingales for very useful discussion including some of the ideas in this talk.)

The Credit Crisis and Cycle-proof Regulation

There is some consensus that the proximate causes of the crisis are: (i) the U.S. financial sector misallocated resources to real estate, financed through the issuance of exotic new financial instruments; (ii) a significant portion of these instruments found their way, directly or indirectly, into commercial and investment bank balance sheets; (iii) these investments were largely financed with short-term debt; (iv) the mix was potent, and imploded starting in 2007. On these, there is broad agreement. But let us dig a little deeper.

This is a crisis born in some ways from previous financial crises. A wave of crises swept through the emerging markets in the late 1990s: East Asian economies collapsed, Russia defaulted, and Argentina, Brazil, and Turkey faced severe stress. In response to these problems, emerging markets became far more circumspect about borrowing from abroad to finance domestic demand. Instead, their corporations, governments, and households cut back on investment and reduced consumption.

From net absorbers of financial capital from the rest of the world, a number of these countries became net exporters of financial capital. When combined with the savings of habitual exporters like Germany and Japan, there was what Chairman Bernanke referred to as a global savings glut.

Clearly, the net financial savings generated in one part of the world have to be absorbed by deficits elsewhere. Industrial country corporations initially absorbed these savings by expanding investment, especially in information technology. But this proved unsustainable, and investment was cut back sharply following the collapse of the Information Technology bubble.

Extremely accommodative monetary policy by the world's central banks, led by the Federal Reserve, ensured the world did not suffer a deep recession. Instead, the low interest rates in a number of countries ignited demand in interest-sensitive sectors such as automobiles and housing. House prices started rising as did housing investment.

The United States was not by any means the highest in terms of price growth. Housing prices reached higher values relative to rent or incomes in Ireland, Spain, the Netherlands, the United Kingdom, and New Zealand, for example. Then, why did the crisis first manifest itself in the United States? Probably because the U.S. went further on financial innovation, thus drawing more marginal-credit-quality buyers into the market!

A home mortgage loan is very hard for an international investor to hold directly because it requires servicing, is of uncertain credit quality, and has a high propensity to default. Securitization dealt with some of these concerns. If the mortgage was packaged together with mortgages from other areas, diversification would reduce the risk. Furthermore, the riskiest claims against the package could be sold to those who had the capacity to evaluate them and had an appetite for bearing the risk, while the safest AAA-rated portions could be held by international investors.

Indeed, because of the demand from international investors for AAA paper, securitization became focused on squeezing out the most AAA paper from an underlying package of mortgages; the lower quality securities issued against the initial package of mortgages were packaged together once again with similar securities from other packages, and a new range of securities, including a large quantity rated AAA, issued by this 'Collateralized Debt Obligation'.

The 'originate-to-securitize' process had the unintended consequence of reducing the due diligence undertaken by originators. Of course, originators could not completely ignore the true quality of borrowers since they were held responsible for initial defaults, but because house prices were rising steadily over this period, even this source of discipline weakened. If the buyer could not make even the nominal payments involved on the initial low mortgage teaser rates, the lender could repossess the house, sell it quickly in the hot market, and recoup any losses through the price appreciation. In the liquid housing market, so long as the buyer could scrawl X on the dotted line, she could own.

The slicing and dicing through repeated securitization of the original package of mortgages created very complicated securities. The problems in valuing these securities were not obvious when house prices were rising and defaults were few. But as the house prices stopped rising and defaults started increasing, the valuation of these securities became very complicated.

It was not entirely surprising that bad investments would be made in the housing boom. What was surprising was that the originators of these complex securities, the financial institutions, who should have understood the deterioration of the underlying quality of mortgages, held on to so many of the mortgage-backed securities (MBS) in their own portfolios. Why did the sausage-makers, who knew what was in the sausage, keep so many sausages for personal consumption?

The explanation has to be that at least one arm of the bank thought these securities were worthwhile investments, despite their risk. Investment in MBS seemed to be part of a culture of excessive risk-taking that had overtaken banks. A key factor contributing to this culture is that, over short periods of time, it is very hard, especially in the case of new products, to tell whether a financial manager is generating true excess returns adjusting for risk, or whether the current returns are simply compensation for a risk that has not yet shown itself but that will eventually materialize. This could engender excess risk taking both at the top and within the firm.

For instance, the performance of CEOs is evaluated based in part on the earnings they generate relative to their peers. To the extent that some leading banks can generate legitimately high returns, this puts pressure on other banks to keep up. Follower-bank bosses may end up taking excessive risks in order to boost various observable measures of performance.

Indeed, even if managers recognize that this type of strategy is not truly value-creating, a desire to pump up their stock prices and their personal reputations may nevertheless make it the most attractive option for them. There is anecdotal evidence of such pressure on top management – perhaps most famously, Citigroup Chairman Chuck Prince, describing why his bank continued financing buyouts despite mounting risks, said: 'When the music stops, in terms of liquidity, things will be complicated. But, as long as the music is playing, you've got to get up and dance. We're still dancing.' *Financial Times*, 9 July 2007.

Even if top management wants to maximize long-term bank value, it may find it difficult to create incentives and control systems that steer subordinates in this direction. Given the competition for talent, traders have to be paid generously based on performance. But, many of the compensation schemes paid for short-term risk-adjusted performance. This gave traders an incentive to take risks that were not recognized by the system, so they could generate income that appeared to stem from their superior abilities, even though it was in fact only a market-risk premium.

The classic case of such behaviour is to write insurance on infrequent events such as defaults, taking on what is termed 'tail' risk. If a trader is allowed to boost her bonus by treating the entire insurance premium as income, instead of setting aside a significant fraction as a reserve for an eventual payout, she will have an excessive incentive to engage in this sort of trade.

Indeed, traders who bought AAA MBS were essentially getting the additional spread on these instruments relative to corporate AAA securities (the spread being the insurance premium) while ignoring the additional default risk entailed in these untested securities.

The traders in AIG's Financial Products Division just took all this to an extreme by writing credit default swaps, pocketing the premiums as bonus, and not bothering to set aside reserves in case the bonds that were covered by the swaps actually defaulted.

This is not to say that risk managers in a financial institution are unaware of such incentives. However, they may be unable to fully control them, because 'tail' risks are by their nature rare, and therefore hard to quantify with precision before they occur. While they could try and impose crude limits on the activities of the traders taking maximum risk, these traders are likely to have been very profitable (before the risk actually is realized), and such actions are unlikely to sit well with a top management that is being pressured for profits.

Finally, all these shaky assets were financed with short-term debt. This is because in good times, short-term debt seems relatively cheap compared to long-term capital, and the market is willing to supply it because the costs of illiquidity appear remote. Markets seem to favour a bank capital structure that is heavy on short-term leverage. In bad times, though, the costs of illiquidity seem to be more salient, while risk-averse (and burnt) bankers are unlikely to take on excessive risk. The markets then encourage a capital structure that is heavy on capital.

Given the proximate causes of high bank holdings of mortgage-backed securities, as well as other risky loans, such as those to private equity, financed with a capital structure heavy on short-term debt, the crisis had a certain degree of inevitability. As house prices stopped rising, and indeed started falling, mortgage defaults started increasing. Mortgage-backed securities fell in value, became more difficult to price, and their prices became more volatile. They became hard to borrow against, even short term. Banks became illiquid, and eventually insolvent. Only heavy intervention has kept the financial system afloat, and though the market seems to believe that the worst is over, its relief may be premature.

Who is to blame for the financial crisis? As the above discussion

suggests, there are many possible suspects – the exporting countries who still do not understand that their thrift is a burden and not a blessing to the rest of the world, the U.S. household that has spent way beyond its means in recent years, the monetary and fiscal authorities who were excessively ready to intervene to prevent short-term pain, even though they only postponed problems into the future, the bankers who took the upside and left the downside to the taxpayer, the politician who tried to expand his vote bank by extending home-ownership to even those who could not afford it, the markets that tolerated high leverage in the boom only to become risk averse in the bust...

There are plenty of suspects, and enough blame to spread. But if all are to blame, though, should we also not admit they all had a willing accomplice – the euphoria generated by the boom. After all, who is there to stand for stability and against the prosperity and growth in a boom?

Internal risk managers, having repeatedly pointed to risks that never materialized during an upswing, have little credibility and influence – that is if they still have jobs. It is also very hard for contrarian investors to bet against the boom – as Keynes said, the market can stay irrational longer than investors can stay solvent. Politicians have an incentive to ride the boom, indeed to abet it through the deregulation sought by bankers. After all, bankers not only have the money to influence legislation but also have the moral authority conferred by prosperity.

And what of regulators? When everyone is for the boom, how can regulators stand against it? They are reduced to rationalizing why it would be technically impossible for them to stop it. Everyone is therefore complicit in the crisis because, ultimately, they are aided and abetted by cyclical euphoria. And unless we recognize this, the next crisis will be hard to prevent.

For we typically regulate in the midst of a bust when righteous politicians feel the need to do something, when bankers' frail balance sheets and vivid memories makes them eschew any risk, and when regulators have backbones stiffened by public disapproval of past laxity.

But we reform under the delusion that the regulated, and

the markets they operate in, are static and passive, and that the regulatory environment will not vary with the cycle. Ironically, faith in draconian regulation is strongest at the bottom of the cycle, when there is little need for participants to be regulated. By contrast, the misconception that markets will take care of themselves is most widespread at the top of the cycle, at the point of maximum danger to the system. We need to acknowledge these differences and enact cycle-proof regulation, for a regulation set against the cycle will not stand.

Consider the dangers of ignoring this point. Recent reports have argued for 'countercyclical' capital requirements – raising bank capital requirements significantly in good times, while allowing them to fall somewhat in bad times. While sensible prima facie, these proposals may be far less effective than intended.

To see why, recognize that in boom times, the market demands very low levels of capital from financial intermediaries, in part because euphoria makes losses seem remote. So when regulated financial intermediaries are forced to hold more costly capital than the market requires, they have an incentive to shift activity to unregulated intermediaries, as did banks in setting up SIVs and conduits during the current crisis. Even if regulators are strengthened to detect and prevent this shift in activity, banks can subvert capital requirements by taking on risk the regulators do not see, or do not penalize adequately with capital requirements.

Attempts to reduce capital requirements in busts are equally fraught. The risk-averse market wants banks to hold a lot more capital than regulators require, and its will naturally prevails.

Even the requirements themselves may not be immune to the cycle. Once memories of the current crisis fade, and once the ideological cycle turns, there will be enormous political pressure to soften capital requirements or their enforcement.

To have a better chance of creating stability through the cycle – of being cycle-proof – new regulations should be comprehensive, contingent, and cost-effective. Regulations that apply comprehensively to all levered financial institutions are less likely to encourage the drift of activities from heavily regulated to lightly regulated institutions over the boom, a source of instability

since the damaging consequences of such drift come back to hit the heavily regulated institutions in the bust, through channels that no one foresees.

Regulations should also be contingent so they have maximum force when the private sector is most likely to do itself harm but bind less the rest of the time. This will make regulations more cost-effective, which will make them less prone to arbitrage or dilution.

Consider some examples of such regulations. First, instead of asking institutions to raise permanent capital, ask them to arrange for capital to be infused when the institution or the system is in trouble. Because these 'contingent capital' arrangements will be contracted in good times when the chances of a downturn seem remote, they will be relatively cheap (compared to raising new capital in the midst of a recession) and thus easier to enforce. Also, because the infusion is seen as an unlikely possibility, firms cannot go out and increase their risks, using the future capital as backing. Finally, because the infusions come in bad times when capital is really needed, they protect the system and the taxpayer in the right contingencies.

One version of contingent capital is for banks to issue debt which would automatically convert to equity when two conditions are met; first, the system is in crisis, either based on an assessment by regulators or based on objective indicators, and second, the bank's capital ratio falls below a certain value. The first condition ensures that banks that do badly because of their own idiosyncratic errors, and not when the system is in trouble, don't get to avoid the disciplinary effects of debt. The second condition rewards well-capitalized banks by allowing them to avoid the forced conversion (the number of shares the debt converts to will be set at a level so as dilute the value of old equity substantially), while also giving banks that anticipate losses an incentive to raise new equity well in time.

Another version of contingent capital is to require that systemically important levered financial institutions buy fully collateralized insurance policies (from unlevered institutions, foreigners, or the government) that will infuse capital into these institutions when the system is in trouble.

Here is one way it could operate. Megabank would issue capital insurance bonds, say to sovereign wealth funds. It would invest the proceeds in Treasury bonds, which would then be placed in a custodial account in State Street Bank. Every quarter, Megabank would pay a pre-agreed insurance premium (contracted at the time the capital insurance bond is issued) which, together with the interest accumulated on the Treasury bonds held in the custodial account, would be paid to the sovereign fund.

If the aggregate losses of the banking system exceed a certain pre-specified amount, Megabank would start getting a payout from the custodial account to bolster its capital. The sovereign wealth fund will now face losses on the principal it has invested, but on average, it will have been compensated by the insurance premium.

Consider next regulations aimed at 'too-big-to-fail' institutions. Regulations to limit their size and activities will become very onerous when growth is high, thus increasing the incentive to dilute them. Perhaps, instead, a more cyclically sustainable regulation would be to make these institutions easier to close. What if systemically important financial institutions were required to develop a plan that would enable them to be resolved over a weekend? Such a 'shelf bankruptcy' plan would require banks to track, and document, their exposures much more carefully and in a timely manner, probably through much better use of technology. The plan will need to be stress tested by regulators periodically and supported by enabling legislation – such as one facilitating an orderly transfer of the institution's swap books to pre-committed partners. Not only will the need to develop a plan give these institutions the incentive to reduce unnecessary complexity and improve management, it will not be much more onerous in the boom, and may indeed force management to think the unthinkable at such times.

Let me conclude. A crisis offers us a rare window of opportunity to implement reforms – it is a terrible thing to waste. The temptation will be to over-regulate, as we have done in the past. This creates its own perverse dynamic.

For as we start eliminating senseless regulations once the

recovery takes hold, we will find deregulation adds so much economic value that it further empowers the deregulatory camp. Eventually, though, the deregulatory momentum causes us to eliminate regulatory muscle rather than fat. Perhaps rather than swinging maniacally between too much and too little regulation, it would be better to think of cycle-proof regulation.

Postscript: These ideas (I cannot claim originality because these were in the air) made their way into post-crisis regulation as contingent convertible bonds (CoCos) and living wills.

In 2012, I wrote a longer piece in *Foreign Affairs* summarizing my views on the reasons for the build-up in debt before the crisis and the post-crisis recovery measures.

The True Lessons of the Great Recession

According to the conventional interpretation of the global economic recession, growth has ground to a halt in the West because demand has collapsed, a casualty of the massive amount of debt accumulated before the crisis.

Households and countries are not spending because they can't borrow the funds to do so, and the best way to revive growth, the argument goes, is to find ways to get the money flowing again. Governments that still can should run up even larger deficits, and central banks should push interest rates even lower to encourage thrifty households to buy rather than save. Leaders should worry about the accumulated debt later, once their economies have picked up again.

This narrative – the standard Keynesian line, modified for a debt crisis – is the one to which most Western officials, central bankers, and Wall Street economists subscribe today. As the United States has shown signs of recovery, Keynesian pundits have been quick to claim success for their policies, pointing to Europe's emerging recession as proof of the folly of government austerity. But it is hard to tie recovery (or the lack of it) to specific policy interventions. Until recently, these same pundits were complaining that the stimulus packages in the United States were too small. So they could have claimed credit for Keynesian stimulus even if the recovery had not materialized, saying, 'We

euro was introduced, Italy's unemployment rate was 11 per cent, Greece's was 12 per cent, and Spain's was 16 per cent. The resulting drain on government coffers made it difficult to save for future spending on health care and pensions, promises made even more onerous by rapidly aging populations.

In countries that did reform, deregulation was not an unmitigated blessing. It did boost entrepreneurship and innovation, increase competition, and force existing firms to focus on efficiency, all of which gave consumers cheaper and better products. But it also had the unintended consequence of increasing income inequality – creating a gap that, by and large, governments dealt with not by preparing their work forces for a knowledge economy but by giving them access to cheap credit.

DISRUPTING THE STATUS QUO

For the United States, the world's largest economy, deregulation has been a mixed bag. Over the past few decades, the competition it has induced has widened the income gap between the rich and the poor and made it harder for the average American to find a stable, well-paying job with good benefits. But that competition has also led to a flood of cheap consumer goods, which has meant that any income he or she gets now goes further than ever before.

During the postwar era of heavy regulation and limited competition, established firms in the United States had grown fat and happy, enjoying massive quasi-monopolistic profits. They shared these returns with their shareholders and their workers. For banks, this was the age of the '3-6-3' formula: borrow at 3 per cent, lend at 6 per cent, and head off to the golf course at 3 p.m. Banks were profitable, safe, and boring, and the price was paid by depositors, who got the occasional toaster instead of market interest rates. Unions fought for well-paying jobs with good benefits, and firms were happy to accommodate them to secure industrial peace – after all, there were plenty of profits to be shared.

In the 1980s and 1990s, the dismantling of regulations and trade barriers put an end to this cozy life. New entrepreneurs with better products challenged their slower-moving competitors, and the variety and quality of consumer products improved radically, altering peoples' lives largely for the better. Personal computers, connected through the Internet, have allowed users to entertain, inform, and shop for themselves, and cell phones have let people stay in constant contact with friends (and bosses). The shipping container, meanwhile, has enabled small foreign manufacturers to ship products speedily to faraway consumers. Relative to incomes, cotton shirts and canned peaches have never been cheaper.

At the same time as regular consumers' purchasing power grew, so did Wall Street payouts. Because companies' profits were under pressure, they began to innovate more and take greater risks, and doing so required financiers who could understand those risks, price them accurately, and distribute them judiciously. Banking was no longer boring; indeed, it became the command centre of the economy, financing one company's expansion here while putting another into bankruptcy there.

Meanwhile, the best companies became more meritocratic, and they paid more to attract top talent. The top 1 per cent of households had obtained only 8.9 per cent of the total income generated in the United States in 1976, but by 2007 this had increased to nearly 25 per cent. Even as the salaries of upper management grew, however, its ranks diversified. Compared with executives in 1980, corporate leaders in the United States in 2001 were younger, more likely to be women, and less likely to have Ivy League degrees (although they had more advanced degrees). It was no longer as important to belong to the right country club to reach the top; what mattered was having a good education and the right skills.

It is tempting to blame the ever-widening income gap on skewed corporate incentives and misguided tax policies, but neither explanation is sufficient. If the rise in executive salaries were just the result of bad corporate governance, as some have claimed, then doctors, lawyers, and academics would not have also seen their salaries grow as much as they have in recent years. And although the top tax rates were indeed lowered during the presidency of George W. Bush, these cuts weren't the primary source of the inequality, either, since inequality in before-tax incomes also rose. This is not to say that all top salaries are deserved – it is not hard to find the pliant board overpaying the underperforming CEO – but most are simply reflections of the value of skills in a competitive world.

In fact, since the 1980s, the income gap has widened not just between CEOs and the rest of society but across the economy, too, as routine tasks have been automated or outsourced. With the aid of technology and capital, one skilled worker can displace many unskilled workers. Think of it this way: when factories used mechanical lathes, university-educated Joe and high-school-educated Moe were no different and earned similar paychecks. But when factories upgraded to computerized lathes, not only was Joe more useful; Moe was no longer needed.

Not all low-skilled jobs have disappeared. Non-routine, low-paying service jobs that are hard to automate or outsource, such as taxi driving, hairdressing, or gardening, remain plentiful. So the U.S. workforce has bifurcated into low-paying professions that require few skills and high-paying ones that call for creativity and credentials. Comfortable, routine jobs that require moderate skills and offer good benefits have disappeared, and the laid-off workers have had to either upgrade their skills or take lower-paying service jobs.

Unfortunately, for various reasons – inadequate early schooling, dysfunctional families and communities, the high cost of university education – far too many Americans have not gotten the education or skills they need. Others have spent too much time in shrinking industries, such as auto manufacturing, instead of acquiring skills in growing sectors, such as medical technology. As the economists Claudia Goldin and Lawrence Katz have put it, in 'the race between technology and education' in the United States in the last few decades, education has fallen behind.

As Americans' skills have lagged, the gap between the wages of the well educated and the wages of the moderately educated has grown even further. Since the early 1980s, the difference between the incomes of the top 10 per cent of earners (who typically hold university degrees) and those of the middle (most of whom have only a high school diploma) has grown steadily. By contrast, the difference between median incomes and incomes of the bottom 10 per cent has barely budged. The top is running away from the middle, and the middle is merging with the bottom.

The statistics are alarming. In the United States, 35 per cent of those aged 25 to 54 with no high school diploma have no job, and high school dropouts are three times as likely to be unemployed as university graduates. What is more, Americans between the ages of 25 and 34 are less likely to have a degree than those between 45 and 54, even though degrees have become more valuable in the labour market. Most troubling, however, is that in recent years, the children of rich parents have been far more likely to get college degrees than were similar children in the past, whereas college completion rates for children in poor households have stayed consistently low. The income divide created by the educational divide is becoming entrenched.

THE POLITICIANS RESPOND

In the years before the crisis, the everyday reality for middle-class Americans was a paycheck that refused to grow and a job that became less secure every year, even while the upper-middle class and the very rich got richer. Well-paying, low-skilled jobs with good benefits were becoming harder and harder to find, except perhaps in the government.

Rather than address the underlying reasons for this trend, American politicians opted for easy answers. Their response may be understandable; after all, it is not easy to upgrade workers' skills quickly. But the resulting fixes did more damage than good. Politicians sought to boost consumption, hoping that if middle-class voters felt like they were keeping up with their richer neighbours – if they could afford a new car every few years and the occasional exotic holiday – they might pay less attention to the fact that their salaries weren't growing. One easy way to do that was to enhance the public's access to credit.

Accordingly, starting in the early 1990s, U.S. leaders encouraged the financial sector to lend more to households, especially lower-middle class ones. In 1992, Congress passed the Federal Housing Enterprises Financial Safety and Soundness Act, partly to gain more control over Fannie Mae and Freddie Mac, the giant private mortgage agencies, and partly to promote affordable homeownership for low-income groups.

Such policies helped money flow to lower-middle-class households and raised their spending – so much so that consumption inequality rose much less than income inequality in the years before the crisis. These policies were also politically popular. Unlike when it came to an expansion in government welfare transfers, few groups opposed expanding credit to the lower-middle class – not the politicians who wanted more growth and happy constituents, not the bankers and brokers who profited from the mortgage fees, not the borrowers who could now buy their dream houses with virtually no money down, and not the laissez-faire bank regulators who thought they could pick up the pieces if the housing market collapsed. Cynical as it may seem, easy credit was used as a palliative by successive administrations unable or unwilling to directly address the deeper problems with the economy or the anxieties of the middle class.

The Federal Reserve abetted these short-sighted policies. In 2001, in response to the dot-com bust, the Fed cut short-term interest rates to the bone. Even though the overstretched corporations that were meant to be stimulated were not interested in investing, artificially low interest rates acted as a tremendous subsidy to the parts of the economy that relied on debt, such as housing and finance. This led to an expansion in housing construction (and related services, such as real estate brokerage and mortgage lending), which created jobs, especially for the unskilled. Progressive economists applauded this process, arguing that the housing boom would lift the economy out of the doldrums. But the Fed-supported bubble proved unsustainable. Many construction workers have lost their jobs and are now in deeper trouble than before, having also borrowed to buy unaffordable houses.

Bankers obviously deserve a large share of the blame for the crisis. Some of the financial sector's activities were clearly predatory, if not outright criminal. But the role that the politically induced expansion of credit played cannot be ignored; it is the main reason the usual checks and balances on financial risk-taking broke down.

Outside the United States, other governments responded differently to slowing growth in the 1990s. Some countries focused on making themselves more competitive. Fiscally conservative Germany, for example, reduced unemployment benefits even while reducing worker protections. Wages grew slowly even as productivity increased, and Germany became one of the most competitive manufacturers in the world. But some other European countries, such as Greece and Italy, had little incentive to reform, as the inflow of easy credit after their accession to the eurozone kept growth going and helped bring down unemployment. The Greek government borrowed to create high-paying but unproductive government jobs, and unemployment came down sharply. But eventually, Greece could borrow no more, and its GDP is now shrinking fast. Not all European countries in trouble relied on federal borrowing and spending. In Spain, a combination of a construction boom and spending by local governments created jobs. In Ireland, it was primarily a housing bubble that did the trick. Regardless, the common thread was that debt-fuelled growth was unsustainable.

WHAT CAN BE DONE?

Since the growth before the crisis was distorted in fundamental ways, it is hard to imagine that governments could restore demand quickly – or that doing so would be enough to get the global economy back on track. The status quo ante is not a good place to return to because bloated finance, residential construction, and government sectors need to shrink, and workers need to move to more productive work. The way out of the crisis cannot be still more borrowing and spending, especially if the spending does not build lasting assets that will help future generations pay off the debts that they will be saddled with. Instead, the best short-term policy response is to focus on long-term sustainable growth.

Countries that don't have the option of running higher deficits, such as Greece, Italy, and Spain, should shrink the size of their governments and improve their tax collection. They must allow freer entry into such professions as accounting, law, and pharmaceuticals, while exposing sectors such as transportation to more competition, and they should reduce employment protections – moves that would create more private sector jobs for laid-off government workers and unemployed youth. Fiscal austerity is not painless and will probably subtract from growth in the short run. It would be far better to phase reforms in over time, yet it is precisely because governments did not act in good times that they are forced to do so, and quickly, in bad times. Indeed, there is a case to be made for doing what is necessary quickly and across the board so that everyone feels that the pain is shared, rather than spreading it over time and risking dissipating the political will. Governments should not, however, underestimate the pain that these measures will cause to the elderly, the youth, and the poor, and where possible, they should enact targeted legislation to alleviate the measures' impact.

The United States, for its part, can take some comfort in the powerful forces that should help create more productive jobs in the future: better information and communications technology, lower-cost clean energy, and sharply rising demand in emerging markets for higher-value-added goods. But it also needs to take decisive action now so that it can be ready to take advantage of these forces. The United States must improve the capabilities of its workforce, preserve an environment for innovation, and regulate finance better so as to prevent excess.

None of this will be easy, of course. Consider how hard it is to improve the match between skills and jobs. Since the housing and financial sectors will not employ the numbers they did during the pre-crisis credit boom any time soon, people who worked in, or depended on, those sectors will have to change careers. That takes time and is not always possible; the housing industry, in particular, employed many low-skilled workers, who are hard to place. Government programmes aimed at skill building have a checkered history. Even government attempts to help students finance their educations have not always worked; some predatory private colleges have lured students with access to government financing into expensive degrees that have little value in the job market. Instead, much of the initiative has to come from people themselves.

That is not to say that Washington should be passive. Although educational reform and universal health care are long overdue, it can do more on other fronts. More information on job prospects in various career tracks, along with better counselling about educational and training programmes, can help people make better decisions before they enrol in expensive but useless programmes. In areas with high youth unemployment, subsidies for firms to hire first-time young workers may get youth into the labour force and help them understand what it takes to hold a job. The government could support older unemployed workers more – paying for child care and training – so that they can retrain even while looking for work. Some portion of employed workers' unemployment insurance fees could accumulate in training and job-search accounts that could help them acquire skills or look for work if they get laid off.

At the same time, since new business ventures are what will create the innovation that is necessary for growth, the United States has to preserve its entrepreneurial environment. Although the political right is probably alarmist about the downsides of somewhat higher income taxes, significantly higher taxes can reduce the returns for entrepreneurship and skill acquisition considerably – for the rich and the poor alike. Far better to reform the tax system, eliminating the loopholes and tax subsidies that accountants are so fond of finding in order to keep marginal income tax rates from rising too much.

Culture also matters. Although it is important to shine the spotlight on egregious unearned salaries, clubbing all high earners into an undifferentiated mass – as the '1 per cent' label does – could denigrate the wealth creation that has served the country so well. The debate on inequality should focus on how the United States can level up rather than on how it should level down.

Finally, even though the country should never forget that

financial excess tipped the world over into crisis, politicians must not lobotomize banking through regulation to make it boring again. Finance needs to be vibrant to make possible the entrepreneurship and innovation that the world sorely needs. At the same time, legislation such as the Dodd-Frank Act, which overhauled financial regulation, although much derided for the burdens it imposes, needs to be given the chance to do its job of channelling the private sector's energies away from excess risk taking. As the experience with these new regulations builds, they can be altered if they are too onerous. Americans should remain alert to the reality that regulations are shaped by incumbents to benefit themselves. They should also remember the role political mandates and Federal Reserve policies played in the crisis and watch out for a repeat.

The industrial countries have a choice. They can act as if all is well except that their consumers are in a funk and so what John Maynard Keynes called 'animal spirits' must be revived through stimulus measures. Or they can treat the crisis as a wake-up call and move to fix all that has been papered over in the last few decades and thus put themselves in a better position to take advantage of coming opportunities. For better or worse, the narrative that persuades these countries' governments and publics will determine their futures – and that of the global economy.

I returned to academia in January 2007 after a three and a half year stint at the Fund. What follows are a sampling of my pieces including but not speeches. The following was delivered in February 2007, just before the crisis.

Financial Conditions, Asset Management, and Political Risks: Trying to Make Sense of Our Times

Despite widespread strong productivity growth, nominal investment, especially corporate investment, has remained relatively weak for the world as a whole, while desired savings is strong; all this is savings glut (as the Chairman Bernanke of investment restraint, as did the IMF), the net effect is an imbalance between desired savings and realized investment. Consequently, real long-term interest rates have been low for some time. Interestingly, even as the Federal Reserve raised policy rates during 2006, long-term interest rates fell further – in slowing domestic demand in the United States, markets may believe the Fed is aggravating the worldwide excess of desired savings over realized investment further.

Current conditions are unlikely to be permanent. Given aging

Section III

OCCASIONAL PIECES

I

This piece, written with Luigi Zingales (also a University of Chicago professor and my co-author for *Saving Capitalism from the Capitalists*), was published in the early days of the Iraq occupation in 2003. It is quite sceptical about the prospects of building democracy in Iraq.

Capitalism Does Not Rhyme with Colonialism

The end of the Cold War marked the triumph of market democracies over socialism and the ascendance of the United States to the position of the sole world superpower. While this occurred more than a decade ago, only now with Operation Iraqi Freedom are the geopolitical implications becoming clearer. The military power now enjoyed by the United States is similar to that Western Europe had during the second half of the 19th century. Back then European powers went on a hunt for colonies, partly because of economic self-interest, partly in an attempt to 'civilize' the rest of the world. While history is not so boring as to repeat itself, some in U.S. policy circles genuinely believe that by deposing rogue regimes like Iraq and planting the seeds of democracy and capitalism in those countries, the United States can also infect neighbouring countries and eventually remake the world in its own image. While these policy makers would reject any parallels in motives with colonialism, they exist nonetheless: a mix of self-interest – the world will become safer for the United States – and idealism – it will also make the world more prosperous and liberal. But can these policies work?

The reasoning is not without merit. Dictators like Saddam

Hussein hold such a grip on power that internal change is all but impossible. In such situations, an outside power that truly has the interests of the people at heart can effect a change that the people themselves cannot manage easily. Without foreign intervention, the Franco dictatorship in Spain lasted forty years. By contrast, military defeat brought Mussolini's and Hitler's regimes to a quicker end. If the United States can overthrow a bloody dictator like Saddam Hussein in the space of weeks and free his people, why not do it? This logic would favour an intervention in every dictatorial country, from Cuba to North Korea, from Venezuela to Zaire, constrained only by crass budgetary constraints.

Overthrowing a dictator, however, is only the first and easiest step toward building a democracy. If the United States simply left Iraq at this point after holding elections, or with a puppet government in place, there would be little to safeguard the Iraqi people from the emergence of a new tyrant. Countries do not fall prey to dictatorial regimes simply because of bad luck. Such countries often have power structures in place that facilitate dictatorships: typically, dictators are the face of a narrow elite, which has captured both political and economic power. Change is possible only if the power structure is changed and becomes more broad-based. Without that, any political revolution will only replace the old tyrants with new ones.

Japan is often mentioned as a successful example of democracy imposed by outside forces. The origins of that success, however, have to be found in the sweeping reforms imposed by Douglas MacArthur. Before his reforms, land holdings in Japan were concentrated and economic power was held by a few large industrial and financial combines called the Zaibatsus. MacArthur saw these agrarian and industrial elites gave backbone to the Japanese Nationalist government, which had taken Japan to war. For this reason, he tried to undermine their power. The post-war land reforms did expand and widen the land-owning class, in the process fostering an agricultural revival, and making Japanese democracy more stable. But even though MacArthur started to break up the Zaibatsus, he did not have the necessary time to carry it out. The need for reliable suppliers during the Korean

War forced the government to compromise with the Zaibatsus. This failure explains in part why the Japanese domestic market is still so uncompetitive even though Japanese democracy is vibrant.

Nevertheless, MacArthur accomplished a lot. In part, he was helped by the complete collapse of Japan and the utter exhaustion of its people. There was virtually no armed resistance to the occupying authority. The Japanese held their domestic elites responsible for initiating and prolonging the disastrous war, and attempts to cut them down to size were not resisted, and even welcomed by the citizenry.

The problem with a situation like Iraq's is that the occupying forces face a people who are neither completely subdued nor completely convinced of the legitimacy of the occupation. Without popular legitimacy any major reform may not stick. Worse, the exigencies of an unpopular occupation can perpetuate (and even strengthen) the power of existing elites.

If it does not obtain the citizenry's support, the occupying authority will have to seek allies to control the territory – else the costs of armed occupation will become prohibitive. These allies are typically found among powerful local bosses, who are often the very same ones who made possible the previous regime. In return, these bosses will seek economic favours such as government contracts and local monopolies. In other words, if the occupying authority does not have widespread popular support – and few foreign rulers, no matter how noble their intentions, will have such support – its natural tendency will be to allow mutually dependent concentrations of power to build up. If this seems much like the concentrations of power that surrounded the previous dictatorship, it is because of natural parallels: the dictator was also an unpopular occupier who ruled largely by distributing privileges to a supportive few. Under these conditions of concentrated power, it is hard for either democracy or markets to take root.

All this is not idle theorizing. Studies show that colonies like the United States, Canada, and Australia, where Europeans (typically the British) settled in large numbers, often displacing or driving out native populations, developed many of the institutions necessary for a market democracy. Government was relatively benign, and even democratic, in large part because it did not have to keep a native population under control. By contrast, in colonies like India where there was too large a population to be displaced, or where disease prevented large-scale European migration, a small body of Europeans had to keep a large native population under check. Typically, this was done by co-opting the domestic elites, such as the native rajas and big landlords, and supporting their power so long as they repaid the compliment. Under these circumstances, democratic and market institutions did not emerge. Studies show that regions in India where these arrangements were particularly predominant have, even today, underdeveloped social and market infrastructure.

In sum, the end of the Cold War gives the United States both the power and the interest to spread democracy and capitalism by force. But history suggests that democracy and free markets are hard to impose, no matter how beneficial they are. Rarely did an occupying outside power, unconnected by the bonds of ethnicity, culture, and national origin with the ruled citizenry, leave behind the conditions that would foster both democracy and markets. Even in the 21st century, capitalism does not rhyme with colonialism!

II

This is another of the quarterly columns for *Straight Talk*, written while I was at the International Monetary Fund in 2004. It reflects my general unease with 'magic bullet' or quick-fix solutions to complex problems. I find that 'magic bullets' often have overlooked collateral effects. The role of the pragmatic economist is to point them out.

Clever Solution: But Will It Work?

Knotty problems abound in economics: For example, how can the poor obtain access to credit? How can international economic and financial policies help to cut short the duration of kleptocratic, despotic regimes? How can we eliminate bank runs? And clever solutions keep bubbling up. Give the poor formal title to their land because that will give them collateral against which to borrow. Declare the debt issued by terrible regimes 'odious' and unenforceable so that investors will be unwilling to finance such regimes in the future. Force banks to hold only liquid, marketable instruments so that they can meet the demands of depositors. The solutions seem ingenious, low-cost responses to the problems posed. Yet they are rarely implemented.

Often, this is not because there is a conspiracy to ignore the solutions, but because both the underlying causes of the problem and the ramifications of the proposed solution are broader than have been allowed for. Not only can the clever proposal not solve the problem, but it also has the unintended consequence of detracting from less attractive, painful reform that is ultimately necessary to solve it. This is not necessarily to say that one shouldn't propose clever ideas or try to implement them, but one should be aware that to have a high probability of working, solutions have to be robust, that is, allow for the possibility that the underlying problem is not the obvious one. Many clever solutions are not robust. Consider the following example.

DOLLARIZATION AND ORIGINAL SIN

The dollarization of liabilities has become widespread in recent years. More and more countries, banks, and firms in emerging markets issue debt denominated in a foreign currency (typically the dollar), even though they don't have large dollar revenues. When a country's currency depreciates, the resulting currency mismatch between revenues and obligations can lead to serious consequences – sovereign defaults, banking system meltdowns, and widespread corporate bankruptcy.

Given these risks, why do countries persist in borrowing in foreign currencies? One reason – referred to as the 'original sin' hypothesis – is that not only do countries not have any choice now but also they can't do anything about it in the future. Many years ago, the country committed a horrible 'original sin' and ever since, investors have feared that country, refusing to accept paper denominated in its currency. In other words, no matter how good the country's fiscal and monetary situation becomes, it has little hope of escaping the rejection, albeit irrational, of the market (I should note that there are more rational explanations for 'original sin' now – it is a moving target).

But recent studies show the empirical basis for this argument is shaky. Its logic is also particularly problematic when we see investors returning to lend to Latin American economies that had defaulted on them just a few years before. Such historical experience suggests that investors have short memories, certainly not ones extending over centuries or even decades. Nevertheless, the original sin argument is politically attractive because it absolves countries of responsibility for their current condition.

A related but more plausible explanation for the steady increase in dollarized debt is that countries are forced into this position because their monetary policies lack credibility. If a country issued debt in domestic currency, the argument goes, it would have an incentive to inflate its way out of debt and would be viewed as likely to succumb to that temptation even though its policies have recently been on the straight and narrow. But with dollarized debt, the country wouldn't have this incentive, and so investors would be more willing to lend to it.

What is the clever solution? Some suggest that the World Bank or IMF issue bonds in the country's domestic currency and then lend the proceeds to the country with repayment also denominated in the domestic currency. These international financial institutions (IFI) are presumably more sensible than market investors and aren't fazed by original sin or misleading reputations. They can also serve as guarantors that the country will not inflate its way out of trouble, giving investors reasons to hold domestic currency debt that they have issued (alternatively, the IFIs can issue debt indexed to inflation). Such proposals have been floated in a number of forms with varying degrees of sophistication and varying objectives. Some of the most reasonable are those by Barry Eichengreen and Ricardo Hausmann ('How to eliminate original financial sin', *Financial Times*, 22 November 2002) and by Eduardo Levy Yeyati ('Financial de-dollarization and the role of IFIs: De-dollarizing multilateral credit', mimeo, Universidad Torcuato Di Tella).

Would the clever solution work? The key question is whether the phenomenon of dollarization is driven purely by bad reputations from the past. History suggests that countries have graduated from issuing foreign currency debt to issuing debt denominated in domestic currency, and they have typically done so by fixing fundamental problems like excessive deficits or a tendency to inflate, rather than by obtaining absolution for sins from a higher power.

DOLLARIZATION AND FEAR PREMIUMS

To see whether this solution is robust, consider another explanation for dollarization of liabilities. Typically, a country's debt isn't sold only to foreigners but also to locals. This is natural, especially given that locals are more likely than foreigners to believe they can enforce repayment. The marginal domestic investor will care about the pattern of returns the debt offers. Finance theory indicates that he or she will be prepared to pay more for (accept lower returns from) a security that is expected to retain its value or go up in bad economic times relative to a security that is expected to plummet in value. The former security provides more insurance.

What do citizens in these investing countries want insurance against? One major problem in an emerging market is that it's prone to adverse economic shocks that cause foreign lenders to stop lending, forcing a real currency depreciation as well as high inflation in the country. Economic activity tends to collapse, causing immense hardship for the people. Consider what happens to the securities at this time. As long as the country doesn't default, dollar-denominated debt goes up in value because of the real depreciation, while debt denominated in local currency falls because of inflation and depreciation. Domestic investors who wanted protection against such crises caused by sudden stops would prefer dollar-denominated debt because it provides valuable insurance, and thus be willing to accept a lower rate of interest on it. (Of course, such debt is valuable only under the reasonable belief that the government wouldn't default on its debt or that, even if it defaulted, it would repay in proportion to its outstanding obligations.)

This doesn't immediately imply that domestic issuers would rush to issue such debt, for they would have to pay more in bad times. But even though in a perfect world issuers would be indifferent between dollar and domestic currency debt, in the real world, ministers, bankers, and industrial managers might not be. Given an expected revenue stream with which to repay, the lower-interest dollar debt will allow the minister more borrowing upfront. If the country finds itself greatly constrained in its borrowing, dollar debt might be attractive even if a minister isn't myopic. If one adds the very real possibility that he doesn't look beyond his short term of office, a minister might be extra willing to accept the uncertain longer-run risk for the certain short-run budgetary flexibility. Similarly for bankers and chief executive officers of industrial firms.

In these circumstances, will the clever solution work? Absolutely not. The IMF and the World Bank would have to pay the same risk premium when they issue domestic currency-denominated debt as does the country. If the country borrowed in local currency through these institutions, it would simply add a costly layer of intermediation to its borrowing costs. That said, if international financial institutions were willing to step in to such an extent that the country didn't need to borrow from its own citizens – an extremely unlikely scenario – then the holders of the country's debt would all be foreigners and the country wouldn't need to pay a premium.

One should also be careful about condemning dollarization out of hand: banning it might seem another clever solution. Although a currency mismatch is a severe problem in the midst of a crisis, one cannot judge the merit of actions that led to it simply by looking at outcomes. There may be costs of banning dollarization – such as a lower ability for a country or firm to borrow or lower hedging possibilities. These have to be traded off against the potentially distorted incentives for issuers to raise excessive amounts of dollar debt.

Without a clear sense of the costs and benefits, a prudent policy might be to work on fixing the deep underlying causes while taking measures to limit the obvious risks. The big fixes would include boosting the private saving rate so that a country becomes less dependent on outside capital, strengthening revenue collection and cutting expenditures in good times so a country accumulates spare capacity for bad times and reduces the need to inflate, and increasing a country's ability to export its way out of sudden capital inflow stoppages. Such a policy of 'living with dollarization' may be neither clever nor quick but, in the long run, it is more likely to work. Of course, such a policy is not robust if 'original sin' is the true problem. Fortunately, history suggests it works.

In the following piece in 2004 in *Straight Talk*, I worried about the starting point for economic models, and why it was unrealistic. Models are, by their very nature, abstractions from reality, but we always have to ask whether in the process of abstraction we are throwing important features of the real world away.

Assume Anarchy?

Institutions are all the rage. The absence of institutions – such as efficient and impartial judiciaries, legal systems to protect intellectual property, tax administrations that are efficient and free of corruption, and credible central banks – is offered as an explanation for some of the central puzzles in development economics, including why so many countries do not grow fast enough to vanquish poverty. But unfortunately, economic theory offers us little guidance on how strong institutions are created and nurtured. And, unless we develop a better understanding, simply reciting the mantra 'institutions' offers little in the way of constructive policy advice to less developed countries, leaving the policy arena open to other, more dubious, views. A tremendous amount of research is now being conducted on the provenance of institutions (including whether they are a proxy for deeper forces) but my focus here is on why mainstream economists have neglected this in the past. In particular, I want to ask how much blame for this neglect should be attached to the canonical model in economics, the complete markets model.

In this theoretical model, which every graduate economics student encounters in some form or other, everyone is fully informed; every eventuality is anticipated in contracts; all contracts are enforced by omniscient, incorruptible courts; and governments automatically take care of all the public goods and interfere in none of the private ones. Clearly this is an abstraction even in relation to the developed world. Yet it is regarded as a useful starting point for a number of reasons. First, it is argued, the model is in important respects a reasonable approximation of reality. Second, it usefully serves as a common point of departure, deviations from which – and the fewer the better – have to be justified. This disciplines research, preventing original but muddled thinkers from generating results simply by making unorthodox assumptions. This enables economists to talk to each other rather than past each other, and to see the implications of their favourite deviation by comparing the conclusions from the model incorporating it with the outcomes from the complete markets model. This methodical one-step deviation approach enhances debate and understanding (and makes refereeing for scholarly publications easier). Third, the model is mathematically tractable and allows elegant theorems and proofs.

The point of building models is to learn about the real world by abstracting from details that are irrelevant to the issue being considered. Without models, we would just have descriptions. But while some abstraction is important, gross abstraction can make a model irrelevant. And for many situations, at least in the developing world, the complete markets model is too far distanced from reality to be useful. Take, for example, armed conflict, which plagues many poor countries. It is usually viewed as wasting resources and therefore being economically inefficient. There is no room for conflict in the complete markets paradigm: with complete markets, we would simply anticipate all possible situations of conflict and contract them away. But in truth, an important reason for continued conflicts in some countries is that there is simply no credible mechanism to enforce contracts. Warlords may sign peace treaties, but knowing they will not be enforced, exploit the ensuing peace to prepare for the next war.

How to build commitment against predation and enforce contracts at the national level are first-order economic issues.

Early economists, like Hobbes and Locke, reflected on them, but with a few notable exceptions, economists neglected them for many decades, in part, perhaps, because many were trained in developed countries where the complete markets model is somewhat less absurd. Only recently have economists returned to these questions.

Although the complete markets model can be a useful abstraction in some circumstances, it is an intellectual straitjacket when applied universally, particularly because it ignores the costs of contracting and enforcement. Requiring card-carrying economists to stay within a few standard deviations of the model may greatly hinder their ability to focus on what is essential in environments different from the one that gave birth to the model. I say this even though several important breakthroughs in economics in the last three decades have come from one-step deviations, such as assuming that not everyone has the same information (known in the jargon as 'asymmetric information'), or that economic activity is carried out by organizations where employees may not share the goals of the organization (known in the jargon as 'agency').

One problem with relying on models that are within a few standard deviations of the complete market model to guide policy in a poor country is that solutions may seem far easier than they actually are. For example, in these countries some contracts are inflexible or do not exist. The facile policy prescription from the model is to advocate greater flexibility or to create the missing contract. Yet there may be far deeper deficiencies that need to be addressed in order to rectify the problem.

For example, the inflexibility of labour contracts – in particular the difficulty of firing employees – is seen as inefficient because it does not permit firms to react quickly to business conditions. Often, these prohibitions are ascribed to overly strong unions that hold the economy to ransom. But if courts are slow and corrupt, so that a worker who is wrongfully fired has no redress, perhaps the prohibition of firing – because violations are so easily and publicly observable – is the only way to protect workers from arbitrary decisions by employers. Job tenure may also act as a form of social security, necessary because the government does a miserable job providing a safety net, and private insurance markets do not exist. Admittedly, these explanations are speculative, and the truth may lie elsewhere. But my point is that crude, inefficient prohibitions on firing may be a robust response to a number of deficiencies in the system, many of which reinforce each other in subtle ways. If so, unions may command strong popular support because of deficiencies in the system rather than be the cause of them. This is not to say that inflexible contracts are without cost, but that altering them may require deep-rooted reform.

Consider another example. Small entrepreneurs in developed countries often have to pledge property as collateral for a loan. The poor in developing countries often lack clear title to their assets – such as the land they occupy. So, some analysts suggest, a way to give them access to finance is to give them clear title. In practice, however, this suggestion is hard to implement when so much else does not work. For one thing, how is the tenuous protection of existing private property affected when squatters obtain property rights? How will informal ways of establishing ownership by determining the historical antecedents of a particular piece of property be misused when local thugs and politicians can coerce the citizenry? Instead of analysing the effects of introducing contracts in a world where everything else works, a better approach might be to investigate the effects of introducing a legitimate contract in a world where nothing works. Our analysis would be better informed by assuming anarchy as a starting point rather than a pristine world of complete contracts!

I am not suggesting that policy makers do actually analyse problems with a complete markets model in mind. They do, of course, make adjustments for the world they confront. But their world view is naturally influenced by the frameworks they were taught. And because those frameworks assume so much that is unrealistic, how confident can policy makers be in their recommendations?

Nor am I arguing for undisciplined economic thinking, for an 'anything-goes' school of theory. Economics has come a long way in the past half century, and much that we have learnt is of great relevance. Respectable economists such as Oliver Hart and Jack Hirshleifer have escaped the straitjacket of the complete markets model without sacrificing sensible economics. But a sizeable group of economists still thinks there is only one model, and complete markets is its name. One cannot but help suspect that elegance rather than relevance is its appeal.

Institution building is one area where international financial institutions and policy makers have learned from experience and used common sense to devise practical approaches, without much guidance from academia. And there is hope, supported by a growing body of research work, that more students of development are realizing that a better starting point for analysis than a world with only minor blemishes may be a world where nothing is enforceable, where property and individual rights are totally insecure, and the enforcement apparatus for every contract must be derived from first principles – the world that Hobbes so vividly depicted. Not only will this kind of work more closely approximate reality in the poorest, conflict-ridden countries, but it could also lead to more sensible policy.

IV

Another *Straight Talk* column, which appeared in December
2004, this time pointing out the difficulties with a clever
proposal to declare debt taken on by unpleasant regimes
unpayable.

Odious or Just Malodorous?

Something terribly wrong happens when debt is incurred by
a sovereign government that does not have good claim to
represent the will of the people of the country, and its proceeds
are not used for their benefit. Take the case of South Africa
under the apartheid regime, which borrowed, in part, to finance
a military machine that was used to repress the majority African
population. The debt thus incurred was doubly odious, for not
only were the proceeds used to suppress the African majority
and keep the apartheid regime in power but the suppressed also
eventually ended up being responsible for the debt repayment.
The post-apartheid government accepted that responsibility.
Yet, the case seems to have all the hallmarks of a situation
where 'something ought to have been done' to remove the 'odious
debt.'

But what should be done in such a case? One suggestion is
to institute an international commission (say under the United
Nations) that will determine which regimes have neither popular
legitimacy, nor the interests of their people at heart. Once the
commission declares the regime and its debt odious, successor
regimes could be absolved, through international agreement,
of having to repay the debt incurred by the odious regime.
Also, creditor country laws could be altered so as to make it

difficult for creditors from that country to enforce debt payment from another country once that country's debt is declared to be odious.

The possibilities of such a mechanism are dramatic. If a commission had declared Mobutu Sese Seko odious early on in his regime, he would not have been able to build up Zaire's debt to $12 billion, or to use $4 billion of it in building his own personal assets. He might not even have lasted long in power if he had not been able to borrow to keep his regime afloat. Certainly, the objectives of those advocating mechanisms to declare debt 'odious' are compelling (see Kremer and Jayachandran in *F&D*, June 2002, p. 36).

Unfortunately, the mechanism would not work as precisely as this example suggests – it would be more of a neutron bomb than a laser-guided missile. Not only would it make it more difficult for odious regimes to borrow, but it would also make borrowing more difficult for any legitimate regime that had even a remote possibility of being succeeded by an odious regime. A fledgling democratic regime, struggling to borrow to avoid the consequences of drought, might find the going even harder if creditors were also attempting to judge the possibility that the regime might collapse. If the regime gave way to a nasty successor, the debt would be declared odious, imposing huge losses on the creditors. Anticipating this, the creditors would not lend, making regime change more likely. How, then, does one prevent the odour of future odious debt from polluting all prior debt and making borrowing more difficult for all countries that have even a remote possibility of future regime change?

A clever proposal is simply to restrict odium to future debt (Kremer and Jayachandran, 2003). In other words, successor regimes could legitimately escape repayment only of the debt that is issued after the commission declares a regime's debt odious. The beauty of this idea is that markets would not be left guessing about whether their debt would be legitimate. Moreover, to the extent that the regime could not borrow to finance theft or build monuments to its own glory, resources would be preserved to service the old debt, thus enhancing its value.

But would it work? The trouble is that implementation of the proposal could have other, unintended, consequences. Though creditors would not be forced to guess whether the loan they made to a country would be viewed as legitimate, they might still be left guessing whether it would be valuable. Here is why: few developing countries or expanding firms can repay all the debt they have contracted or even generate substantial income unless they have access to further financing. This is because countries and firms rely on growth – a steady stream of new projects and continuing old projects to provide both the cash flows to service debt incurred to set up those projects as well as a residual amount – to service older debt. Countries and firms typically grow their way out of debt.

But if future debt were declared odious, the country would no longer be able to borrow to continue old projects, let alone finance new ones (assuming, of course, that the odious regime was not bent on driving the country into immediate economic collapse – if it were so destructive, few would be willing to lend in the first place, and there would be no need for a special procedure to declare its debt odious). Even if the odious regime had the intention of servicing its debt, the declaration that the regime's future debt was odious would make it very difficult for it to do so. When coupled with the fact that the incentives to repay debt come, in part, from the attraction of continuing to be able to borrow, it might well be that the regime defaults on existing debt as soon as it is declared odious, with adverse consequences for its valuation. The proposal to declare only future debt odious might mitigate some of the concerns associated with the original odious debt mechanisms, but it would not eliminate them by any means.

Another variant is to single out past debt that was used for nefarious purposes such as repression or theft and declare only that odious and uncollectible (see for example, 'Iraq's Odious Debts' by Patricia Adams, *Policy Analysis*, 28 September 2004, Cato Institute). Such a mechanism would make lenders responsible for the end use of their funds. But this suggestion is also not without problems. For one, it is hard to know whether steel that is being imported will be used to make cradles or cannons. Even guns and bullets may have legitimate uses if the police use them to combat crime. If lenders were held responsible for end use, they would shy away from financing a large number of legitimate activities. Moreover, this proposal assumes that money is not fungible. What is to prevent the government from funding roads and ports with foreign loans while using taxpayer funds to buy tanks and submarines?

If there are potential costs to such proposals, then a re-examination of the benefits becomes important. Would dictators really be stopped in their tracks? Would the truly corrupt not simply sell the country's existing assets at bargain basement prices for cash? Would we not see an increase in trafficking in antiques, endangered animals, wood, and drugs? Is it possible that the country could be worse off if the dictator stole through unusual channels than if he stole by building up debt?

The point is that while the odious debt proposal is well motivated, it is unlikely to provide a panacea. We have to recognize there will be trade-offs – the upfront costs to any fragile democracy from the odour of possible future odium, weighed against the possible benefits of curbing corrupt dictators financed by overeager bankers. If there are many odious regimes today but little chance that currently democratic regimes will switch to being odious, the benefits of the proposal outweigh the costs. If there are few odious regimes today, and many possible switches, the reverse is true.

In sum then, one does not need conspiracy theories to explain why the odious debt proposal has not gone anywhere, or why newly legitimate governments like that of post-apartheid South Africa have accepted the responsibility of servicing the potentially odious debts they inherited. The concern that debt markets might be disrupted is well-founded. But there are also potential benefits that deserve further investigation. If researchers had their way, we would pick one petty dictator through a random draw, declare his debt odious, and watch what happened. This suggestion is unlikely to find many takers – the notion of experimenting with countries seems repugnant to most. So in the absence of research that will use existing data cleverly to inform us, or fortuitous natural experiments, it is not surprising nor even unfair that the odious debt proposal is likely to stay in cold storage.

Many of the facts in this article are drawn from 'Odious Debt,' a working paper by Michael Kremer and Seema Jayachandran, published by the National Bureau of Economic Research in the U.S. in May 2002.

V

One of my research forays at the IMF was into the costs and benefits of foreign aid. This was work done with Arvind Subramanian, the Indian government's current Chief Economic Advisor. This work was controversial because it went against the received wisdom in developmental institutions that aid was tremendously beneficial. This 2005 piece reports on that joint research.

Aid and Growth: The Policy Challenge

Now that developed countries and international financial institutions have committed themselves to writing off the debt of highly indebted poor countries, the challenge will be to convert these resources into actual growth and faster progress toward the Millennium Development Goals. While for some it may seem that the war against poverty can be won simply by getting rich countries to provide more debt relief and aid, the view of experts – including those behind recent reports by the UK Commission for Africa and the Millennium Project – is that this is just one of the necessary ingredients. It is early days yet in the campaign to make poverty history. If it is to succeed, we have to recognize the failures of the past as well as be open-minded about the solutions for the future. And the first thing to recognize is the checkered history of aid.

AID AND GROWTH

The best way to get the poor in low-income countries out of poverty is to strengthen economic growth in those countries.

To the layperson, this may just mean sending these countries more aid. Yet one point about which there is general agreement amongst economists is that there is little evidence of a robust unconditional effect of aid on growth.

Before going further, let me say that the word 'effect' implies causality. This is different from correlation. It is possible to find in the data a negative correlation between aid and economic growth, but this doesn't mean that more aid causes less growth. For instance, if aid tends to go to countries that are doing badly, you would get aid and growth being negatively correlated even though aid does not cause poor growth: the direction of causation is the reverse. This is why economists use a technique called instrumental variables analysis to tell causality from simple correlation. In recent papers that I have written with Arvind Subramanian of the IMF's Research Department, we describe how we found a negative correlation between aid and growth when we did not use instrumental variables, but how this essentially disappeared once we used the technique (Rajan and Subramanian 2005 a and b). This means that aid sceptics may have been mistaken in viewing negative correlations found in the past as supporting their view. But unfortunately, we don't find a robust, significant positive correlation either.

Does this mean that aid cannot, in any circumstances, boost growth? Of course not! The layperson's thinking does, of course, have some significant basis. Poor countries are short of resources and ought to be able to put aid inflows to good use. There are case studies of countries that have grown using aid, and specific aid projects that have helped the poor enormously. What we economists have not identified is a reliable set of economic circumstances in which we can say that aid has helped countries grow. And this is not for want of trying.

For example, an influential study suggested that aid leads to growth, but only in countries that have good governance (Burnside and Dollar 2000). This certainly seemed a very reasonable conclusion – a necessary condition for aid to help growth is obviously that aid receipts should not be spirited away to Swiss bank accounts. Unfortunately, however, it doesn't seem to be a sufficient condition for aid to help growth, as follow-up studies suggest the finding is not robust (Easterly, Levine, and Roodman 2004). It would appear that other levers are needed in addition to reasonable governance for aid to be effective.

A recent study (Clemens, Radelet and Bhavnani 2004) takes another crack at parsing the data, working from the assumption that not all aid is alike in its impact on growth. Again, the rationale is plausible. Why, for instance, should we expect humanitarian aid to result in growth, or why should we expect aid devoted to education (children are a long-term project if ever there was one) to produce growth in the short run? The study indeed shows that aid likely to have a short-term economic impact (for instance, aid used to build roads or support agriculture directly) is positively correlated with short-term growth. Here again, however, I'm not fully persuaded. The authors of this study argue that the reason to focus on short-impact aid is because the literature focuses on country growth rates over four-year periods. So I presume it follows that if one were to depart from the literature and look at long-run growth (say growth over decades, which is what we really care about), economic aid (as contrasted with, say, humanitarian aid) cumulated during the period should have a discernible effect on growth (and there would be no need to separate out short-impact aid from long-impact aid). My work with Subramanian suggests that economic aid does not have a robust positive correlation with long-run growth.

Despite my own convictions about what the past tells us, I will acknowledge that the debate about aid effectiveness is one where little is settled. Unfortunately, further cross-country research along existing lines may not yield credible answers. We can continue trying to find some variable that will select out those countries that have received aid and also grown (or attempt to find some form of aid that is positively correlated with growth). But what do we conclude once we do that? Put another way, when the same data are pored over many times, there is a danger we will find patterns that are there by accident. This is why many economists have become sceptical that cross-country studies can tell us much more.

Of course, the layperson would despair of econometrics long before the economist. It should, however, be of concern to the layperson that the best example we have of aid working systematically for a group of countries is the Marshall Plan, whereby the ravaged countries of post-war Western Europe were returned to the ranks of the rich. The reason it worked so well might be that these countries' institutions, including the education of their people, were probably capable of sustaining much higher per capita GDP than their post-war low. Perhaps this is why one might see a country emerging from conflict experience a substantial period of catch-up growth, where aid is very effective – Mozambique or Uganda might be more recent examples. Nevertheless, it should be sobering that the canonical recent example of a country clawing itself out of poverty into the ranks of the rich is South Korea. South Korea was indeed ravaged by war, but its spectacular growth started approximately when aid inflows tapered off.

DODGING 'DUTCH DISEASE'

According to some, there is a better way – to focus on what we know works. Specifically, funding should support micro-interventions or programmes, validated through evaluations and experimentation, that might be very helpful, say, in furthering education and health care, which undoubtedly lead to growth. Here, we have learned a lot from work by Abhijit Banerjee of MIT, Michael Kremer at Harvard, and their students, as well as from the World Bank, including its *World Development Report 2004*.

We know that providing services to the poor isn't just about money. One can build spanking new schools and pay teachers a good wage, yet they may not come in to teach. One can provide free drugs to the hospitals, intended for the poor, but the druggist may simply sell them on the black market. This is not to say that schools and hospitals aren't necessary, but bricks and mortar are often the easy part. Policy makers also need to create the right incentives for the service provider and the poor client, as well as the right allocation of power and information between them to ensure that reasonable quality services are provided. And we know that the law of unintended consequences is always at work. This means that few programmes ever operate as the designers intended, so we need abundant experimentation, frequent monitoring and evaluation, and a sharing of best practices so that these targeted interventions can have their intended effect.

Unfortunately, I am not sure that even if each micro-intervention works well by itself, they will all work well together. Interventions could affect each other and come in each other's way or vie for the same resources. They could also have adverse spillover effects on the rest of the economy.

The last is not just a possibility. Suppose a lot of aid flows in to support interventions in education, health care, and other social services. The recipient country quickly hires many educated workers as teachers, clerks, nurses, foremen (to build the schools), engineers, and government and aid administrators. Because well-educated people will be in high demand, their wages will tend to rise and may well go up rapidly. In turn, factories will have to escalate the wages they pay to managers, engineers, and supervisors. Now factories that produce for the domestic market and don't face competition can pass their higher costs on. But factories that export cannot, so they will cut down on operations and even start shutting down. This is one example of a phenomenon called Dutch Disease, which makes aid recipients less competitive. Subramanian and I show that in countries that received more aid in the 1980s and 1990s, the export-oriented, labour-intensive industries not only grew more slowly than other industries – suggesting that aid did in fact create Dutch Disease – but the manufacturing sector as a whole also grew more slowly. Again it's sobering to think that by constraining the growth of manufacturing, aid inflows may have prevented poor countries from taking the path to growth followed first by the East Asian tigers and now by China.

That said, Dutch Disease is not a terminal condition. It can be mitigated through sensible policies. But to do so, one must first acknowledge its existence and its pernicious effects. Similarly for other possible diseases caused by aid.

THERE IS HOPE

To ignore the past, or to read only rosy lessons from it, is to condemn oneself to relive it. While it would be churlish to deny that many poor countries have made tremendous progress in creating the conditions for sustained growth, it doesn't serve the citizens of poor countries either if we say that all the problems of the past are well and truly in the past. While no one has the 'magic bullet' for growth, there are some things that do seem important. These include sensible macroeconomic management, with fiscal discipline, moderate inflation, and a reasonably competitive exchange rate; laws and policies that create an environment conducive to private sector activity with low transaction costs; and an economy open for international trade. In addition, investments in health and education, which create a population that not only lives a better life but also sees opportunities in growth and competition, ought to be encouraged.

One way rich countries and international financial institutions can help is by making policies that broadly meet these requirements an essential condition for aid. They should, however, resist micromanaging and overlaying broad economic conditionality with too many detailed economic prescriptions, or with social and political conditionality. Once a country has the necessary broad environment in place, it should have the freedom to chart its own path. After all, the failure of past grand theories of growth should make us wary of becoming overly prescriptive.

Rich countries can also help by reducing the impediments they place in the way of poor country exports, and by coaxing these countries to lower their own trade barriers, including barriers to other poor countries. They can spend more to foster research on drugs and agricultural technologies that would benefit the poorest countries. They can be more active in ensuring that their companies and officials don't grease the wheels of corruption in poor countries (see Birdsall, Rodrik, and Subramanian 2005 for other suggestions). And they should never hesitate to give humanitarian aid in the face of a disaster.

Let us draw hope from the willingness of the outside world to provide more, and better, aid. Ultimately, though, poor countries hold their future in their own hands. It is only through their own will and actions that the good intentions of the outside world can be used to truly make poverty history.

As the IMF embarked on debt relief in 2005, this article tried to lay out the circumstances under which that made sense.

Debt Relief and Growth

In a number of developed countries, debt relief for low-income countries has become an important political issue. Rock stars and politicians rightly point to the overwhelming burden borne by poor countries who have to set aside a significant fraction of their national income to repay creditors. Worse still, they argue, much of this debt is 'odious,' built up by past corrupt dictators who whisked the money to Swiss bank accounts. Furthermore, evidence that countries with high debt tend to have low growth suggests that debt relief can help poor countries grow.

Several debt relief proposals are on the table, but there is little agreement among donors on which one makes the most sense. The proposals typically have a one-size-fits-all flavour, in part because uniform treatment would avoid politicking by potential recipients. But would poor countries benefit from uniform treatment? This article tries to clarify some of the broad principles that could lead to an optimal debt relief proposal.

NET FLOWS, NOT DEBT RELIEF, MATTER

Consider a poor country that has to repay $100 million to official creditors such as developed countries or international financial institutions in the current period. Assume it earns $50 million in foreign exchange in this period and has no other resources.

Clearly, it cannot repay the debt fully out of its own resources. Now consider three alternative proposals. First, the creditors do not forgive the debt, but lend $120 million to the country. Second, creditors forgive the debt down to $50 million, but lend nothing. Third, creditors forgive the entire debt and lend nothing. Which alternative is best for the country?

Assuming this country has no access to private capital markets, the answer seems obvious: full debt forgiveness, which would be twice as good as half debt forgiveness and surely better than a loan that is not much bigger than the full debt amount. Yet when viewed in terms of net resources available to the country during the period, under the first proposal these would amount to $70 million (the loan of $120 million plus inflows of $50 million, less the repayment of $100 million), under the second they would amount to nothing, while under the third they would amount to $50 million. Of immediate importance to a resource-starved poor country is the amount of additional resources it gets in the current period (termed 'additionality'). The best proposal in terms of additionality is the first, which offers no debt relief.

The point is that if official creditors take with one hand (collecting debt service) but give more with the other (in the form of a loan), the poor country may have more financing in the short run than with debt forgiveness. And debt forgiveness may actually be problematic if it exhausts donor aid budgets. Of course, without forgiveness, in the long run, the country will have more debt on its books, which may become unsustainable. In the three proposals, the country will end the period owing $120 million, $50 million, and nothing, respectively. However, high or unsustainable debt is a problem only if it hurts the country's growth. Let us turn to that.

High debt can be detrimental to a country's growth. It can increase the risk of financial distress or crisis, when foreign creditors rush to cash in their claims, resulting in the failure of banks and firms. However, if official creditors hold the bulk of the poor country's debt, it is unlikely they will precipitate a crisis, so the country will not experience a meltdown no matter what its level of debt.

A second reason why a high level of debt might hurt is that it can create a debt overhang problem. For instance, when a country has high debt outstanding, private investors may be reluctant to invest for fear that the debt will eventually be repaid by levying extra taxes on corporations. Similarly, the government may hesitate to invest because the returns will largely go to service debt. Hence, high debt can impair investment and thus growth, and reducing debt may be necessary to jump-start growth. Compelling as these arguments may be in the case of emerging markets, I am not convinced they are important for poor developing countries. Investors in poor countries face other, more significant impediments to investment, such as a discouraging business climate and uneven regulation. A reduction in the level of government debt, without any additional resources or policy change, is unlikely to jump-start investment.

Some analysts have indeed found a negative correlation between debt and growth in poor countries, but there are other possible explanations. For instance, the causality could run from low growth to high debt, with countries that have weak growth (which may be due to poor policies) running larger deficits, and thus borrowing more. If this is the direction of causality, then debt forgiveness will not spur more growth, and I have yet to see compelling evidence against this possibility. This means that for poor countries borrowing primarily from official creditors, the extent of debt forgiveness matters only in that it increases net resources. Sometimes more additionality – at least in the short term – can be obtained with no debt relief, especially if forgiveness impairs donor aid budgets. And the 'unsustainable' outstanding debt can eventually be dealt with through some mix of repayment and forgiveness (when donors have more budget room).

A POSSIBLE ROLE FOR DEBT RELIEF

This is not to say debt relief never makes sense. Debt relief could effectively provide predictable additional resources directly to the budget (via the repayments that no longer have to be made) and could offer a way to force coordination on conditionality among donors. Equally important, debt relief could allow a poor country to obtain access to loans from private foreign investors. Private investors may be unwilling to lend to a highly indebted country for fear that the country will be unable to repay, but if official debt is completely forgiven, they will jump in to lend, because even the worst debtor can be trusted to service small amounts of debt. Thus, official creditors may be able to expand a country's access to private resources through debt forgiveness.

Would such additional resources from the private sector be beneficial? That depends on how much official debt is left on the books, on the nature of the recipient government, and on whether projects have a commercial or social orientation. Clearly, if most of the official debt is forgiven, the private sector has little need to be careful in its lending. Moreover, if the poor country's government is irresponsible it can build up debt again by spending on worthless projects. As a result, the citizens of the recipient country will not benefit from this renewed debt build-up. In addition, donor countries will likely suffer from 'forgiveness fatigue' the next time around. By contrast, moderate debt forgiveness can lead to higher-quality investment as the private sector will have to evaluate the profitability of projects carefully, which in turn can help improve the quality of commercial projects. Of course, if projects produce a social return but no commercial one, the private sector will likely not provide any funds, and official aid will be necessary.

DIFFERENT SITUATIONS, DIFFERENT APPROACHES

Let us then summarize where logic leads us. If a poor country has no access to private markets, and the investment climate is bleak, financial distress or debt overhang are unlikely to result from high debt. A focus on debt forgiveness – as opposed to the net incremental resources available in the short run (that is, additionality) – is misplaced. Debt forgiveness makes sense if it generates more resources from the private sector, but the country authorities must have the incentive to use resources well and the private sector to lend responsibly. Interestingly, this means that depending on the country's situation, the status quo, as well as any one of the three proposals I outlined, could be the best approach for the country.

If the country's government is thoroughly corrupt, then the status quo – no forgiveness and no additional aid – is best, for it gives the government no official resources to misuse and limits its ability to raise private sector funds. Aid in this case should be distributed directly to nongovernmental organizations. If the country has a reasonably committed government, look at the country's primary need. When social sector projects top the list, then what matters is the extent of official sector net funding. Here, the first alternative – debt is not forgiven but official creditors lend more – is best. But if most projects are commercially viable, the second alternative – some relief but leaving enough outstanding official debt that foreign private investors lend responsibly – may be optimal. Finally, substantial debt forgiveness is prudent if the risk of financial distress really is a serious problem – an unlikely eventuality. But there must be an assurance that the country does not borrow up again from private creditors and game the system to get further debt relief. Donor-imposed limits on borrowing may be needed.

Political momentum in the developed world is building for offering some form of debt relief, and while no developing country situation will fit neatly into these categories, debt-relief proposals can be better crafted. One-size-fits-all proposals, while politically more convenient, are unlikely to benefit recipient countries as much as proposals that tie debt relief and additional aid to a country's specific situation. Of course, the more transparent the proposals and the more quickly they can be implemented, the better off the recipients will be.

Countries, including India, have often tried to argue for buying stakes in commodity producers in faraway lands as a way of ensuring national security. This article in *Straight Talk* in December 2006 explains why that is mistaken.

The Great Game Again?

Some commentators see the desperate search by countries to acquire commodity-producing firms in other (typically poor, developing) countries as a repeat of the Great Game – the tussle among powers like Britain and Russia for influence in the Middle East and Central Asia during the 19th century. In this view, those that acquire the greatest share of commodity producers early on will enjoy the greatest economic security in the future, as growth in China, India, and other populous developing countries creates shortages of commodity resources. Economic security is the new justification for purchases, such as minority stakes in opaque companies in poorly governed countries, that would otherwise make little business sense. In this replayed Great Game, will those who move fastest and farthest acquire the most economic protection? Does the gain from economic security trump common business sense?

A QUESTIONABLE BUYING SPREE

I'll leave aside the question of whether we're inevitably headed for a sustained period of commodity demand outstripping supply, even though in the past such predictions have proved unfounded. Let me take as given that such an eventuality is possible. To simplify the argument, I'll assume that state-owned companies undertake the acquisitions and that all income and value obtained flow directly to the citizens of the acquiring state – a questionable assumption at best. Even under these strong assumptions, should a country go on an acquisition spree to protect itself?

Precisely how an incipient imbalance between demand and supply would play out matters. Consider the most likely situation, where a world market for a commodity – let's use the example of oil in what follows – continues to operate. If there's an incipient imbalance and oil is in fixed supply in the short run, the market price for oil will shoot up so that demand is brought down to equal supply.

How does ownership of foreign oil assets help? One might think that a country that owns foreign oil can use the profits from sales to keep its domestic price low and thus insulate the economy from high oil prices. But this doesn't make economic sense. The market price of oil reflects its opportunity cost. Rather than subsidize the price in the domestic oil market (and thus give domestic manufacturers and consumers the incentive to use too much oil, given its true cost), it would make far better sense to let the domestic price rise to the international price and distribute the windfall profits from oil sales to the population.

Put differently, suppose the country exported widgets that it manufactured in an energy-intensive way. It would be politically convenient to avoid layoffs and continue competing in the widget market by subsidizing the oil price, using the financial leeway from foreign oil assets. But this would eat up the oil windfall by subsidizing both inefficient manufacturing and foreign widget buyers. A more economical decision would be to shrink widget manufacturing (or shift to new technologies) and use the windfall to make transfers to citizens, especially those most affected by high prices. These citizens would thus receive additional income when the price of oil rose: they would be hedged.

The key point is that fundamental economic decisions shouldn't be affected by the ownership of additional foreign oil assets. However, because of pressure exerted by small, powerful, affected interest groups, politics will intervene and oil windfalls will inevitably be spent in unwise subsidies. As a result, the acquiring country will, if anything, make suboptimal economic decisions because of the financial windfall available through hedging.

But let's assume the country always makes the right economic decisions. Does hedging lead to more financial security? A hedge will always look beneficial if one looks backward after the price has risen. But if the price of oil had fallen, citizens would have suffered a loss of income and wealth from having bought foreign oil assets (relative to having instead invested the money elsewhere). Assuming the foreign oil assets were priced fairly at the time of purchase, the country benefits only when the hedge helps smooth its income and wealth. This isn't obviously true even for a country that relies heavily on oil.

For instance, in a large country like the United States or China, which account for a significant portion of world demand, the world price of oil is likely to be high when the country is growing strongly and citizens have lots of income, whereas the price is likely to be low when the country is doing poorly. Foreign oil assets are a bad hedge in such a case for they subtract from citizens' income when it's already low and add to it when it's high. Indeed – and this may seem heretical – the country might be better off selling its domestic oil assets to foreigners and investing the proceeds in non-oil assets.

Even if owning oil assets is a useful hedge (as in a small, oil-consuming country), it's not clear that buying stakes in opaque companies in poorly governed foreign countries is the way to go. As the oil price increases, a poorly governed country is more tempted to expropriate foreign owners of its oil industry through extortionary taxation or nationalization – especially if the domestic public feels, with the benefit of hindsight and populist egging, that the assets had been sold too cheaply in the past. The security of a country's ownership of oil assets in poorly governed foreign countries likely diminishes when the oil price rises.

PLANNING FOR A BLEAK WORLD

How then should a small country hedge oil price risk? Liquid, oil-linked financial securities in well-governed financial markets, such as oil futures traded in developed markets, make the most sense, but not enough is available very far out. There do, however, exist liquid, long-dated, oil-linked securities – the equity of large oil companies. So, without being facetious, perhaps the best advice I could offer countries seeking to hedge oil price risk is 'Buy Exxon shares!'

If economic security isn't the reason, why would a country want to buy large interests in poorly managed oil companies in dangerous locations? It might make good business sense – the target is poorly managed and can benefit from the know-how and management the acquirer provides. But, then, this is a sound business case for buying the asset untainted by specious claims of enhancing national security. It's important that the target's price not fully discount these future managerial improvements. For instance, targets in countries that are international pariahs may be attractive for acquiring countries that are still willing to do business with them because the acquisition price may be extremely low. Otherwise, it's hard to see how the acquirer will escape the customary fate of acquisitions: they typically overpay and lose money in the long run.

Other reasons are less good. One is that countries fear a total market breakdown and descent into an autarkic 'Mad Max' world in which oil is scarce, no country is willing to allow trade in what it has, and there's no world market clearing price. It's not clear that, if such a situation were to come to pass, ownership of oil assets abroad would help. Most likely, the governments within whose borders those assets lay would expropriate the assets. Each country would have only oil assets that are physically within its political borders. Indeed, to protect against such a bleak world, a country would do well to increase exploration, the use of alternative energy sources, consumption and production efficiency, and the storage of reserves within its own borders (regardless of who owns the assets) while increasing the economy's flexibility to respond to oil supply disruptions.

Even in such a bleak world, it's hard to imagine the market breaking down totally or for long. Indeed, one can imagine black marketers and smugglers buying where oil is cheap and transporting it to sell to countries where oil is costly. Unless governments build leakproof barriers around their countries – the costs would likely be prohibitive – an implicit world price would be re-established. We would then be back to the case we've already examined.

Another bad motive might be that state-owned commodity companies are flush with profits that they'd otherwise have to return to the government. What better way for management to spend those profits than to build foreign empires, justifying the acquisitions with the time-honoured 'it's in the national interest'? Of course, sweetening any such rationale would be any 'under the table' payments to acquiring managers if the transaction is non-transparent.

*

The best way to secure the supply of a commodity is to ensure that the world market for that commodity is well informed and competitive and that the business environment is transparent and predictable. Information on reserves and investments helps market participants make sound business decisions. Competition keeps participants honest and prices informative, and allows consumers to reap the benefits. A predictable business environment allows businesses to invest for the long term. Transparency not only reduces the costs associated with corruption but also protects businesses from future accusations of having obtained overly sweet deals.

The bottom line is that the new mercantilism – I own more of others than they own of me – appealing as it may be, is not going to lead to more national security. Countries are collectively most secure if the control of productive assets is in the hands of those who can manage them best. Indeed, anyone who takes or keeps control of an asset that someone else can manage more productively is contributing to both individual and collective insecurity. The Great Game exacerbated insecurity even as each power tried to secure itself. Let's hope that better sense will prevail this time.

AFTERWORD

NOTE TO THE PARLIAMENTARY ESTIMATES
COMMITTEE ON BANK NPAs

This note was prepared by Raghuram G. Rajan on
6 September 2018 on the request of the Chairman of
the Parliament Estimates Committee, Dr Murli Manohar
Joshi, MP. The committee was set up to examine the
issue of burgeoning bank NPAs.

1. Why did the NPAs occur?

I have not seen a study that has unearthed the precise weight of all the factors responsible, but here is a list of the main ones.

OVER-OPTIMISM

A larger number of bad loans were originated in the period 2006-08 when economic growth was strong, and previous infrastructure projects such as power plants had been completed on time and within budget. It is at such times that banks make mistakes. They extrapolate past growth and performance to the future. So they are willing to accept higher leverage in projects, and less promoter equity. Indeed, sometimes banks signed up to lend based on project reports by the promoter's investment bank, without doing their own due diligence. One promoter told me about how he was pursued then by banks waving cheque books, asking him to name the amount he wanted. This is the historic phenomenon of irrational exuberance, common across countries at such a phase in the cycle.

313

Slow Growth

Unfortunately, growth does not always take place as expected. The years of strong global growth before the global financial crisis were followed by a slowdown, which extended even to India, showing how much more integrated we had become with the world. Strong demand projections for various projects were shown to be increasingly unrealistic as domestic demand slowed down.

Government Permissions and Foot-Dragging

A variety of governance problems such as the suspect allocation of coal mines coupled with the fear of investigation slowed down government decision making in Delhi, both in the UPA and the subsequent NDA governments. Project cost overruns escalated for stalled projects and they became increasingly unable to service debt. The continuing travails of the stranded power plants, even though India is short of power, suggests government decision making has not picked up sufficient pace to date.

Loss of Promoter and Banker Interest

Once projects got delayed enough that the promoter had little equity left in the project, he lost interest. Ideally, projects should be restructured at such times, with banks writing down bank debt that is uncollectable, and promoters bringing in more equity, under the threat that they would otherwise lose their project. Unfortunately, until the Bankruptcy Code was enacted, bankers had little ability to threaten promoters (see later), even incompetent or unscrupulous ones, with loss of their project. Writing down the debt was then simply a gift to promoters, and no banker wanted to take the risk of doing so and inviting the attention of the investigative agencies. Stalled projects continued as 'zombie' projects, neither dead nor alive ('zombie' is a technical term used in the banking literature).

It was in everyone's interest to extend the loan by making additional loans to enable the promoter to pay interest and pretend it was performing. The promoter had no need to bring in equity, the banker did not have to restructure and recognize losses or declare the loan NPA and spoil his profitability, the government had no need to infuse capital. In reality, though, because the loan was actually non-performing, bank profitability was illusory, and losses on its balance sheet were ballooning because no interest was actually coming in. Unless the project miraculously recovered on its own – and with only a few exceptions, no one was seriously trying to put it back on track – this was deceptive accounting. It postponed the day of reckoning into the future, but there would be such a day.

MALFEASANCE

How important was malfeasance and corruption in the NPA problem? Undoubtedly, there was some, but it is hard to tell banker exuberance, incompetence and corruption apart. Clearly, bankers were overconfident and probably did too little due diligence for some of these loans. Many did no independent analysis, and placed excessive reliance on SBI Caps and IDBI to do the necessary due diligence. Such outsourcing of analysis is a weakness in the system, and multiplies the possibilities for undue influence.

Banker performance after the initial loans were made was also not up to the mark. Unscrupulous promoters who inflated the cost of capital equipment through over-invoicing were rarely checked. Public sector bankers continued financing promoters even while private sector banks were getting out, suggesting their monitoring of promoter and project health was inadequate. Too many bankers put yet more money for additional 'balancing' equipment, even though the initial project was heavily underwater, and the promoter's intent suspect. Finally, too many loans were made to well-connected promoters who have a history of defaulting on their loans.

Yet, unless we can determine the unaccounted wealth of bankers, I hesitate to say a significant element was corruption. Rather than attempting to hold bankers responsible for specific loans, I think bank boards and investigative agencies must look for a pattern of bad loans that bank CEOs were responsible for – some banks went from healthy to critically undercapitalized under the term of a single CEO. Then they must look for unaccounted assets with that CEO. Only then should there be a presumption that there was corruption.

FRAUD

The size of frauds in the public sector banking system has been increasing, though still small relative to the overall volume of NPAs. Frauds are different from normal NPAs in that the loss is because of a patently illegal action, by either the borrower or the banker. Unfortunately, the system has been singularly ineffective in bringing even a single high-profile fraudster to book. As a result, fraud is not discouraged.

The investigative agencies blame the banks for labelling frauds much after the fraud has actually taken place, and the bankers are slow because they know that once they call a transaction a fraud, they will be subject to harassment by the investigative agencies, without substantial progress in catching the crooks. The RBI set up a fraud monitoring cell when I was Governor to coordinate the early reporting of fraud cases to the investigative agencies. I also sent a list of high-profile cases to the PMO urging that we coordinate action to bring at least one or two to book. I am not aware of progress on this front. This is a matter that should be addressed with urgency.

2. Why did the RBI set up various schemes to restructure debt and how effective were they?

When I took office it was clear that bankers had very little power to recover from large promoters. The Debts Recovery Tribunals (DRTs) were set up under the Recovery of Debts Due to Banks and Financial Institutions (RDDBFI) Act, 1993, to help banks and financial institutions recover their dues speedily without being subject to the lengthy procedures of usual civil courts. The Securitization and Reconstruction of Financial Assets and Enforcement of Security Interests (SARFAESI) Act, 2002, went a step further by enabling banks and some financial institutions to enforce their security interest and recover dues even without approaching the DRTs.

Yet the amount banks recovered from defaulted debt was both meagre and long delayed. The amount recovered from cases decided in 2013-14 under DRTs was Rs 30,590 crore while the outstanding value of debt sought to be recovered was a huge Rs 2,36,600 crore. Thus, recovery was only 13 per cent of the amount at stake. Worse, even though the law indicated that cases before the DRT should be disposed of in six months, only about a fourth of the cases pending at the beginning of the year were disposed of during the year – suggesting a four-year wait even if the tribunals focused only on old cases. However, in 2013-14, the number of new cases filed during the year was about one and a half times the cases disposed of during the year. Thus, backlogs and delays were growing, not coming down. A cautionary point as we welcome the National Company Law Tribunal's (NCLT) efforts is that the DRTs and SARFAESI were initially successful, before they became overburdened as large promoters understood how to game them.

The inefficient loan recovery system gave promoters tremendous power over lenders. Not only could they play one lender off against another by threatening to divert payments to the favoured bank, they could also refuse to pay unless the lender brought in more money, especially if the lender feared the loan becoming an NPA. Sometimes promoters offered low one-time settlements (OTS), knowing that the system would allow the banks to collect even secured loans only after years. Effectively, bank loans in such a system become equity, with a tough promoter enjoying the upside in good times, and forcing banks to absorb losses in bad times, even while he holds on to his equity.

The RBI decided we needed to empower the banks and improve on the ineffective CDR system then in place. Our first task was to make sure that all banks had information on who had lent to a borrower. So we created a large loan database

(CRILC – Central Repository of Information on Large Credits) that included all loans over Rs 5 crore, which we shared with all the banks. The CRILC data included the status of each loan – reflecting whether it was performing, already an NPA or going towards NPA. That database allowed banks to identify early warning signs of distress in a borrower such as habitual late payments to a segment of lenders.

The next step was to coordinate the lenders through a Joint Lenders' Forum (JLF) once such early signals were seen. The JLF was tasked with deciding on an approach for resolution, much as a bankruptcy forum does. Incentives were given to banks for reaching quick decisions. We also tried to make the forum more effective by reducing the need for everyone to agree, even while giving those who were unconvinced by the joint decision the opportunity to exit.

We also wanted to stop ever-greening of projects by banks that want to avoid recognizing losses – so we ended forbearance, the ability of banks to restructure projects without calling them NPA, in April 2015. At the same time, a number of long-duration projects such as roads had been structured with overly rapid required repayments, even though cash flows continued to be available decades from now. So we allowed such project payments to be restructured through the 5/25 scheme, provided the long dated future cash flows could be reliably established. Of course, there was always the possibility of banks using this scheme to ever-green, so we monitored how it worked in practice, and continued tweaking the scheme where necessary so that it achieved its objectives.

Because promoters were often unable to bring in new funds, and because the judicial system often protected those with equity ownership, together with the Securities and Exchange Board of India (SEBI) we introduced the Strategic Debt Restructuring (SDR) scheme so as to enable banks to displace weak promoters by converting debt to equity. We did not want banks to own projects indefinitely, so we indicated a timeline by which they had to find a new promoter.

We adjusted the schemes with experience. Each scheme's effectiveness, while seemingly obvious when designing, had to be monitored in light of the distorted incentives in the system. As we learnt, we adapted regulation. Our objective was not to be theoretical but to be pragmatic, even while subjecting the system to increasing discipline and transparency.

All these new tools (including some I do not have the space to describe here) effectively created a resolution system that replicated an out-of-court bankruptcy. Banks now had the power to resolve distress, so we could push them to exercise these powers by requiring recognition. The schemes were a step forward, and enabled some resolution and recovery, but far less than we thought was possible. Incentives to conclude deals were unfortunately too weak.

3. Why recognize bad loans?

There are two polar approaches to loan stress. One is to apply band aids to keep the loan current, and hope that time and growth will set the project back on track. Sometimes this works. But most of the time, the low growth that precipitated the stress persists. Lending intended to keep the original loan current (also called 'ever-greening') grows. Facing large and potentially unpayable debt, the promoter loses interest, does little to fix existing problems, and the project goes into further losses.

An alternative approach is to try to put the stressed project back on track rather than simply applying band aids. This may require deep surgery. Existing loans may have to be written down somewhat because of the changed circumstances since they were sanctioned. If loans are written down, the promoter brings in more equity, and other stakeholders like the tariff authorities or the local government chip in, the project may have a strong chance of revival, and the promoter will be incentivized to try his utmost to put it back on track.

But to do deep surgery such as restructuring or writing down loans, the bank has to recognize it has a problem – classify the asset as a Non Performing Asset (NPA). Think therefore of the NPA classification as an anaesthetic that allows the bank to perform extensive necessary surgery to set the project back on its feet. If the bank wants to pretend that everything is all right with the loan, it can only apply band aids – for any more drastic action would require NPA classification.

Loan classification is merely good accounting – it reflects what the true value of the loan might be. It is accompanied by provisioning, which ensures the bank sets aside a buffer to absorb likely losses. If the losses do not materialize, the bank can write back provisioning to profits. If the losses do materialize, the bank does not have to suddenly declare a big loss, it can set the losses against the prudential provisions it has made. Thus, the bank balance sheet then represents a true and fair picture of the bank's health, as a bank balance sheet is meant to. Of course, we can postpone the day of reckoning with regulatory forbearance. But unless conditions in the industry improve suddenly and dramatically, the bank balance sheets present a distorted picture of health, and the eventual hole becomes bigger.

4. Did the RBI create the NPAs?

Bankers, promoters, or their backers in government sometimes turn around and accuse regulators of creating the bad loan problem. The truth is bankers, promoters, and circumstances create the bad loan problem. The regulator cannot substitute for the banker's commercial decisions or micromanage them or even investigate them when they are being made. Instead, in most situations, the regulator can at best warn about poor lending practices when they are being undertaken, and demand banks hold adequate risk buffers. The RBI is primarily a referee, not a player in the process of commercial lending. Its nominees on bank boards have no commercial lending experience and can only try and make sure that processes are followed. They offer an illusion that the regulator is in control, which is why nearly every RBI Governor has asked the government for permission to withdraw them from bank boards.

The important duty of the regulator is to force timely recognition of NPAs and their disclosure when they happen, followed by requiring adequate bank capitalization. This is done through the RBI's regular supervision of banks.

5. Why did the RBI initiate the Asset Quality Review?

Once we had created enough ways for banks to recover, we decided to not prolong forbearance beyond when it was scheduled to end. Banks were simply not recognizing bad loans. They were not following uniform procedures – a loan that was non-performing in one bank was shown as performing in others. They were not making adequate provisions for loans that had stayed NPA for a long time. Equally problematic, they were doing little to put projects back on track. They had also slowed credit growth. What any student of banking history will tell you is that the sooner banks are cleaned up, the faster the banks will be able to resume credit. We proceeded to ensure in our bank inspections in 2015 that every bank followed the same norms on every stressed loan. We especially looked for signs of ever-greening. A dedicated team of supervisors ensured that the Asset Quality Review (AQR), completed in October 2015 and subsequently shared with banks, was fair and conducted without favour. The government was kept informed and consulted every step of the way, after the initial supervision was done.

6. Did NPA recognition slow credit growth and, hence, economic growth?

The RBI has been accused of slowing the economy by forcing NPA recognition. I actually gave a speech in July 2016 on this issue before I demitted office, knowing it was only a matter of time before vested interests that wanted to torpedo the clean-up started attacking the RBI on the growth issue.

Simply eye-balling the evidence suggests the claim is ludicrous, and made by people who have not done their homework. Let us start by looking at public sector bank credit growth compared with the growth in credit by the new private banks. As the trend in non-food credit growth shows (Chart 1), public sector bank non-food credit growth was falling relative to credit growth from the new private sector banks (Axis, HDFC, ICICI, and IndusInd) since early 2014.

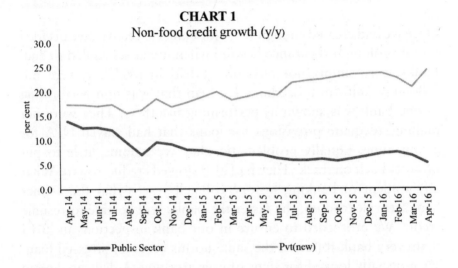

CHART 1
Non-food credit growth (y/y)

This is reflected not only in credit to industry (Chart 2), but also in credit to micro and small enterprise credit (Chart 3).[*]

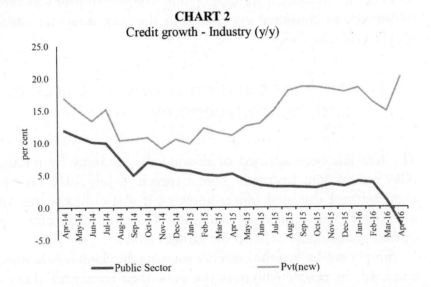

CHART 2
Credit growth - Industry (y/y)

---

[*] In Chart 2, the negative growth in April 2016 may be an aberration because of UDAY (Ujwal DISCOM Assurance Yojana) bonds being transferred from bank loan books to investments.

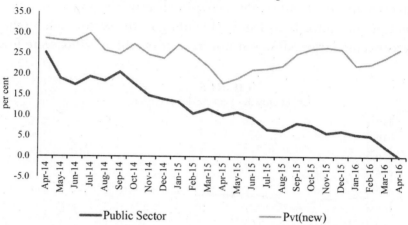

CHART 3
Credit growth - Micro & Small Enterprises

The relative slowdown in credit growth, albeit not so dramatic, is also seen in agriculture (Chart 4), though public sector bank credit growth picked up once again in October 2015.

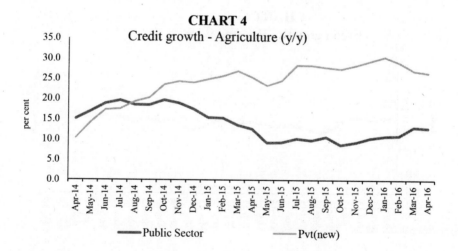

CHART 4
Credit growth - Agriculture (y/y)

Whenever one sees a slowdown in lending, one can conclude there is no demand for credit – firms are not investing. But what we see here is a slowdown in lending by public sector banks vis-à-vis private sector banks.

Interestingly, if we look at personal loan growth (Chart 5), and specifically housing loans (Chart 6), public sector bank loan growth approaches private sector bank growth. So the reality is that public sector banks slowed lending to the sectors where they were seeing large NPAs but not in sectors where NPAs were low.

CHART 5
Credit growth - Personal loans (y/y)

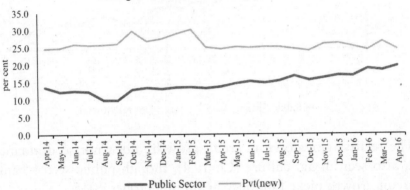

CHART 6
Credit growth - Housing (y/y)

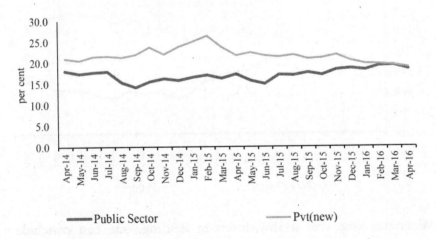

The fact that the public sector bank credit slowdown to industry dates from early 2014 suggests that the bank clean-up, which started in earnest in the second half of fiscal year 2015, was not the cause. Indeed, the slowdown is best attributed to over-burdened public sector bank balance sheets and growing risk aversion in public sector bankers. Their aversion to increasing their activity can be seen in the rapid slowdown of their deposit growth also, relative to private sector banks (see Chart 7). After all, why would public sector banks raise deposits aggressively if they are unwilling to lend?

CHART 7
Bank Group-wise Deposit Growth
(y-o-y, per cent)

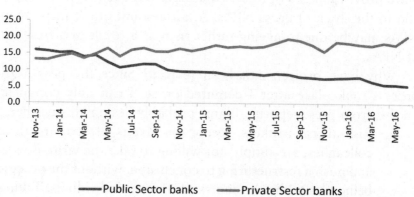

━━━Public Sector banks   ━━━Private Sector banks

In sum, the Indian evidence, supported by the experiences from other parts of the world such as Europe and Japan, suggests that what we were seeing was classic behaviour by a banking system with balance sheet problems. We were able to identify the effects because parts of our banking system – the private banks – did not suffer as much from such problems. The obvious remedy to anyone with an open mind would be to tackle the source of the problem – to clean the balance sheets of public sector banks, a remedy that has worked well in other countries where it has been implemented. This is not a 'foreign' solution, it is an economically sensible solution. It is something that has been repeatedly flagged by the government's own Economic Survey, under the guidance of the respected Dr Arvind Subramanian. Clean-up was part of the solution, not the problem.

7. Why do NPAs continue mounting even after the AQR is over?

The AQR was meant to stop the ever-greening and concealment of bad loans, and force banks to revive stalled projects. The hope was that once the mass of bad loans was disclosed, the banks, with the aid of the government, would undertake the surgery that was necessary to put the projects back on track. Unfortunately, this process has not played out as well. As NPAs age, they require more provisioning, so projects that have not been revived simply add to the stock of gross NPAs. A fair amount of the increase in NPAs may be due to ageing rather than as a result of a fresh lot of NPAs.

Why have projects not been revived? Since the post-AQR process took place after I demitted office, I can only comment on this from press reports. Blame probably lies on all sides here.

a. Risk-averse bankers, seeing the arrests of some of their colleagues, are simply not willing to take the write-downs and push a restructuring to conclusion, without the process being blessed by the courts or eminent individuals. Taking every restructuring to an eminent persons' group or court simply delays the process endlessly.

b. Until the Bankruptcy Code was enacted, promoters never believed they were under serious threat of losing their firms. Even after it was enacted, some still are playing the process, hoping to regain control through a proxy bidder, at a much lower price. So many have not engaged seriously with the banks.

c. The government has dragged its feet on project revival – the continuing problems in the power sector are just one example. The steps on reforming governance of public sector banks, or on protecting bank commercial decisions from second guessing by the investigative agencies, have been limited and ineffective. Sometimes even basic steps such as appointing CEOs on time have been found wanting. Finally, the government has not recapitalized banks with the urgency that the matter needed (though without governance reform, recapitalization is also not likely to be as useful).

d. The Bankruptcy Code is being tested by the large promoters with continuous and sometimes frivolous appeals. It is very important that the integrity of the process be maintained, and bankruptcy resolution be speedy, without the promoter inserting a bid by an associate at the auction, and acquiring the firm at a bargain-basement price. Given our conditions, the promoter should have every chance of concluding a deal before the firm goes to auction, but not after. Higher courts must resist the temptation to intervene routinely in these cases, and appeals must be limited once points of law are settled.

That said, the judicial process is simply not equipped to handle every NPA through a bankruptcy process. Banks and promoters have to strike deals outside of bankruptcy, or if promoters prove uncooperative, bankers should have the ability to proceed without them. Bankruptcy Court should be a final threat, and much loan renegotiation should be done under the shadow of the Bankruptcy Court, not in it. This requires fixing the factors mentioned in (a) that make bankers risk-averse and in (b) that make promoters uncooperative.

We need concentrated attention by a high-level empowered and responsible group set up by the government on cleaning up the banks. Otherwise the same non-solutions (bad bank management teams to take over stressed assets, bank mergers, new infrastructure lending institution) keep coming up and nothing really moves. Public sector banks are losing market share as non-bank finance companies, the private sector banks, and some of the newly licensed banks are expanding.

8. What could the regulator have done better?

It is hard to offer an objective self-assessment. However, the RBI should probably have raised more flags about the quality of lending in the early days of banking exuberance. With the benefit of hindsight, we should probably not have agreed to forbearance, though without the tools to clean up, it is not clear what the banks would have done. Forbearance was a bet that growth would revive, and projects would come back on track. That it did not work out does not mean that it was not the right decision at the time it was initiated. Also, we should have initiated the new tools earlier, and pushed for a more rapid enactment of the Bankruptcy Code. If so, we could have started the AQR process earlier. Finally, the RBI could have been more decisive in enforcing penalties on non-compliant banks. Fortunately, this culture of leniency has been changing in recent years. Hindsight, of course, is 20/20.

9. How should we prevent recurrence?

- Improve governance of public sector banks and distance them from the government.
  i. Public sector bank boards are still not adequately professionalized, and the government rather than a more independent body still decides board appointments, with the inevitable politicization. The government could follow the P.J. Naik Committee report more carefully. Eventually, strong boards should be entrusted with all decisions but held responsible for them.
  ii. Pending the change above, there is absolutely no excuse for banks to be left leaderless for long periods of time, as has been the case in recent years. The date of retirement of CEOs is well known and the government should be prepared well in advance with succession plans. Indeed, it would be good for the old CEO and the successor to overlap for a few months while they exchange notes. All the more reason to delegate appointments entirely to an entity like the Bank Board Bureau, and not retain it in government.

iii. Outside talent has been brought in in very limited ways into top management in public sector banks. There is already a talent deficit in internal PSB candidates in coming years because of a hiatus in recruitment in the past. This needs to be taken up urgently. Compensation structures in PSBs also need rethinking, especially for high-level outside hires. Internal parity will need to be maintained. There will be internal resistance, but lakhs of crores of national assets cannot be held hostage to the career concerns of a few.

iv. Risk management processes still need substantial improvement in PSBs. Compliance is still not adequate, and cyber risk needs greater attention.

- Improve the process of project evaluation and monitoring to lower the risk of project NPAs.

  i. Significantly more in-house expertise can be brought to project evaluation, including understanding demand projections for the project's output, likely competition, and the expertise and reliability of the promoter. Bankers will have to develop industry knowledge in key areas since consultants can be biased.

  ii. Real risks have to be mitigated where possible, and shared where not. Real risk mitigation requires ensuring that key permissions for land acquisition and construction are in place up front, while key inputs and customers are tied up through purchase agreements. Where these risks cannot be mitigated, they should be shared contractually between the promoter and financiers, or a transparent arbitration system agreed upon. So, for instance, if demand falls below projections, perhaps an agreement among promoters and financier can indicate when new equity will be brought in and by whom.

  iii. An appropriately flexible capital structure should be in place. The capital structure has to be related to residual risks of the project. The more the risks, the more the equity component should be (genuine promoter equity, not borrowed equity, of course), and the greater the flexibility in the debt structure. Promoters should be incentivized to deliver, with significant rewards for on-time execution and debt repayment. Where possible, corporate debt markets, either through direct issues or securitized project loan portfolios, should be used to absorb some of the initial project risk. More such arm's length debt should typically refinance bank debt when construction is over.

iv. Financiers should put in a robust system of project monitoring and appraisal, including, where possible, careful real-time monitoring of costs. For example, can project input costs be monitored and compared with comparable inputs elsewhere using IT, so that suspicious transactions suggesting over-invoicing are flagged? Projects that are going off track should be restructured quickly, before they become unviable.

v. And finally, the incentive structure for bankers should be worked out so that they evaluate, design, and monitor projects carefully, and get significant rewards if these work out. This means that even while committees may take the final loan decision, some senior banker ought to put her name on the proposal, taking responsibility for recommending the loan. IT systems within banks should be able to pull up overall performance records of loans recommended by individual bankers easily, and this should be an input into their promotion and pay.

- Strengthen the recovery process further.
  i. Both the out-of-court restructuring process and the bankruptcy process need to be strengthened and made speedy. The former requires protecting the ability of bankers to make commercial decisions without subjecting them to inquiry. The latter requires steady modifications where necessary to the bankruptcy code

so that it is effective, transparent, and not gamed by unscrupulous promoters.

- The government should focus on sources of the next crisis, not just the last one. In particular, the government should refrain from setting ambitious credit targets or waiving loans.

  i. Credit targets are sometimes achieved by abandoning appropriate due diligence, creating the environment for future NPAs. Both MUDRA (Micro Units Development and Refinance Agency) loans as well as the Kisan Credit Card, while popular, have to be examined more closely for potential credit risk. The Credit Guarantee Scheme for MSME (CGTMSE) run by SIDBI (Small Industries Development Bank of India) is a growing contingent liability and needs to be examined with urgency.

  ii. Loan waivers, as RBI has repeatedly argued, vitiate the credit culture, and stress the budgets of the waiving state or central government. They are poorly targeted, and eventually reduce the flow of credit. Agriculture needs serious attention, but not through loan waivers. An all-party agreement to this effect would be in the nation's interest, especially given the impending elections.

INDEX

ABOUT THE AUTHOR

RAGHURAM G. RAJAN is a world-renowned Indian economist who is currently a distinguished service professor at the University of Chicago Booth School of Business. His past policy positions include governor of the Reserve Bank of India and chief economist at the International Monetary Fund. His books include *Fault Lines* (winner of the Financial Times Business Book of the Year Award), *I Do What I Do*, *The Third Pillar*, *Saving Capitalism from the Capitalists* (with Luigi Zingales) and *Breaking the Mould* (with Rohit Lamba). His widely cited research focuses on the underpinnings of economic growth. His numerous awards include the Fischer Black Prize and the Deutsche Bank Prize for financial economics, Euromoney's Central Banker of the Year award and the Banker's Global Central Banker Award.